Study Skills

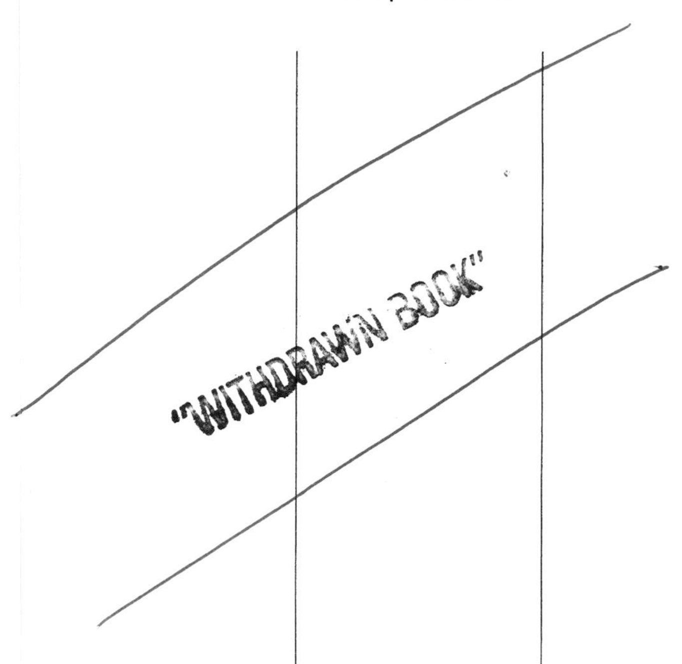

Study Skills

for

Language Students

A PRACTICAL GUIDE

SYDNEY G. DONALD

Senior Lecturer in German, University of Leeds

PAULINE E. KNEALE

Senior Lecturer in Geography, University of Leeds

A Member of the Hodder Headline Group
LONDON
Co-published in the United States of America by
Oxford University Press Inc., New York

First published in Great Britain in 2001 by
Arnold, a member of the Hodder Headline Group
338 Euston Road, London NW1 3BH

http://www.arnoldpublishers.com

Co-published in the United States of America by
Oxford University Press Inc.,
198 Madison Avenue, New York, NY10016

British Library Cataloguing in Publication Data
A catalogue record for this book is available from the British Library

Library of Congress Cataloging-in-Publication Data
A catalog record for this book is available from the Library of Congress

ISBN 0 340 76308 6 (pb)

1 2 3 4 5 6 7 8 9 10

Production Editor: Lauren McAllister
Production Controller: Martin Kerans
Cover Design: Terry Griffiths

Typeset in Palatino and Gill Sans by Phoenix Photosetting, Chatham, Kent
Printed and bound in Great Britain by Redwood Books, Trowbridge, Wiltshire

What do you think about this book? Or any other Arnold title?
Please send your comments to feedback.arnold@hodder.co.uk

CONTENTS

ACKNOWLEDGEMENTS

Many thanks to colleagues in the University of Leeds, Department of German, particularly Michael Beddow, Ingo Cornils, Verena Jung, Sibylle Metzger, Ingrid Sharp, John Tailby, and students, especially Christina Irvine, Katarina Jånsson, Anne Macdonald and Carly McKay. Thanks to Mark Ogden, Language Centre, Chris Todd, Department of French, Lee Davidson, Department of Linguistics and Phonetics, Alec McAllister, Information Systems Services, and Ann Serjeantson. To Sylvie Collins, School of Psychology for contributions that first appeared in *Study Skills for Psychology Students*, extensive proof reading and good ideas. To Mark Newcombe, School of Geography for the graphics. Lynne Shaw for crossword proofing. Members of Leeds University Careers Service, especially Clair Souter, Sue Hawksworth, Paul Jackson, Jane Conway and Val Butcher. Members of Leeds University Staff and Student Development Unit, particularly Chris Butcher, Maggie Boyle and Penny Hatton.

Thanks are due to the following for permission to reproduce diagrams and extracts:

Arnold for extracts from *Language Teaching Research*, *The Modern Language Review*, and *Second Language Research*. The Bibliographisches Institut & F.A. Brockhaus AG for the picture and text of *Weberei* of the Duden Oxford Bildwörterbuch Deutsch-Englisch.

Faites nein error. C'est di mega fantåstico livre en história du monde. It's stampato en multi-colôre, avec vorsprung durch technik. Recordar, nous sommes ne pas born hier. Morelle: La skillö ist neder miks die L2s.

PREFACE

This book is for undergraduate and masters students who want information about studying and researching modern languages in Higher Education. It is designed to defuse confusion and build confidence as you develop your L2 (foreign or target language skills) and assumes that most students would rather spend extra time honing their colloquial language skills in bistros, Kneipen and trattorias, than in the library. Most people using self-help books or on training courses find that 90+ per cent of the material is already familiar, but the few, new elements make it worthwhile. The 90 per cent increases your confidence that you are on the right track, and the remainder, hopefully, sparks some rethinking, reassessment and refining. The trick with university study is to find a combination of ideas that suits you, promotes your research and learning, and adds self-confidence. As with all texts, not all the answers are here, but who said study would be a doddle? This text is intended for reference throughout your degree; some items will seem irrelevant at first but become important later. There is a real difference between reading about a skill and applying the ideas in your degree. The **Try This** activities are designed to make the link between skills and their practical application, and to give you an opportunity to practise either mentally, or mentally and physically.

We hope you will enjoy some of the humour: this is not meant to be a solemn book, but it has serious points to make. The crosswords follow the style familiar to readers of UK broadsheet newspapers, quick crosswords and cryptic; all the answers have vaguely language related connections. Remember, you should be enjoying studying languages at university, it is supposed to be exciting and it can be fun as well as a challenge.

KEEP SMILING!

Chat up
Librarians

1 LET'S THINK ABOUT LANGUAGE LEARNING

Be careful not to let education get in the way of your learning

This book discusses the skills needed to study and do research in languages at university or college. Some of the motivation for assembling it came from a student who said, 'The problem with first year was I didn't know what I didn't know, and even when I thought there was something I was supposed to know I didn't know what to do about it'. University can seem confusing; you are expected to learn independently rather than being taught, but there is limited information about how to learn. This book might help. It is deliberately 'hands-on', making lots of practical '**Try This**' suggestions. It aims to add to your self-confidence in your research and study abilities, and save you time by acting as an on-going resource. Rather than worrying about what will happen in a seminar, how to do an on-line search, or reference an essay, look it up and carry on. You are already skilled in many areas like thinking, listening, note-making and writing, BUT reviewing your approach and refining your skills should prove beneficial. The language and tone of the book is deliberately light-hearted, with some games for light relief. There are some terrible jokes, although being written down inevitably diminishes humour, so keep smiling as you groan. Light relief is vital in study. If deep thinking leads to deep kipping, have a coffee, solve an anagram, but remember to go back to thinking after your break!

University is part of life-long learning; you start to control what and how you learn. There is a departmental teaching agenda to follow, and time to explore other avenues. If, in the process, these equip you for later life, that is a bonus.

You have multiple skills already in your L1 (native language) and have decided to study another, L2, (foreign or target language). For a Languages degree, like any other, you need to exploit your current skills and add more. Recognize that a languages degree has two elements:

- **The knowledge element**, including all the vocabulary and grammatical knowledge necessary to enable you to communicate at or near the level of an educated native speaker over an extensive range of topics and in a wide variety of registers, but also a knowledge and understanding of the culture and people who actually speak the language. Learning your L2 is a lifelong process, as languages evolve and change over time. The sheer statistics about languages are pretty daunting with perhaps 6000 different languages being spoken around the globe. Yet in the twenty-first century communication is recognized to be the single most vital factor in conducting business and

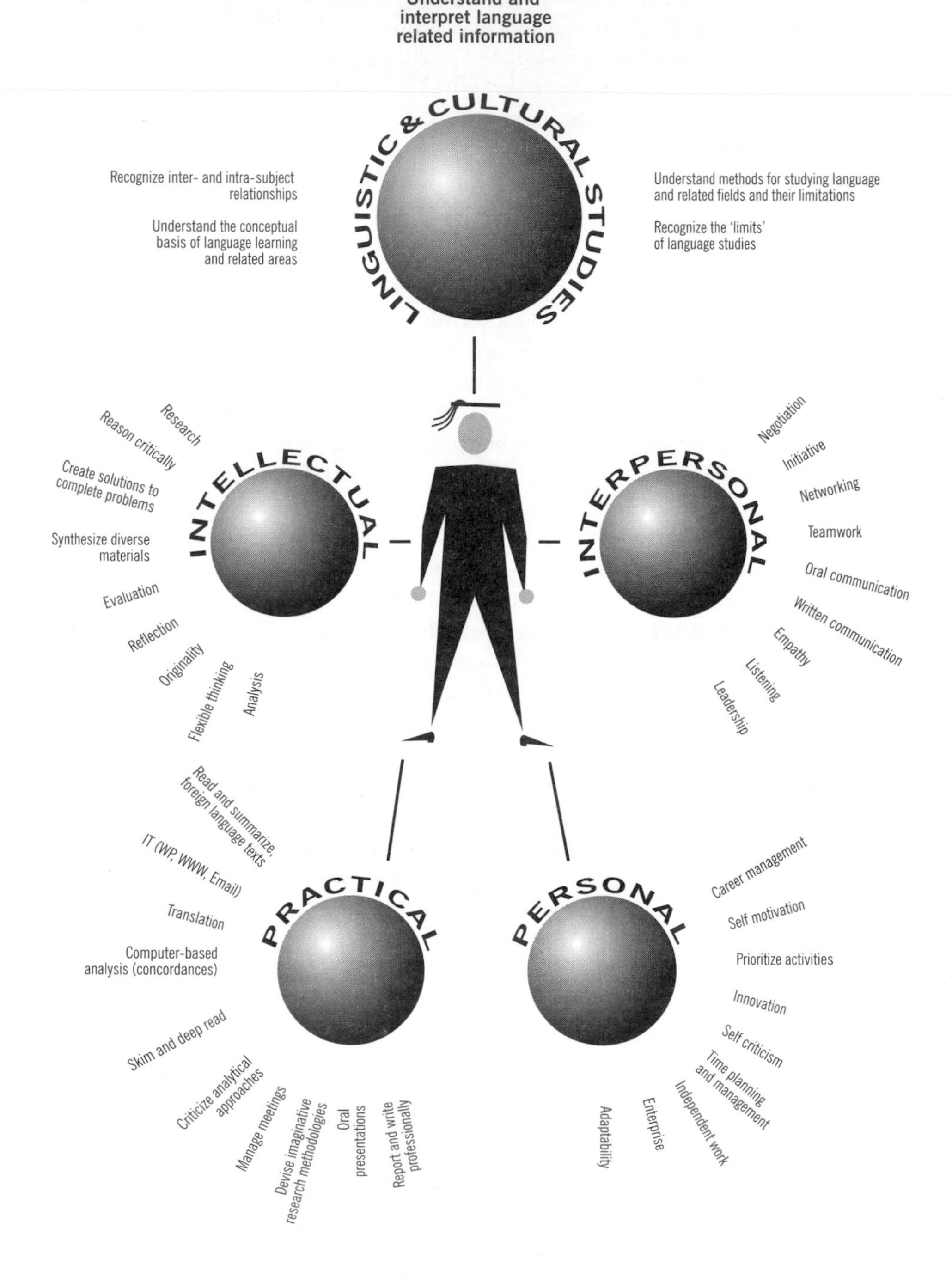

Figure 1.1 Skills and attributes of a Modern Languages or Linguistics graduate.

professional activities of all kinds around the world, and an ability to function in the language of your colleagues abroad, or even more importantly, your competitors, is a truly valuable asset. As Willy Brandt allegedly said: 'I sell to you in English but I buy from you in German'. The scope for learning languages is global because, of course, 'linguists do it world-wide'.

- **The skills element.** Often called *transferable skills*, these enable linguists to be efficient researchers, which will be of long-term benefit in the workplace. Most language students acquire practical experience of the skills and attributes shown in Figure 1.1. Some are absorbed by osmosis whilst others are taught at varying levels of detail.

In the last years of the twentieth century, UK student numbers expanded and the emphasis switched from lecturers teaching to students learning. Self-motivated learning is vital in life, enabling you to keep abreast of developments and initiatives. Employment is unpredictable. Job market and company requirements change rapidly. An employer needs individuals who are flexible about their careers. An effective graduate is someone who sees their career as a process of work and learning, mixing them to extend skills and experience. This is the essence of lifelong learning. The Nuffield Inquiry into Modern Languages (NLI 2000) firmly endorsed the importance of foreign language skills, so your degree course is mega-valuable, combining skills for life and for language.

In the jargon of career management and personal development, the phrase 'transferable skills' is readily quoted. To add value to your degree, you need to recognize and reflect on what you do every day in your course (Chapter 4), and understand where these skills have market value. Employers claim to be happy with the academic skills students acquire, such as researching, collating and synthesizing new material, but they also want graduates with skills like listening, negotiating and presenting. Any strengthening of your skills and experience of skill-based activities should add to your self-confidence and improve your performance as a linguist and as a potential employee.

In addition to traditional language skills, your degree will give you the opportunity to experience the latest developments in information technology including tele-working, surfing the world wide web (www), electronic journals, video-conferencing, tandem e-mail, bulletin-boards, databases, spreadsheets and digital video. University encourages you to get wired, get trained and build your own electronic resource base. The technology may seem daunting but it is fun too. (And if some five-year-old proto-anorak wearer can manage, so can you!)

The importance of graduates acquiring skills as well as knowledge was reinforced by the Dearing Report (NCIHE, 1997), which defined four key graduate skills, and happily, language degrees are awash with them (see Table 1.1). However, these four need some unpacking to show what is involved.

Making Applications, Graduate Careers Information (AGCAS, 1997) lists the self-reliance skills that organizations and companies desire. Most elements involve communication, IT and 'learning how to learn' and are as follows:

Graduate Skills (NCIHE 1997)	In Modern Languages or Linguistics Degrees
Communication	All modules. Oral and written communication in seminars, tutorials, workshops, debates, group work and all assessments.
Numeracy	All modules involving interpreting numerical and statistical information. Data handling in concordances and linguistic studies
Use of Information Technology	Most modules. On-line research activities. Word processing. Modules using graphics, spreadsheets, databases, programming for linguistics and language information systems.
Learning how to Learn	All modules. Taking personal responsibility for learning as an individual, and in group research, projects and dissertation.

Table 1.1 Where to find NCIHE skills in action.

- Communication skills: written and oral, and the ability to listen to others.
- Interpersonal or social skills: the capacity to establish good, professional working relationships with clients and colleagues.
- Organizational skills: planning ahead, meeting deadlines, managing yourself and co-ordinating others.
- Problem analysis and solution: the ability to identify key issues, reconcile conflicts, devise workable solutions, be clear and logical in thinking, prioritize and work under pressure.
- Intellect: judged by how effectively you translate your ideas into action.
- Leadership: many graduates eventually reach senior positions managing and leading people.
- Teamwork: working effectively in formal and informal teams.
- Adaptability: being able to initiate and respond to changing circumstances, and to continue to develop one's knowledge, interests and attitudes to adapt to changing demands.
- Technical capability: the capacity to acquire appropriate technical skills including scheduling, IT, statistics, computing, data analysis and to update these as appropriate.

- Achievement: the ability to set and achieve goals for oneself and for others, to keep an organization developing.

By graduation you should feel confident in listing these skills on a *curriculum vitae* (CV), and be able to explain where in the degree these abilities were practised and demonstrated.

This book recognizes that language learners in Higher Education come in a variety of shapes and sizes, each with their own objectives and needs. Examples of students will include:

- Native speakers of English who are studying for a language degree, either as a single-subject, or by combining a language with another subject – e.g. business studies, chemistry, tourism, history or another language.
- Students with little or no prior knowledge of their chosen language on *ab initio* programmes. These involve intensive language studies to bring you up to the level of students entering with A-level or equivalent, in a short space of time, typically one year.
- Students from overseas who are studying a foreign language at a university in Britain.
- Students taking modules in one or more foreign languages as part of completely unrelated degree programmes.

Most of the ideas and suggestions in the book apply to all types of language learner, but first-time, *ab initio* language learners might find Chapter 23 a useful starting point.

1.1 LEARNING ACTIVITIES AT UNIVERSITY; WHAT TO EXPECT, AND SPOTTING THE SKILLS!

Modern Language degrees are usually taught over three years called either Years 1, 2 and 3, or Levels 1, 2 and 3, and most incorporate a fourth year working or studying abroad. The university year is typically divided into 10 or 12 teaching blocks called modules or units, each addressing an aspect of language or some other topic related to the student's particular programme. Language degrees are usually progressive, which means that the standards and difficulty increase each year, and modules in later years build on experience and learning in earlier years. This section outlines the main activities at university and some of the skills practised during them.

Lectures

Believing any of the following statements will seriously damage your learning from lectures:

- In good lectures the lecturer speaks, the audience takes very rapid notes and silence reigns.
- The success of a lecture is all down to the lecturer.
- A great lecturer speaks slowly so students can take beautifully written, *verbatim* notes.
- Everything you need to know to get a first class degree will be mentioned in a lecture.
- Lectures are attended by students who work alone.

Lectures are the traditional teaching method, usually about 50 minutes long, with one lecturer and loads of students. If your lectures involve 100+ students they may seem impersonal and asking questions is difficult. Top tips for managing lectures include:

☺ Get there early and find a seat where you can see and hear.

☺ Have a supply of paper, pens and pencils ready.

☺ Get your brain in gear by thinking, 'I know I will enjoy this lecture, it will be good. I really want to know about ...'; 'Last week s/he discussed ...., now I want to find out about...'.

☺ Before the lecture, read the notes from the last session, and maybe some library material too. Even 5–10 minutes will get the brain in gear.

☺ Look at handouts carefully. Many lecturers give summary sheets with lecture outlines, main points, diagrams and reading. Use these to plan reading, revision and preparation for the next session.

☺ Think critically about the material presented.

☺ Revise and summarize notes soon after a lecture; it will help you recall material later. Decide what follow up reading is required.

☺ Ask questions.

Skills acquired during lectures include understanding language, historical or cultural issues, recognizing research frontiers and subject limitations. They also include, crucially, knowing how to listen, knowing how and when to take notes, and knowing when NOT just to follow the flow of the argument. WITHOUT taking notes.

Tutorials: What are they? What do you do?

Usually tutorials are a 50-minute discussion meeting with an academic or postgraduate tutor and 4–8 students. The style of tutorials varies between departments, but there is normally a set topic involving preparation. You might be asked to prepare a short talk, write an essay, write outline essays, prepare material for a debate, review a paper, and share your information with the group. The aim is to discuss and evaluate issues in a group that is small enough for everyone to take part. Other tutorial activities include discussing a set text, brainstorming examination answers, comparing note styles, planning a research activity, evaluating dissertation possibilities, and the list goes on.

The tutor's role is NOT to talk all the time, is NOT to teach, and is NOT to dominate the discussion. A good tutor will set the topic and style for the session well in advance, so everyone knows what they are doing. S/he will let a discussion flow, watch the time, encourage use of your L2 rather than L1 language in discussion, make sure everyone gets a fair share of the conversation, assist when the group is stuck, and sum up if there is no summarizer to do so as part of the assignment. A good tutor will comment on your activities, but tutorials are YOUR time.

Sometimes tutors ask you to run tutorials in their absence, and to report the outcomes. This is not because tutors are lazy, but because generating independence is an important part of university training. Student-led and managed tutorials demonstrate skills in the management of group and personal work. When a tutor is ill, continuing unsupervised uses the time effectively. A tutor may assign or ask for volunteer chairpersons, timekeepers and reporters to manage and document discussions.

Your role is to arrive at tutorials fully prepared to discuss the topic NO MATTER HOW UNINTERESTED YOU ARE. Use tutorials to develop listening and discussion skills, to become familiar with talking around language-related issues and build up experience of arguing about ideas.

Top Tips

- ✔ Taking time to prepare for tutorials will stop (or reduce) nerves, and you will learn more by understanding something about the topic in advance.
- ✔ Reviewing notes and reading relevant books and articles will increase your confidence in discussions.
- ✔ Asking questions is a good way of saying something without having to know the answer.
- ✔ Have a couple of questions or points prepared in advance, and use them early on – get stuck in!
- ✔ Taking notes in tutorials is vital. Other people's views, especially when different to your own, broaden your ideas about a topic, but they are impossible to recall later unless noted at the time. Tutorial notes make good revision material.

Tutorial skills include communication, presentation, critical reasoning, analysis, synthesis, networking and negotiation.

Seminars

Seminars are a slightly more formal version of a tutorial, with 8–25 people. One or more people make a presentation for about half the allotted period, leaving ample time for group discussion. Seminars are a great opportunity to brainstorm and note the ideas and attitudes of colleagues. Spot extra examples and approaches to consider later. Take notes.

Even if you are not a main speaker, you need to prepare in advance. In the week you speak, you will be enormously grateful to everyone who contributes to the discussion. To benefit from this kind of co-operation you need to prepare and contribute in the weeks when you are not the main presenter.

ONLY TO BE READ BY THE NERVOUS. If you are worried, nervous or terrified then volunteer to do an early seminar. It gets it out of the way before someone else does something brilliant (well, moderately reasonable) and upsets you! Acquiring and strengthening skills builds your confidence so seminars appear less of a nightmare. Alternatively (depending on your temperament), by the third week you will know people and be less worried.

Seminar skills include discussion, listening, analysis, teamwork, giving a professional performance and networking more connections than BT.

Workshops or large group tutorials

Workshops are classes with 12–35 students, which support lectures and practical modules. They have very varied formats. They may be called 'large group tutorials', 'support classes' or 'revision classes'. There will usually be preparation work and a group activity. Tutors act as facilitators, not as teachers. Expect a tutor to break large groups into sub-groups for brainstorming and discussion. These sessions present a great opportunity to widen your circle of friends and to find colleagues with similar and diverse views.

Workshop skills are the same as for tutorials and seminars with wider networking and listening opportunities.

Written and spoken language classes

Oral and written language practice are the central, 'hands on' skills element of a language degree, and are discussed in Chapter 2.

Assessment

Assessments come like Christmas presents, regularly and in all sorts of shapes. Assessments should be regarded as helpful because they develop your understanding. There are two forms:

- ✔ Within-module assessment of progress (sometimes called 'monitoring'), where the marks do not count (formative), and usually involve some feedback.

- ✔ Assessments where the marks do count (summative). Feedback may or may not happen, depending on the test and system. The results eventually appear on your degree result notification for the edification of your first employer who wants written confirmation of your university prowess.

There is a slight tendency for the average student to pay less attention to formative, within-module assessments, where the marks do not count. Staff design formative tests because they know 99 per cent (± 1 per cent) of students need an opportunity to 'have a go', to get an insight into procedures and expected standards, when marks are not an issue.

Assessments are very varied: examinations, essays, oral presentations, written language assignments, seminars, discussion contributions, debates, reports, reviews of books and papers, project designs, critical learning log, year abroad placement report, multiple choice tests ... . It is a matter of time management to organize your life (Chapter 3). You should make it your business to know in advance exactly how each module is assessed and what each element is worth. Many modules have mixed assessments, so those who do very well in examinations or essay writing are not consistently advantaged. Many departments have standard assessment criteria. Get hold of your own departmental versions or see examples for essays (Table 14.1, Figure 14.2), oral presentations (Figure 11.2), dissertations (Figure 20.2) and posters (Figure 19.3). If you cover all the criteria then the marks come rolling in.

Amongst the many skills enhanced by assessments are thinking, synthesis, evaluation, originality and communication.

Non-academic learning

Do not underestimate what you know! In your years at university you also acquire loads of personal skills, like negotiating with landlords, debt crisis management, charming bank staff, juggling time to keep a term-time job and still deliver essays on time, being flexible over who does the washing up and handling flat mates and tutors.

1.2 The research process

All students are 'reading' for a degree, finding out for themselves, the research process. Taught activities involve 20–50 per cent of the timetable, leaving 80–50 per cent for personal research into sub-topics, and study activities which reinforce understanding. The scope of Language degrees is vast, and covering all aspects is impossible. Every linguist is aiming to maximize the return on their research activities, to broaden and deepen their knowledge of the country and the culture whose language they are studying, and to expand their language knowledge, all within the constraints of time, facilities and energy. Consequently, working in a group (see Chapter 16) can be seriously beneficial.

Language issues are not simple. The lecturer may set the topic in its linguistic, historical or cultural context and provide a framework of what is known, generally assumed or already well understood, before moving on to discuss in greater detail those areas of the subject where there is less consensus, perhaps outlining conflicting theories or arguments and directing the students towards aspects worthy of further investigation. Most language issues are highly interlocking and multidimensional. Linguists' greatest strengths, in addition to specific L2 knowledge and related topics, lie in their ability to assimilate and weigh up unclear, and at times contradictory, information from a wide range of sources and in synthesizing it to make sense of the wider picture.

By the time you graduate you should have (besides high-level language skills) an enhanced knowledge of, and/or ability to identify and analyse critically, the historical and cultural background of the country in question, its current political, economic and ecological makeup and concerns, and the systems and administrative frameworks (educational, legal, etc.) which underpin its society. Some exposure to its literature, music and art is also a feature of the educated linguist. You should also have learned to recognize what you as an individual know and do not know; and (perhaps this is paramount for today's society) you should understand how and where to find the information you need. Recognizing the boundaries of one's own expertise is a relevant life skill. University learning is not about recalling a full set of lecture notes. It is about understanding issues and being able to relate and apply them in different contexts.

Recognizing the links between Languages and other disciplines will enhance your research ability. Some language students have no formal background in the subject. If you are one of these students, remember this is not a disadvantage, you are clearly interested in language, and all topics are fresh and not confused by half-remembered notes (see Chapter 23). Language studies draw on many subjects for theory and insights, and you can profitably use the background information and skills you have from other subjects to strengthen your language research. Mature students, with longer experience of life, politics, social conditions and general knowledge have a particularly extensive skills base to build on.

1.3 How to handle this book?

No single idea is going to make a magical difference to your learning, but taking time to think about the way you approach tasks like reading and thinking, listening and writing, researching and presenting should help your efficiency rate. Studying is a personal activity. There are no 'right' ways, just tips, techniques, short-cuts and long-cuts.

If you attempt to read the whole book in one go you are likely to feel got at and preached at. **This is not the idea**. Look through the chapter headings and index. If you are concerned or stuck, we hope there is a useful section. Use it as a handbook

START FIRST YEAR
(Unaware of the rules?)

AWARENESS
(Could be better?)

LOADS
OF PRACTICE

PRACTICAL

ACTIVITIES

Improvement

REINFORCEMENT

INFORMED
ability

CONFIDENT
CAREER
Application

MULTI-SKILLED TRAINED
LINGUIST

Figure 1.2 The skills route.

throughout your degree. Some parts are relevant for Level 1, others like the dissertation advice (see Chapter 20), will matter more in the final year. When you have an essay or book review to write, look at the relevant chapters. The key is to view it as encouragement (see Figure 1.2). Build on your existing skills. There are lots of **Try This** opportunities suggesting ways of practising or applying your skills. We predict that most people will ignore most of them initially. Adapt them to your needs when you want them. Treat them as part of your Languages learning rather than as an isolated skill exercise. Experience is built on doing things, not on watching them.

The aim of the book is to encourage and build your self-confidence in your skills, and to show where they are transferable and marketable. Your task is to decide to what extent you agree with the ideas in the book, and apply them for your own purposes. In some ways this is like a cookery book, many of the **Try This** activities are recipes, BUT adapt, garnish, modify and extend them. Be inventive with the ingredients! University research is a creative activity, like cooking. Some statements are deliberately controversial, designed to encourage thinking. Most of the figures and examples are deliberately 'less than perfect'. You are asked to consider how they can be improved, and what needs changing, as a way into active criticism. Universities provide IT facilities and gymnasiums, but getting more skilled means 'working out'. The first year is a good time to practise and enhance skills, but it is important to keep practising and reflecting throughout your degree.

1.4 References and Further Reading

AGCAS (1997) *Making Applications, Graduate Careers Information.* London: Association of Graduate Careers Advisory Services.

Buzan, T. (1995) *Use your Head.* (rev. edn). London: BBC Books.

Chambers, E. and Northedge, A. (1997) *The Arts Good Study Guide.* Milton Keynes: Open University.

Crystal, D. (1987) *The Cambridge Encyclopedia of Language.* Cambridge: Cambridge University Press.

Dufeu, B. (1994) *Teaching Myself.* Oxford: Oxford University Press.

Jones, R. (1991) *Languages and How to Master Them.* Cambridge: Allborough Publishing.

Lewis, M. (1999) *How to Study Foreign Languages.* Basingstoke and London: Macmillan Study Guides.

NCIHE (1997) *Higher Education in the Learning Society,* Report of the National Committee of Inquiry into Higher Education. Norwich: HMSO.

NLI (2000) *Nuffield Languages Inquiry* http://www.nuffieldfoundation.org/language/index.html Accessed 15 October 2000.

Rubin, J. and Thompson, I. (1994) *How to be a More Successful Language Learner.* Boston MA: Heinle and Heinle.

For further skills texts and www links see http://www.german. leeds.ac.uk/ skillsbook/index.htm

Anagrams I

Try these Language anagrams, answers p. 271

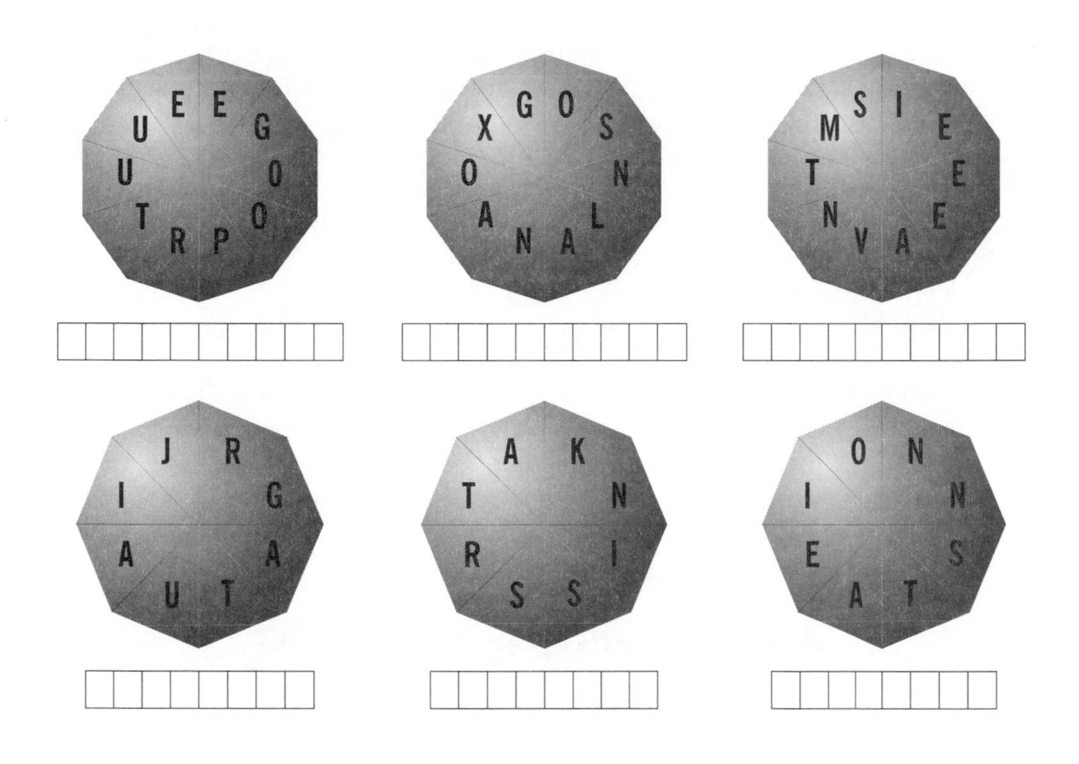

2 WORKING WITH LANGUAGES: THE FOUR SKILLS

I've forgotten the German for four, said Stefano, fearlessly

Language teachers conventionally distinguish between four aspects of language which are mastered by means of the 'four skills': listening, speaking, reading, writing. Listening and reading might be thought of as primarily 'passive', 'receptive' or 'input' skills, whilst speaking and writing are their 'active', 'productive' or 'output' counterparts. The trick is to balance building up all four skills. In practice you will be working on all four skills virtually all the time. The Chinese you hear in conversation, or on television, or at the cinema, is the raw material for your own spoken Chinese; and you can't remotely hope to write correct Portuguese without reading a lot of it as well.

So how do you go about mastering the four skills? It requires the sort of push–pull effort that accordion players are familiar with. Considerately, your department will have arranged a few helpful classes. Most language courses split learning activities into 'written' and 'spoken' language, with one or more classes per week on each aspect (Ho Hum – another reason to get up). This chapter aims to encourage you to recognize the different skills and to organize a balance between the four activities.

2.1 THE ART OF LISTENING

Tapes

Arguably this is the most important skill of all, yet in many ways it is also the hardest. Unless you are listening to a tape, you cannot control the vocabulary, style, accent or pace. Speech is ephemeral, so by far the best way to build up your listening skills and boost your confidence is to use recorded material which you can play and re-play over and over again. College language centres bulge with tapes at graded levels of difficulty and on every imaginable topic. Get these in your machines. Start with material which interests you and that you know something about; later you should choose new subjects to broaden your knowledge and to provide a greater challenge. Try and also get tapes with 'non-standard' speech – to train your ear to male and female, children and adult, educated and uneducated, and regional accents.

Can you get addicted to foreign soaps? These may be accessible via satellite or cable, or in your language centre. Brilliantly (?) the same set of characters appear in every episode using bang up-to-the-minute colloquial language, and repetitive and constrained lexis (technical term for the vocabulary of a language) on limited topics; this aids comprehension and helps to reinforce vocabulary (within this limited range). The same is true to a certain extent of news broadcasts – EU currency, refugees, local politics . . . each have their own rhetorical language and structure, and re-appear nightly.

Add cinematic 'thrills and spills' by checking out the video list in your language centre. Book out must-see films and documentaries, and plan some viewing time into your timetable (and ask your mates). On your personal stereo you can practise listening to audio-tapes, use dead time such as the bus ride to and from college. Who else can you borrow tapes from – library, tutors, class mates? Record programmes off-air and listen to them when you like. Share your tapes. Remember to include watching and listening to tapes in your work schedule (Chapter 3), and marvel at your progress! Only language students can give themselves learning credits for watching Sly Stallone dubbed into Spanish.

Listening is tough, it may help to take some notes. The more often you play a tape, the more of it you will understand, but even the first time around there are plenty of clues to help your comprehension:

✔ the topic itself (you can expect certain content to be covered and certain vocabulary to come up);

✔ the general flow of conversation (to a degree, you can anticipate what is coming next from what has been said previously);

✔ the speaker (a doctor, say, or a member of a political party);

✔ the type of material (a play, or a speech, a news item, or perhaps a travel programme);

✔ the speaker's tone of voice.

All of this applies to videos as well of course, but then you have the added bonuses of the setting and the speaker's movements, facial expressions and body language. Conversely, you will also encounter obstacles to comprehension, in particular:

✘ the speed of delivery;

✘ the use of exceptionally idiomatic, slang, technical or otherwise obscure lexis;

✘ slurred or otherwise unclear speech;

✘ unfamiliar dialects or accents.

Replaying a difficult section and, if necessary, pausing to look up the more elusive words, will help greatly, and the mere fact of extended listening will gradually acclimatize you to even the most challenging of accents. Approach it like a cryptic crossword puzzle.

The first time you play a tape, concentrate on identifying key words or phrases.

Home in on nouns and verbs first, they determine the meaning of a passage, then on the modifiers/qualifiers (adjectives and adverbs), followed by the other parts of speech. Most speakers point out the key elements in a sentence by placing stress on them. Listen to stress and intonation patterns and note the word order preferences of a variety of speakers. OK, easier said than done, but it comes with practice – use **Try This 2.1**.

TRY THIS 2.1 – Tape Games 1

With audio or video tapes listen for different things each time you play them:

- ☺ List new words or phrases, and new constructions.
- ☺ List unusual figures of speech, colloquialisms.
- ☺ List technical terms.
- ☺ List new proverbs or sayings.
- ☺ Mini-dictation: play a 300--500 words section once, then play it again one sentence at a time, pausing to write down the text. Play it again to check your copy for errors, and then compare your work against the transcript (if available).

Don't expect, or even try, to pick up every last detail. You can be having a conversation in your native tongue and miss things, and generally it doesn't much matter. When there is background noise, concentration wanders, but you still follow the drift of the discussion and make appropriate responses. After you have practised your tape drills for a few weeks have a go at **Try This 2.2**.

TRY THIS 2.2 – Tape Games 2

Get a new tape. Play it through just once, then write a brief summary of its content. The following day, play it through again a few more times, making fresh, more detailed notes. Compare these with your Day 1 notes to see how much you got right the first time. You will probably find that even from one listening you managed to get the gist and the main points of the conversation.

To understand or to follow?

In conversations bear in mind that understanding and following are not quite the same thing. When you're listening to someone talking, you need to *understand* as much as you can of the individual points **and** *follow* the thread of the conversation **and** make your own contribution to it. Unless you are in a bureaucratic or legal situation (when you would take notes) it is a big mistake to try to remember a conversation *verbatim*. Your brain processes information by sifting out the significant elements, recasting or filing them alongside connected information, and throwing the rest away. Let your brain do this for you; if you concentrate on remembering everything your brain will overload and you will be left hopelessly behind. Relax, listen for the key words and don't let the detail get you down. If you think you've missed something really crucial in a conversation, you can always ask for it to be repeated. Aim to focus hard on the framework, the theme, or the general thrust of the conversation – you will still be able to follow what is going on even if you miss odd bits.

It should be easier to keep up with a lecture or a themed programme where the topic is announced in advance, and you can prepare for it by looking up some of the relevant vocabulary or reading around the subject. An informal conversation is unstructured and can go off at alarming tangents. Even so, there are plenty of ways in which you can help yourself. Here are just a few:

✔ *Unfamiliar words*? Knowing the basic principles of *word-formation* in your L2 helps you work out their meaning. How are verbs formed from adjectives, for instance? How do particular prefixes or suffixes modify the meaning of the word-stem they are attached to? How can you tell the difference between an adjective and an adverb?

✔ *Little words* make a difference. In English, conversations are dosed liberally with expressions like 'you know', 'admittedly', 'actually', 'nevertheless'. Check out the equivalents in your L2 such as dichiaratamente (It.), reconocidamente (Esp.), indrømmet (Da.). Words like these modify meanings and help the speaker to persuade, concede, create distance, etc. Get your own list ready – understanding and using them properly is essential for authentic language.

✔ *Grammar* matters! The sounder your grammar is, the better you will grasp what is going on. In an inflected language like German, for example, you need to be thoroughly familiar with case endings, and you also need to be clear about, say, the way that the meaning changes when you use certain prepositions with the accusative rather than the dative case.

✔ *Regular phrases and constructions*. Everyday spoken language is in large measure rhetorical and repetitive. Unless you are aiming to be witty or otherwise impress, you generally use stock phrases, – 'good morning', 'happy birthday', 'it's been a great day', 'lousy weather for the time of year', and so on. We all recycle phrases, even within a single dialogue, and build up a stock of conversational phrases and responses. Using them will make you sound more authentic and enable you to look ahead in a conversation and anticipate what is coming next.

Activities like **Try This 2.1** and **Try This 2.2** build up your confidence and you will begin to trust your ability to grasp the gist of a once-heard conversation or speech. Make regular dates to listen to broadcasts and to watch films in your L2 (preferably not dubbed) – as varied in topic and as many as possible. Soon you will be wondering why you ever worried so much about comprehension.

2.2 Getting the most out of spoken language classes

Generally a spoken or oral language class will focus on a particular topic, and one or two students may be asked to lead the group's discussion or make a presentation to start the ball rolling. But an oral class develops a dynamic of its own which can make or mar it. Take a minute to analyse what is actually going on there the next time you are in an oral language group. Does anything need changing? Do you see the class as:

? a forum for conveying and sharing information?

? a chance for everyone to hone their spoken language skills?

? an opportunity to practise listening comprehension?

? a free-for-all?

And what appears to be the tutor's role? Is it to:

? cover a pre-determined topic in a structured fashion, or to allow the conversation to range all over the subject or even drift away from it?

? make sure that everybody has a chance to contribute to the discussion?

? provide exposure to authentic Spanish (or German, or Japanese, or whatever your language of study is)?

Obviously the gains to be had from listening to a native speaker in an oral class are enormous, provided the tutor doesn't speak at the wrong pace, or restrict the conversation to a pet hobby-horse, or do all the talking. If any of these happen, find a polite way of asking him/her to modify the approach. Many language assistants are either students themselves or recent graduates just starting out on their careers, and they will usually welcome constructive, polite feedback. Happy students make for a happy tutor, and classes are run for your benefit!

Part of the oral language tutor's job is to act as facilitator and, if necessary, referee. If someone hogs the conversation the whole time, or sits in a corner imitating wallpaper, the tutor will try to even things out, and to encourage quieter contributors. In addition, though, as a native speaker the tutor is the expert and role-model, not just in what s/he says (knowledge of the country, its culture, its history and its politics) but how s/he says it. This is where you will hear the living language taking spontaneous, idiomatic shape, and you will have plenty of opportunities to respond in kind; but only if you have a game plan.

Good language tutors gear their speech to the ability level of the class; maintain discussion at an appropriate intellectual level; broaden and enrich students' vocabulary and knowledge of structures by deliberately using a wide and varied range of words, phrases and registers; and strike a balance between correcting mistakes and encouraging communication. But even with a good tutor, there are things you can usefully do to make the class as profitable as possible for yourself (and everyone else as well).

- Do you tend to speak without thinking? Chances are that you make your fair share of mistakes in the process, so try putting your last utterance through a quick grammar check before you speak again.
- Do you prefer to listen to the others? Instead of thinking about how to break into the conversation again and what you are going to say next, force yourself to pay closer attention to everyone else. In responding to them, conversation becomes more natural.

If you are shy you probably have well-developed listening skills. Capitalize on this by assimilating the expressions the tutor uses. This provides you with a reservoir of vocabulary and idiom which you *know* to be correct and can trot out with confidence. Keep talking – you know more than you think!

Top Tips

- Come prepared, think about the topic of the class in advance – bear in mind that the subject-matter under discussion is generally secondary to the discussion itself.
- Conversations are messy things, like rugby scrums – be prepared for the unexpected.
- Come prepared to listen.
- Come prepared to talk, and don't worry too much about accuracy – it's important, but less so than actually speaking.
- Build your confidence by planning ahead. Reading around the next topic will help but better still, listen to a radio or TV programme about it. Note the expressions that might come in handy.
- If you are nervous about speaking at length, concentrate on the flow of conversation and ask a question. This gets you into the discussion without having to know the answer.
- Live a little dangerously! Resolve to make at least one off-the-cuff remark in every lesson, regardless of mistakes. Before you know it, you'll be butting in with the best of them. Or as one student said, 'It actually works this language lark, I get a real buzz off it!' Here I am speaking in a language other than my own, being understood!' Stay casual now! The biggest incentive/motivation is success. There's nothing worse than arriving unprepared to a lesson. You feel a fool and will miss out on the buzz.

Improving your spoken language out of class

Equipped with your well-honed listening strategies and skills, and spurred on by your weekly oral language class successes, you are now ready to venture into the uncharted territory of unstructured real-world conversation. Fear not! There are plenty of non-threatening opportunities out there for you to improve your spoken language, and plenty of tricks to help you along.

Probably the easiest way of all to start is – by talking to yourself. Most of us have conversations with ourselves from time to time, so have them in Japanese, or Catalan, or Hebrew, and better still, do it out loud! Record yourself on tape (audio or video) then play it back to yourself.

And when you get bored with listening to your own voice, rope in some of your friends. Whenever two or more language-learners are gathered together – over a coffee, in a pub, back in your hall of residence – in fact, just about anywhere, you can practise speaking in L2. Don't worry about correcting one another's grammar or accent, that's what your classes are for, just concentrate on getting your fluency up and improving your comprehension.

With a friend, and depending on which linguistic level you've reached, practise 'transactional dialogues' (at the hairdresser's, in a bank, buying tickets, talking on the telephone). These 'service exchanges' (Lewis, 1999) have a certain 'ritualistic' or rhetorical element, with set phrases and a limited range of vocabulary, so can be rehearsed in advance. Watch and copy the body language used by native speakers, not only to make your own contribution to a conversation appear more authentic, but because certain signs, e.g. nodding or shaking one's head, are aids to comprehension.

Pronunciation

> *'Her English is too good,' he said, 'which clearly indicates that she is foreign.'*
>
> My Fair Lady.

Your Holy Grail is to be mistaken for a native speaker. Listen to native speakers at every opportunity – on the radio, on TV, giving lectures, chatting over a coffee – and imitate their speech, even if this means (again!) talking to yourself. AND make room in your weekly schedule for a regular listening and speaking slot in the language centre, using a wide variety of tapes. Pay special attention to intonation and stress, both important factors in distinguishing a native from an impostor. Use dictionary information on pronunciation and stress, using the International Phonetic Alphabet. Some languages (e.g. German) are almost entirely phonetic, so your knowledge of the sounds of the language will enable you pronounce any new word on sight.

Don't aim for absolute perfection, the equivalent of 'Oxford English', or you'll sound as though you've learned your language from a textbook. In real conversations people make the odd mistake, which they correct or not as the case may be, they throw in bits of slang, and they slur some of their words, so do likewise – in moderation! And incidentally, don't worry if you end up speaking with a regional accent rather than the received standard pronunciation; being authentic is the name of the game where language acquisition is concerned.

Reading

Chapter 6 discusses reading strategies and techniques, and generally these hold good for any language. Beyond these, becoming a good reader of L2 is no different from becoming a good golfer or a good driver: practice, practice, practice and more practice! Use your local library to find fun books in translation – Pratchett, Asimov, Bridget Jones, Harry Potter. Effective reading in a foreign language isn't only about vocabulary. You are reading connected prose, not isolated words, so the ability to recognize sentence patterns is every bit as important, and the more widely you read, the better you will become at this. Once you have mastered the basic principles and can hold structures in your head (in German, for instance, the sense of a subordinate clause isn't completed until you reach the finite verb at the end), you can branch out to more sophisticated aspects of syntax and style. As you read, note the different clause patterns, sentence structures and paragraph lengths used by, for example, tabloid as opposed to broadsheet journalists; technical writers; novelists, and so on.

2.3 Getting the most out of written language classes

Written assignments come most weeks. They are self, peer or tutor marked and overall you are trying to reduce the red ink on the paper as you progress. The comments should alter in character as your command of the language improves; you will get into more subtle areas of style and idiom where there is room for several alternative 'best options'. You will have crossed the great divide from novice learner to advanced professional, and from here on in your future as a linguist will be concerned more with nuances of meaning and elegance of expression than with genders and endings. (Or so the theory goes.) But language is a living organism (to use one metaphor), or a tool for communication (to use another), and therefore all languages need to grow new bits whilst bits of them die and, in some cases, the whole language dies. Languages adapt by developing or borrowing new terms to meet new situations and describe new inventions, and by discarding terms that have fallen out of use.

> ***Q.*** *How can you really waste your time in written language classes?*
> ***A.*** *Sit back and wait for your tutor to spot all your mistakes.*

This is actually two problems rolled into one: 1) you lose marks, and 2) good linguists learn how to spot their own mistakes. Becoming a linguist really is about becoming an independent learner which involves:

- ✔ Checking your own work, pretending to be your tutor before handing it in. Practise spotting errors.
- ✔ Going through marked exercises *in detail* to (try to) ensure that you don't make the same mistakes again.
- ✔ Checking up on grammar, vocabulary and syntax in reference works to really understand how to get it right next time.
- ✔ Learning how to find your way around dictionaries, grammars and other works of reference, so that you know where to look for assistance when you next need it (Chapter 7).
- ✔ Seizing every opportunity to talk with native speakers of your L2 (foreign language assistants, exchange students, boy/girlfriends).
- ✔ Listening to the radio in L2.
- ✔ Watching foreign television (including soaps, football matches and tennis tournaments, etc.).
- ✔ Making the most of chances to listen to and speak the language even in classes that are not strictly language classes.
- ✔ Reading newspapers and magazines (including, increasingly, online editions: see Chapter 5).
- ✔ Reading secondary literature in L2. Don't take the easy way out by sticking to English.
- ✔ Spending a bit longer on your written language exercises – delight/surprise/amaze your tutors!

A new word a day
... is worth
28 million in the
dictionary

2.4 Effective vocabulary acquisition

A Japanese child learns Japanese by osmosis at its mother's kimono strings. Being abroad for a lengthy period (on your year's foreign placement) gives your language an osmosis boost; but you need other methods when daily language immersion is not possible. Try to make your routine or rote learning more fun! Try to fit in at least one of the following **Try This 2.3** and **Try This 2.4** activities into your weekly schedule.

TRY THIS 2.3 – Memorizing doesn't have to be boring – share it with friends

1. Set a regular date to learn and test new vocabulary. You can cover twice as much ground if you each learn a different set of expressions, and then test one another.
2. To learn a list of words and phrases, write them down in one column with their meanings or equivalents in the other, and cover up one side of the page whilst you work on the other side. Then hand the sheet to your friend for testing.
3. Vary the types of test. For instance, one time try reciting a list exactly as it is written down, another time try random order.
4. Devise games and a system of rewards and penalties.

TRY THIS 2.4 – Newspaper games

Historischer Handschlag in Korea/Zimbabwe/Moscow: Historic Handshake in Korea ...

Most major international stories will appear in your L1 and L2 newspapers. The main phrases and names appear in both. Plan a time each week to look at a L2 newspaper and compare it with your own paper (a broadsheet for UK students). Select a story each week and compare the vocabulary. Note how the 'spin' or 'approach' is different and similar in different reports.

Do it by yourself, but do it systematically. Learning is usually more efficient when you have a framework for the information. The framework for vocabulary-building is the *topic* or *context*, where you cluster words or expressions around a central theme. Figure 7.1 (p. 73) is a pictorial dictionary example of this approach; the same principle works for any subject, even abstract concepts like truth and honesty. Mind maps of associated words are fun too, see **Try This 2.5**. and Buzan and Buzan (1995, pp. 230–31) for two language related mind maps – the second is one for French grammar.

Play newspaper games – use **Try This 2.4** to get started. To maximize the return on your efforts, try to explore as many avenues and connections as time allows. This means

- Racking your brains for linked terms in either language and jotting them down.
- Following up these and any other associated expressions (not just *synonyms*, but *antonyms* as well) in your bilingual dictionary. Language being a tangled web, this will probably lead you into some enchanted areas, but that's all grist to the mill.

- Memorizing every new expression embedded in a phrase or sentence, preferably an amusing one, or one that has some private significance for you, to aid recall.
- Learning material in coherent sets, groups or clusters, e.g. if you're doing a topic on transport, make your assignment an opportunity to gather as full a list of modes of travel and vocabulary associated with transport as you can, in both languages.
- Having learned a little vocab, turn it into a small piece of prose. This way the vocab becomes functional.

There are other types of framework as well. For example *lists of grammatically related* words (strong verbs of a certain class, or prepositions which take a particular case), words used only in a certain *register* (poetic, journalese, slang), or of a particular *type*, such as German nouns ending in the abstract suffixes '-heit' and '-schaft', or French adjectives with the suffix '-esque'; or *clusters* of words (adjective. verb, etc.) related to a common stem. **What are your L2 equivalents?**

Because of their shared origins, European languages have many words in common (cognate) with English and with each other, e.g. German 'Kirche' and Scots dialect 'kirk' (church) are cognates, as are English/French 'table', both derived from Latin 'tabula' (plank, tablet). Exploit these connections to your advantage. But beware of false cognates or *faux amis*, words which look similar but whose meaning has evolved in different directions in English and your L2. The English 'sympathetic' does not mean the same as German 'sympatisch' and French 'sympathique' (likeable, congenial). Similarly, 'ordinaire' in French and 'ordinary' in English may mean pretty much the same thing, but 'ordinär' in German means vulgar, common, coarse or rude. Yet curiously enough, a German 'Ordinarius' is a university professor. Friends like these can let you down!

TRY THIS 2.5 – Developing word mind maps

Take an armchair, dictionary, pile of scrap paper and coloured pens. Choose a new word or phrase and write it in the centre of a piece of paper in your L2. Then think of associated words and phrases; add these in groups to make a map or web of interlinked ideas. Use different colours to highlight different ideas or clusters of ideas. Keep important ideas near the centre and let less related ideas radiate towards the edge. Use lines and arrows to connect groups of words or ideas. Buzan and Buzan (1995) give examples. Use the dictionary to find new words and add these. By the end you will have a colourful drawing with lots of new and associated words.

Various websites show mind maps – see
http://www.buzancentre.com/mm_desc.html
http://world.std.com/~emagic/mindmap.html
http://www.demon.co.uk/mindtool/mindmaps.html for ideas.

TRY THIS 2.6 – Visualizing words and phrases

Recalling new words, phrases or concepts can be more effective when you mentally link them to an image, especially a jokey or funny image:

Visual	Obvious	Jokey
	Bicycle, lycra, speeding	The boy wonder
	Breakfast, roast chicken, broken eggs, omelettes	A chicken and egg situation. Which came first? Treading on eggshells
	Aerobics, lycra, leotard, fitness	Let's get it together. Boxercise.
	Clock, late, on time	I'm late, I'm late for a very important date. Clock watching.
	Flame, wood, logs, fire B-B-Q	The fat is in the fire.
		Singing around the campfire

Try some equivalents in your L2. Sketch your own images, or insert some from the clip art in your word processing package. Build up more complex ideas with multiple images. If you put a top hat on the watch to really capture the Mad Hatter idea you are 90 per cent there, wrap a rabbit round the clock for 100 per cent accuracy. Images don't have to be 'correct', they are aids that help you. Hence a cigarette might prompt 'How was it for you darling' in your L2.

Top Tips

- Your passive vocabulary will always be greater than your active vocabulary. You can recognize far more expressions than you ever use. This applies to your first language as well as your second, BUT make it your business to convert as many words from the back of your mind to the front, from passive reserve to active service.

- Deck your walls with examples of mistakes you repeatedly make, and *really* need to get your head round. These are generally of the 'He's just went for a shower,' type, and well worth sorting before using them to try and chat up others abroad. Learn the appropriate rules, tables of endings, or whatever, off by heart: there are many ways of doing this – reciting out loud; writing lists; – repeat until perfection arrives! There is no such thing as a student of languages who is congenitally incapable of learning adjectival endings or the principal parts of strong verbs, whatever your friends may tell you or you may tell yourself.
- Use *mnemonics*. Invent a memorable sentence or a word containing the first letters of the rule or list you are learning (for example, PAD can help you remember that in German the correct word order for Prepositions is Accusative before Dative). A French example is: *On ouvre un livre et sur une page il y a une image d'un lion dans sa cage qui a la rage. Il sort de sa cage pour aller sur la plage faire de la nage.* All other common nouns ending in -age are masculine.
- Enlist a friend to learn together with, and listen to each other as you recite your rules.
- Many language departments encourage annual student drama performances, and the linguistic – not to mention social – gain from watching (or better still, getting involved in) these productions is not to be missed.
- Attend all social events where you can meet and talk to native speakers.
- Join mentor or buddy schemes – take any chance you get to talk in the L2.

Finally:

Language students aim at blasé, perfect 'native-speaker' fluency and accuracy (in a perfect world) but in practice there nearly always has to be a trade-off between the two. In the early stages of language learning, fluency is usually encouraged even if at the expense of accuracy, because it is considered very important to foster confidence in developing the active skills of speaking and writing. When it comes to the crunch, even at advanced stages of language acquisition, it is better to say or write something inaccurate than to just sit *stumm*, but as you progress, increasingly high standards of *both* accuracy *and* fluency will be expected of you. Provided you follow the course, and your tutors' advice, there is no reason why you should not achieve this.

2.5 References

Buzan Centre of the Great Lakes (1999) *Mind Mapping* [online] http://www.buzancentre.com/mm_desc.html

Buzan, T. and Buzan, B. (1995) *The Mind Map Book*. (rev. edn). London: BBC Books.

Lewis, M. (1999) *How to Study Foreign Languages.* Basingstoke and London: Macmillan Study Guides.

Lingu@net Europa (2000) [online] http://www.linguanet-europa.org/y2/ has extensive links and resources for European languages. Accessed 30 July 2000.

Mind Mapping FAQ (1999) [online] http://world.std.com/~emagic/mindmap.html. Accessed 30 July 2000.

Mind Tools Ltd. (1996) *Mind Tools – Helping you to Think your Way to an Excellent Life!* [online] http://www.demon.co.uk/mindtool/mindmaps.html (Includes a time management mind map as an example).

Works and Authors Wordsearch

12 pairs of literary works and their authors to find. Answers p 271.

L	L	E	S	U	O	H	S	L	L	O	D	A	F	A	R	F	N
A	E	F	I	W	Y	R	T	N	U	O	C	E	H	T	E	A	O
L	O	G	L	A	P	O	T	E	N	N	Y	S	O	N	F	N	O
B	A	P	R	S	L	F	T	C	H	A	R	L	E	S	E	I	N
A	R	G	A	A	S	F	A	S	P	E	M	X	E	H	C	N	E
T	E	W	K	E	H	R	R	S	L	A	N	R	R	E	O	E	S
R	L	O	R	D	L	C	H	E	T	O	E	R	S	A	M	R	B
O	L	D	O	O	M	N	S	O	D	M	T	Y	I	A	M	A	I
S	I	E	S	W	Y	C	H	E	R	L	E	Y	N	K	U	K	N
O	H	H	C	E	I	N	O	E	K	S	T	I	L	D	N	A	I
B	C	O	A	D	O	L	D	R	P	A	F	H	E	B	I	N	T
S	S	U	R	L	U	N	X	S	T	E	T	L	A	N	S	N	S
C	N	S	L	I	I	C	H	R	S	T	A	S	O	R	T	A	U
U	O	E	Z	W	T	E	S	T	A	I	M	R	E	A	D	I	A
R	V	O	Y	P	L	E	O	L	R	M	M	T	P	V	I	Y	E
E	F	D	X	P	B	S	H	E	L	L	E	Y	R	D	E	A	N
S	A	I	D	N	A	M	Y	Z	O	J	U	D	E	T	H	E	A
L	V	A	N	I	T	S	M	A	I	R	O	M	E	M	N	I	J

3 MAXIMIZING FREE TIME

It isn't what you know that matters, it's what you think of in time

University is different from school life and employment. There is ample time to snow-board, play street hockey, act, be elected Union Social Secretary, play the trumpet and socialize, but meeting coursework deadlines can be difficult. Time management techniques are especially vital for those with a heavy sport or social programme, a part-time job in term-time, and part-time and mature students with a job running in parallel with the degree. Developing your time management skills should allow you to do all the boring tasks efficiently, like laundry and essays, leaving free time for other activities. It is unlikely that any one idea will change your life overnight, but a few time-saving short cuts can relieve pressure. Try something. Use reflection and evaluation skills (Chapter 4) to identify what to do next and to assign time to your studies.

Ideally one can envisage research for an essay or a dissertation moving linearly from inception to final report or presentation (Figure 3.1A). Regrettably the research process is rarely this simple. The normal elements of life intervene, and the way you view and treat any topic usually changes as research progresses. This means that a linear research model is not realistic. The reality of normal progress, (Figure 3.1B) requires plenty of time for the research process to evolve. Half-way through your research you may have to go back almost to the start, reconsider your approach and execute a revised programme. Increasing your ability to manage your time, and recognizing and adjusting to changing goal posts, are vital skills improved at university.

Keep fit

3.1 Is there a spare minute?

Start by working out what time is available for research and study by filling out your timetable using **Try This 3.1**. Assume social and sport activities will fill every night, and all weekend, and that arriving at University before 10 a.m. is utterly impossible! The remaining moments are available for research, reading, thinking, planning and writing without touching the weekend or evenings. If you add a couple of evening sessions to the plan it will save money, due to temporary absence from bar or club, and get essays written. Divide this total research time by the number of modules to get a rough target of the hours available for support work per module.

Figure 3.1 The research process.

TRY THIS 3.1 – What spare/research time?

Fill in your timetable: lectures, social ... the works. Block out an hour for lunch and a couple of 30-minute coffee breaks each day. Add up the free hours between 10 a.m. and 5 p.m. to find your Total Research Time.

	Morning		Afternoon		Evening
Monday					
Tuesday					
Wednesday					
Thursday					
Friday					
Saturday					
Sunday					

3.2 What do I do now?

Confused? You will be.

University timetables can be complex, with classes in different places from week to week. So:

Diaries are vital. Managing them is a university and workplace skill.

A weekly skeleton timetable will locate blocks of time for study (**Try This 3.1**). Use it to allocate longer free sessions for tasks that take more concentration, like writing, reading and preparing for a tutorial or seminar. Use shorter, 1 hour sessions to do quick jobs, like tidying files, sorting lecture notes, summarizing the main points from a lecture, reading a paper photocopied for later, looking at vocab, highlighting urgent reading, on-line searches, thinking through an issue and making a list of points that you need to be clearer about. Don't be tempted to timetable every hour. Leave time for catching up when plans slip.

Lists. Sort out what you need to do under four headings: Urgent Now, Urgent Next Week, Weekly and Fun (Figure 3.2). If you tackle part of the non-urgent task list each week, you will be less overwhelmed by Urgent Now tasks at a later date. Have a go at **Try This 3.2**.

Urgent now	Urgent next week	Weekly	Fun
Essay: *Witches and Ghosts in French Supernatural Literature* By Friday: *French oral test! → Lang Lab*	Read for tutorial: *French Cinema* Find out about: *French women's literature*	Footie Ironing Supper	Friday: bungee jumping Party: Ed's birthday, get card and bottles

Figure 3.2 Keeping track of essentials.

TRY THIS 3.2 – Essential or not?

Do a quick version of Figure 3.2 for the next three weeks. Put a * against the items that you want to do in the next four days, and make a plan.

Photocopying a diary template with your regular commitments marked: lectures, tutorials, sport sessions, club and society meetings, gives a weekly skeleton for planning. If weekly planning is too tedious, go for the 30-second breakfast-time, back-of-an-envelope version. It can really assist on:

Chaotic days: Classes for one-hour spread across the day encourage time to disappear. There are free hours but *no time to do anything properly*. Completing short jobs will avoid breaking up days when there is more time. Something like this:

9 Lecture	10 *Coffee Anne and Dan*	11 Seminar	12 *Finish Italian Drama Seminar Reading. Lunch*	2 Italian Drama Seminar	3 *Sort file. Read last week's Culture and Class notes.*	4 *Culture and Class* Seminar	5–9 *Shop. Night Out*

and also on:

Average days: which are easier to manage. Two or more free hours give more research time for concentrated activities. Like this:

10–12 *Notes for Tutorial essay Theatre of Molière*	12 Lecture	1 *Lunch. e-mail*	2 Seminar	3–5 *Notes. Tutorial essay Theatre of Molière*	5–9 *Telly and 'phone calls.*

Knowing what you want to do in your research time, saves time. Deciding in advance to go to the library after a lecture should ensure you head off to the right floor with the notes and reading lists you need. Otherwise you emerge from a lecture, take 10 minutes to decide you would rather read about 'Italian Poets' than 'French film-script writing techniques', discover you haven't got the Italian Poets reading list, so look at the film-scripts list to decide which library and floor to visit. All this takes 45 minutes and the time has gone.

3.3 Tracking deadlines

Deadlines are easily forgotten. For some people a term or semester chart will highlight deadlines that initially seem far away. Figure 3.3 shows two chart styles. Which would suit you? The first is essentially a list, whereas the second one

Module	Assessment	Due date	Personal deadlines
SPAN1030 Lengua Española II	Oral	10 Dec.	*Language Labs, assignments 1–7 by November 25. Practise oral sessions with tutorial group by Dec. 1 and revise for Dec. 10*
PORT1010 Intro to Brazilian History	*Report: Postcolonial Brazil*	16 Dec.	*Sort out the main examples, read by 12 Dec. Write up by 15 Dec.*

Week No./ Date	Start of Teaching	Seminars	Tutorial	Essays
1 Sept. 29				
2 Oct. 6				
3 Oct. 13		Tues.: LING1010 Practical Phonetics	Weds: SLAV1040 Perceptions of Chekhov	Fri: SLAV1040 Pushkin's prose style
10 Dec. 1	Mod. Lang. Soc. Ball Thurs.	Mon: LING1060 Transformational grammar	Tues. ITAL1060 Oral Presentation	Fri: LING1070 Genetic influences on language delays in infancy
11 Dec. 8	End of Term. Xmas shop. Hall Dinner.	Tues: ITAL1060 Summary grammar test		Fri: SLAV1040 Chekhov and the Russian Theatre

Figure 3.3 Sample semester planners.

shows where pressure points build up. In this example weeks 3, 10 and 11 already look full. The essay due on Friday of week 10 needs finishing before the Ball on Thursday! This second style highlights weeks where personal research and reading time is limited by other commitments.

Essay Planning: Run it past yourself, backwards. Assuming the essay is due in seven weeks time. Allow:

a) Week 7: slippage, the worst 'flu ever, final checking and completing references (this is generous, unless you get 'flu).

b) Week 6: Finish final version.

c) Weeks 4 and 5: Read and draft sections, review and revise, repeat library and electronic searches.

d) Weeks 2-3: Brainstorm keywords, do library and Internet search, decide on main focus, highlight lecture notes and references, browse for additional information, start writing.

e) Week 1: Put the main jobs and deadline dates on your Semester plan and Urgent list (Figure 3.3).

OK, the chances of 1:1000 students doing this are small, but it is a good idea!

Dissertations: See the dissertation chapter (Chapter 20). Starting to plan dissertations early is a good idea!

3.4 WHAT NEXT?

Get into the habit of reviewing what you have to do and look at the relative importance of different activities, so you don't miss a deadline. Have a go at **Try This 3.3** as practice in prioritizing.

Tackling **Try This 3.3** might encourage you to use a day planner in Figure 3.4 style. To have a go write a 'to do' list for tomorrow, then order your activities. (2 = indicates an intention to be double tasking, in this case reading while the washing tumbles around.) Put some times against the activities. Ticking off jobs as they are done feels good!

TRY THIS 3.3 – Priorities?

Using yesterday as the example, jot down the time devoted to each task, amending the list to suit your activities. Then reflect on where you could re-jig things to release two lots of 20 minutes. Twenty minutes may not seem much, but if you grab a couple of slots to sort notes, re-read last week's lecture notes or skim an article, that's 40 minutes more than would have happened.

Real Life	Hours	Priority	Language Degree	Hours	Priority
Eating			Reading		
Sleeping			Browsing in the library		
Washing/Dressing			Lecture attendance		
Exercise			Sorting lecture notes		
Travelling			Writing		
TV			Thinking		
Other leisure ...			Planning time		
Reading for fun			On-line searches		
Housework					
Washing/Ironing					

Priority	MUST DO!	When
1	Post Mother's Day card	On way to college
2 =	Read chaps 3–5 of *French Cars* by Myra Neault	10–12
3	Look at translation exercise	12–1
2 =	Visit launderette	10–12
4 =	Check e-mail	After lunch
4 =	Spell check tutorial essay	After lunch
6	Lecture 2.00 in Lecture Theatre	2.00!
5	Sort out oral practice notes	After supper
7	Make a list of jobs for tomorrow	After supper

Figure 3.4 An organizer like this?

If you can do a task immediately and easily, that may be the most efficient approach. Generally it helps to allocate larger tasks to longer time chunks and leave little tasks for days that are broken up. Do not procrastinate: 'I cannot write this essay till I have read …' is a lousy excuse. No one can ever read all the relevant literature, so set a reading limit, then write, then go clubbing.

Top Tips

☺ Get an alarm clock/buzzer watch/timetable/diary.

☺ If the Languages library is full of your best mates wanting to chat, head to the Psychology or Biophysics library. Do tasks requiring total concentration in comfortable conditions where the lighting is good, the atmosphere conducive to study and no-one interrupts.

☺ You cannot learn 500 new Cantonese characters overnight – pace yourself, spread out this type of task over a week or more, use short slots and use memory games (**Try This 2.6**).

☺ Plan weekends well ahead; sport, socializing and shopping are crucial. Having worked hard all week, you need and deserve time off. Following a distracting, socially rich week, maybe there is time for some study. Sunday can be a good time to draft a report, and a great time for reading and thinking as very few people interrupt.

☺ Filing systems '… so many modules, so many handouts, my room should be a recycling depot'. Take 10 minutes each week to sort out notes and papers. Supermarkets let you have strong boxes free. Indexing files helps.

- ☺ Investigate the use of bibliographic databases to organize your references. Exploit your IT skills to save time. Computers and the Internet encourage a positive feeling of hours spent diligently communicating with the universe. It also takes hours. Are you being side-tracked? Ask 'Am I wasting good living time?'
- ☺ Good (OK, some or any) organization can save on stress later. Being stressed usually wastes time. Not all assignments are easy. Recognize that the difficult ones, and especially those everyone dislikes, will take longer and plan more time for them. Divide the tasks into manageable chunks and tackle them separately. Finishing parts of a task ahead of time gives you more opportunity to think around the topic.
- ☺ Vacations. Recover from term. Have a really good holiday. Consider taking a typing course, look at a speed-reading guide, or follow an on-line tutorial to improve IT skills. Think about dissertation possibilities.
- ☺ Time has a habit of drifting away very pleasantly. Can you spot and limit a little lost time when the pressure is on? Minimize walking across campus. Photocopy at lunchtime when you are in the Union anyway. Pick up mail while in the department. Ask 'Is this a trip I need to make?', 'Could I be more time efficient?' Make an agreement with a friend to do something in a certain time and reward yourselves afterwards.
- ☺ View apparently 'dead time', when walking to university or cleaning the bathroom, as a 'thinking opportunity'. Use it to plan an essay, mentally review lecture ideas, listen to a language tape . . .
- ☺ Be realistic. Most days do not map out as planned, things (people) happen, but a plan can make you a little more efficient some of the time.

If you decide to investigate some of these ideas, give them a real go for three weeks. Then re-read this Chapter, consider what helped and what did not, and try something else. Find a routine that suits you and recognize that a routine adopted in first year will evolve in following years. A realistic study timetable has a balance of social and fitness activities. Don't be too ambitious. If there was no reading time last week, finding 30 minutes to read one article is a step forward.

Language Quick Crossword 1

Answers p. 271

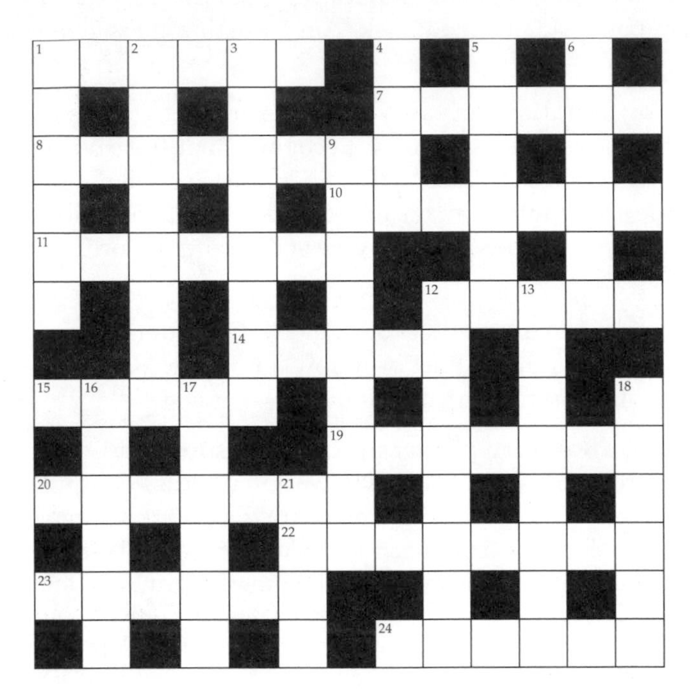

Across

1 Projection . . . in cheek (6)
7 Wilfully absent (6)
8 Place of happiness (8)
10 US tornado (sl.) (7)
11 French hairdresser (7)
12 What was intended (5)
14 A family phrase (5)
15 Write clearly (5)
19 A consonant sound (7)
20 Unresisting voice (7)
22 (A plant) just coming up (8)
23 Record or chronicle (6)
24 Catch in a net (6)

Down

1 Give a classic example (6)
2 Daffodils (8)
3 Not thought of (8)
4 Mixed meat dish (4)
5 Follow up (6)
6 Temporary resident researcher (6)
9 Artful plan (9)
12 One's initials (8)
13 Has an extravagant love of art (8)
16 One who uses books (6)
17 Greek king, toners (anag.) (6)
18 Irregular discolouration (6)
21 An assertive word (4)

4 REFLECTION SKILLS, REVIEWING AND EVALUATING, ADDING VALUE TO YOUR DEGREE

All my real skills are undervalued. I can say Bienvenue, Willkommen, Bienvenido, Benvenuto, Bemvindo, Welkom, Välkommen, Tervetuloa, Velkommen, Welcome too – so all my years of study haven't been wasted!

University language students are asked to become autonomous life-long learners who take responsibility for planning their own learning, deciding what to research and how to operate. This is a complicated way of saying it is up to you decide what to do and when to do it. Degrees involve hundreds of personal decisions about what to read, research, ignore, practise, panic over. . . . Getting your head around reviewing reduces associated worries and provides some sensible options when there are choices, although many decisions are motivated by a looming deadline. Taking control and responsibility for your work can seem scary, and the lack of guidance about academic work is one reason why so many new university students feel that they have been kicked into the melting pot without a lifeline and develop a growing inability to unmix a metaphor from a cliché.

This chapter discusses why evaluation and reflection are useful skills, and how reflection techniques can give you a framework to help your decision making in your studies. There are a variety of **Try This** activities because everyone has their own needs and priorities, and different activities will be relevant at different times of year and in different years of your degree. Most activities benefit from a 'mental and physical (pen in hand)' approach. The knack is to develop this style of thinking so that it becomes automatic; reviewing becomes a process you do while waiting for a cappuccino or defrosting a pizza.

The skill benefits from this chapter are thinking, evaluation, reviewing and reflection. Reflection skills are not easily taught, or acquired overnight. They develop with experience and maturity. They are the outcome of thinking actively about experiences and placing them in a personal context, an iterative process. They are used all the time in business.

4.1 Why reflect?

Adding value to your degree

Some students find it hard to see how parts of their degree course interconnect; this is de-motivating.

'My university course and people were really fun and I enjoyed the different language modules but I had no idea why the lecturers seemed so keen on History and Politics of the Hispanic World and Introduction to Society, Politics and History in the first year, but it did help me to talk to people when I was on the year abroad and understand more about the local issues. Final year modules like The Anarchist Passion and The Mexican Revolution were much more fun and I did much more reading for them.'

The proportion of time spent on literary and contemporary studies varies between courses. Staff aim to get you using your L2 fluently, accurately and appropriately in a variety of occupations and situations. Language graduates should communicate on a high linguistic level and have the cultural and social rapport which is fundamental to successful co-operation in business, administration, education and so on. Take a little time to think about the inter-connections between your modules; it should give more cohesion and be motivating. Try to keep the dual goals of linguistic skills and graduate skills in mind.

Increasing employability

Language graduates start with some skill advantages, their linguistic abilities and cultural awareness being obvious examples, BUT employers also want enthusiastic graduates with powers of articulation and reflection, those who can evaluate their experience and qualities, with examples. Recruiters want to identify people with the awareness and self-motivation to be pro-active about their learning. The ability to teach oneself, to be aware of the need to update one's personal and professional expertise, and to retrain, is vital for effective company or organizational performance and competition (Boud *et al.* 1993, Harvey *et al.* 1997, Hawkins and Winter 1995).

Your excellent grounding in foreign cultures may be of little interest to an employer who is looking for a 'good graduate' (whatever that is) and doesn't care that you also know a great deal about *Film Noir* and 1940s Hollywood. What is relevant is that, faced with the task of researching the market for a new 'dot com' product, you can apply the skills and experience gained through researching film texts and semiotics (thinking, reading, researching, presentation, making connections) to the 'dot com' market. It is your ability to use the skills acquired through school and university in a workplace role that an employer will value.

Remember that an employer is looking for a mix of skills, evidence of your intellectual, practical and interpersonal skills (look back at Figure 1.1). Your linguistic credentials are demonstrated by your degree certificate and international experience. You need also to include your practical, transferable and 'hands-on' skills on your *curriculum vitae* (CV). Keeping a record of your thoughts on forms like those in the **Try This** activities here, or in a diary or journal-style log, will pay off when filling in application forms. They will remind you of what you did and of the skills involved.

If you plan to work in very large multinational companies where skills training is a big budget item and there are many training courses, your life-long learning will be enhanced by company policy. If you want to establish your own business, or to join small and medium-sized enterprises (SMEs) with small numbers of employees and budgets, then your university skills will be directly beneficial. Linguists with 'additional skills' are very valuable employees.

4.2 Getting started

Some businesses require graduate trainees to keep a daily log in their early years of employment. It encourages staff to assess the relative importance of tasks and to be efficient managers of their time. It is a reflective exercise where at 4.50 pm each day, you complete a statement like:

> I have contributed to the organization's success/profits today by ....
>
> ....
>
> I was fully skilled to do ....
>
> I was less capable at ....
>
> Other comments ....

At the end of the week or month, these statements are used to prioritize business planning and one's Continuing Professional Development (CPD). It is an activity that most new employees hate. However, most will admit, later, that it taught them an enormous amount about their time and personal management style, and they wished they had started sooner. In time, this type of structured self-reflection becomes automatic; individuals continually evaluate their personal performance and respond accordingly.

The language student equivalent is to consider:

> I contributed to my language degree today by...
>
> ....
>
> I could have been more efficient at doing this if ....
>
> Tomorrow I am going to ....
>
> ....

Reviewing the whole day may seem too much of a drag. It may be easier to start by responding to statements like:

> What I have learned from this paper/lecture is..
>
> It agrees with ....
>
> It has an approach methodology we could use for...
>
> In future I will...

Reflecting in these three formats is good, BUT which language will you use? This is an opportunity to practise reflection in the language you are studying. Reflection offers an opportunity to develop vocabulary and writing. There are six **Try This** activities in this chapter, each suited to different stages of a degree course. These kinds of forms can be used to build up a learning log, recording your university experience. A learning log can act simply as a diary, somewhere to note activities and skills, but a reflective log asks for a more detailed, reasoned response.

4.3 Reflecting on your degree experience

Try This 4.1 asks you to articulate your feelings about your current, personal approach to learning and your degree course. If you then evaluate your response and decide to do something, you are taking charge.

TRY THIS 4.1 – Personal reflection

This is a random list of degree skills. For those relevant to you now, make a self-assessment of your current position and a reflective explanatory comment. Expand the list to suit your own situation.

Skill	*Current skill level*			*Comment*
	High		*Low*	
Delivering essays on time.			*	*I've had two extensions this semester. I need to sort out the technical problems ahead of the deadline, instead of on the day.*
Speaking in tutorials and seminars.			*	*I hate it. I really need some ways to get more relaxed in tutorials.*
Listening carefully to discussions and responding.	*			*I can do this, but I am still too concerned about whether people agree or not.*
Being efficient in library research.			*	*I spend hours going from one building to the next chasing up materials. I could try looking for alternative books in the same place.*
Knowing when to stop reading.		*		*I read to the last minute, and then rush the writing. Some reading deadlines would help.*
Making notes.				
Using accurate grammar, spelling and punctuation in writing.	*			*Pretty confident about my spelling. I need to find out how a grammar check on the computer works.*

Skill	***Current skill level* *High Low***	***Comment***
Using diagrams to illustrate points.		
Organizing ideas coherently.		
Including relevant information in essays.	*	*I try to include everything in an essay, to show I have done some reading!*
Including accurate information in reports and essays.		
Drawing the threads of an argument together to develop a logical conclusion.	*	*I've had 'weak concluding section' feedback on two essays. I haven't worked out how to address this yet.*
Summarizing information from different sources.		
Putting ideas into my own words.		
Negotiating.	*	*Managed a tricky situation in the group project session this week – feeling pretty good about it.*
Disagreeing in discussion without causing upset or being upset.	*	*Ditto*
Using newspaper databases to research current affairs.	*	*Am fine on* Der Spiegel *and* Le Monde *but haven't tried* Figaro *yet.*
Being more open to new ideas.		
Identifying the important points.	*	*Underlining or highlighting bits in notes would help and not take as long re-writing things.*
Being organized and systematic.	*	*My files are OK. If I used a diary it might help.*
Trying out new ideas.		
Making time to sit down and think about different ideas.	*	*This seems really odd, because you sort of do thinking all the time. It's not really a cool activity. Could try when no one knows – in bed maybe.*
Using IT for word processing.		
Reading appropriate material in another language.		

Try This 4.2 is a self-assessment exercise that you might want to repeat after a term or semester. Please note that when people self-assess a skill before and after an activity, the assessment at the end is frequently lower than that at the start.

Although the skill has been used and improved during the activity, by the end, it is possible to see how further practice and experience will lead to an higher skill or competence level. Now look at **Try This 4.2**. In thinking about your strengths and weaknesses, talk to family and friends and ask what skills you have and what you do well.

TRY THIS 4.2 – Being pro-active about skill development

Having completed **Try This 4.1** go back to the list and highlight three skills you would like to be proactive about in the next three months. Now make some notes about how to be active about these three issues. Like New Year resolutions, this activity can bear re-visiting.

Top Tips

- Reflection is reinforced when you write down your thoughts or speak them aloud.
- Reflection is even more useful in L2.

4.4 Within module reflection

Some modules will have a learning log as part of the assessment process, it may serve the dual purpose of a diary and a reflective statement. Practise by answering some of the questions in **Try This 4.3**. Adapt them for your modules, or for your degree as a whole.

TRY THIS 4.3 – Reflecting on a class or module

Pick a module, or part of it, and answer the questions that are appropriate. Some sample answers from language students are included on pp.271–2.

- What I want to get out of attending this module is..
- In what ways has this module/session helped me to develop a clearer idea of myself, my strengths and weaknesses?

Record your current thinking about the skills you *can* acquire from this module. Tick those you want to develop, and make a plan.

- I have discovered the following about myself with respect to: decision-making . . .; research . . .; thinking . . . .
- How efficiently did I (my group) work?
- How efficiently did I use my language skills?

- What skills did I use well, what skills did other members of the group use well?
- How did preparation for my (the group) presentation progress? What were my concerns?
- What skills were lacking in me (the group) and caused things to go badly?
- How did I (the group) make decisions?
- What have I learned about interview technique? / asking questions? / planning a project?
- What did I enjoy most about the exercise / session / module / degree course?
- What did I enjoy least about the exercise/ session / module / degree course?
- What was the biggest challenge for me in this exercise/ session / module / language degree?
- Give personal examples that illustrate two of the skills and attributes you have gained from this module.

The last four questions in **Try This 4.3** are frequently asked in interviews. Thinking of an answer in advance gives you more chance to enthuse and be positive. You may not have had much experience of some skills, but some experience is better than none.

TRY THIS 4.4 – Reflecting on a day

Brainstorm a list of things that happened (five minutes maximum, just a back-of-an-envelope list) e.g.:

- Went to Tai Kwando.
- Talked in Japanese to Suki for 30 minutes over lunch.
- Went to Dr Leibniz's lecture.
- Talked to Annabel.

Then brainstorm a list of things that made the class/day unsatisfactory, e.g.:

✗ Annabel went on for hours.
✗ Bus was late.
✗ I didn't understand what Dr Leibniz was going on about.
✗ Printer queues were hours long.

Leave the two lists on one side for a couple of hours. Then grab a cup of coffee, a pen, re-read your lists and make a note of where you might have saved time, or done something differently. Consider what might make life more satisfactory if these situations happen again:

✔ Chat to Annabel for an hour MAXIMUM over coffee and leave.
✔ Take a book on the bus.
✔ Have a look at Dr Leibniz's last three lectures. If it still doesn't make sense I will ask my tutor.
✔ Need to take something to read, or do on-line www searches, while printouts are chugging through.

Sometimes one recognizes that a particular lecture, class or day has passed without being of any real benefit to one's degree. Try to identify why; **Try This 4.4** and **Try This 4.5** contain some ideas.

TRY THIS 4.5 – Reflecting on a class

The seminar was: very useful / useful / OK / boring not worth going to.

The good things about it were...

The things that weakened it were..

To make it useful in retrospect I will .... (read ...., check out .... on the www, talk to ....)

In order to get more from the next seminar I will...

Analysing and reflecting on what is happening in a structured manner helps you feel more in control. Following up one in ten of the ideas you have is an improvement on the present. It is possible to review ideas in your head (the bus stop might be a good location) but writing down your list is likely to be more beneficial as this develops your reflective skills, and prompts actions on those reflections. Put your lists somewhere where you will see them again.

4.5 What to do first?

There are many competing demands on your time, what is the next priority? Is it to finish an essay, browse the library shelf for next week's lecture or read a set book? Reflect on who or what takes your time. Some tasks take longer than others, but the proportions should be roughly right. Questions that encourage prioritizing tasks include:

? Why am I doing this now; is it an urgent task (see also Figure 3.2)?

? Is the time allocated to a task matched by the reward? Does a module essay worth 33 per cent deserve five times the time devoted to a tutorial essay worth 20 per cent?

? When and where do I work best? Am I taking advantage of times when my brain is in gear?

? How long did the web search, seminar preparation, monitoring essay take? Were these times in proportion? Which elements deserved more time?

? Am I being interrupted unnecessarily? If I worked somewhere else would that help?

? How can I find another hour a week for study?

4.6 Start on your CV now

Use reflective material to amplify your CV. The thought of leaving university, applying for jobs, and starting a career is probably as far from your mind as the problems of Mexican bean growers. Nevertheless, if you want money from vacation work, having a focused CV could significantly increase your chances of selection for that highly paid shelf-filler or checkout job. Building up a CV as your degree course progresses saves time in the last year. An electronic CV designer may be available on-line; the university Careers Centre should be able to advise you. Reflecting at an early stage can highlight the absence of a particular 'skill'. There is time to get involved in something that will demonstrate you possess that skill before the end of your degree. Use **Try This 4.6**. If you have forgotten what skills your modules involved, look back at the course outline. There are big clues in statements like: 'On completion of the module students should be able to ....'.

TRY THIS 4.6 – Skills from my language degree

Expand and tailor this list for your degree, from your university. Be explicit in articulating the skills and the evidence. Update it each semester. There are a few starter suggestions in the second column.

Skill	Evidence of my ability
Spoken language.	*In addition to classes I meet 3 friends each week for conversation practice.*
Able to meet deadlines – essays, reports, projects etc.	*All essays completed on time.* *Organized group project and planned the mini-deadlines that kept our team on track.*
Team work skills, workshops, group work.	
Communication and presentation skills, tutorials, seminars and presentations.	*Used OHPs and video in tutorial and workshop presentations in Level 2 and PowerPoint in the Finalists' Conference.*
Computing skills.	
IT skills.	*Word processing of essays and 10,000 word dissertation.*
Able to put ideas across.	
Able to work individually.	
Time management skills.	

TRY THIS 2.6 – *Continued*

Skill	**Evidence of my ability**
Organizational skills.	*Final year dissertation. Interview study at local health centre during my foreign placement required co-ordination with GPs, ward staff, and patients.*
Self-motivated.	
Able to prioritize tasks.	
Problem-solving.	

Try This 4.6 does not include skills acquired through leisure pursuits or work experience. Compile a list of these: driving, shorthand, stocktaking, flying, writing for newspaper or magazine, treasurer, secretary and chair of societies, etc. involve skills like time management, negotiation, listening, writing reports. Work experience does not have to be paid; voluntary activities can give you valuable experience that pays dividends on a CV.

4.7 References and Further Reading

On the changing nature of work and the importance of skills, see the following:

Boud, D., Cohen, R. and Walker, D. (1993) *Using Experience for Learning*. Buckingham: Society for Research in Higher Education and Open University Press.

Harvey, L., Moon, S., Geall, V. and Bower, R. (1997) *Graduates' Work: Organisational Change and Students' Attributes*. Birmingham: Centre for Research into Quality and the Association of Graduate Recruiters.

Hawkins, P. and Winter, J. (1995) *Skills for Graduates in the 21st Century*. Birmingham: The Association of Graduate Recruiters.

Purcell, K. and Pitcher, J. (1996) *Great Expectation: The New Diversity of Graduate Skills and Aspirations*. Manchester: Higher Education Careers Services Unit, Careers Service Trust, Institute for Employment Research.

If these are unavailable in your library or Careers Centre, do a library keyword (see p. 50) search using career, lifelong learning, graduate skills and career development.

Wordplay Word Ladder

Change one letter at a time to make new words, each time you move down the ladder. Answers on p. 272.

B	A	R	D		C	A	S	E		C	O	P	Y		M	I	M	E		P	L	A	Y
N	O	D	E		P	O	E	T		P	L	O	T		W	O	R	D		S	T	O	P

5 LIBRARY AND ELECTRONIC RESOURCES

Excite your librarians – chat to them.

Once you discover that all the lecture notes you took so conscientiously are completely unintelligible, or if you did not get to a lecture, using the library might be a good idea. Inconveniently, the texts language students need are often catalogued under history, English, linguistics, politics, philosophy, psychology, sociology as well as under the particular language. This usually means Languages texts are at many locations and sometimes in different buildings. Some departments have their own collections too. Then there are all the electronic resources. Material can be accessed world-wide. Such fun. There is a maze of information, but finding the way around is not always obvious. While it may be way beyond Mulder and Scully, you CAN DO THIS – it is easier than learning the guitar. Skills employed include researching, evaluation, information retrieval, IT, flexible thinking and scheduling.

University libraries can seem scary and confusing. Most people feel very lost for the first few visits. This chapter gives information about library resources and research strategies, tips and hints that will, hopefully, reduce the mystery.

5.1 Library resources

For most library visits you need a library card to get in and out, cash or credit card for photocopying, paper for notes – and watch your bags; the opportunist thief finds a library attractive as people often leave bags while searching the shelves. Joining guided tours, watching videos and on-line explanations of your library's resources, and tips on accessing library and on-line documents will save hours of inefficient searching. Use the library staff. Ask them to show you how the catalogues and search engines work. Find out where the newspapers and periodicals are and where the collections for the other linked subjects you might need to refer to, and the collections for your option subjects, are kept.

Books and journals

You need to read academic journals as well as literature texts. Journals contain collections of articles written by experts, published in every area of academic study. They are the way in which academics communicate their thoughts, ideas, theories and results. The considerable advantage of a journal over a book is that its publication time is comparatively brief, usually one to two years. Recent journals contain the most recent research ideas. Check the location of:

- Recent issues of journals or periodicals, often stored in a separate area of the library. At the end of the year they will be bound and join the rest of the collection. Reading recent issues can give a real feel for the subject and topics of current research interest.
- The leading newspapers and periodicals in the language(s) you are studying.
- Oversized books – they do not readily fit on shelves, and are usually filed as Quartos at the end of a section. They are easy to miss.
- Stack collections containing less commonly used books and journals.

Catalogues

Universities have their own cataloguing systems. Happily, every library has handouts explaining how to retrieve material. Library information is accessed either via an on-line computer catalogue, which shows where the book should be shelved and whether the copies are on loan or not, or from a card index. Before searching, highlight the papers and books on the reading list you want to read. If the books are out check at the shelf references for alternative texts. If the on-line catalogue is accessible from any networked campus computer, you can do bibliographic searches and mark up reading lists while the library is shut.

How do you know which items on a Reading List are journals and which are books?

There is a convention in citing references, used in most texts and articles, that distinguishes journal articles from books, and from chapters in edited books. Traditionally, a book has its *TITLE* in italics (or underlined in hand written text); a journal article has the title of the *JOURNAL* in italics, and where the article is a chapter in an edited book the *BOOK TITLE* is in italics:

Lloyd, R. (1979) *Baudelaire et Hoffmann: Affinités et Influences.* Cambridge: Cambridge University Press.

Johnson, A. (1999) Reading Roberto Schwarz: Outside Out-of-place Ideas, *Journal of Latin American Cultural Studies*, 8, 1, 21–33.

Hughes, A. (1993) Gender Issues. In Cook, M. (Ed.) *French Culture Since 1945.* London: Longman.

For example, to find the Hughes article, search for Cook (1993). This convention eases library searches because, as a rule of thumb, you search for the italicized item first. You will never find the title of a journal article in a library main catalogue, but you will find the journal title and its library shelf location. In spotting journals look for numbers, as here 8, 1, 21–33, indicating volume 8, number or issue 1, and pages 21–33; books do not have this clue. Where there are no italics the game is more fun, you have to work out whether it is a journal or book you are chasing. (All students play this game; it's a university tradition.)

Unfortunately you cannot take out all the books at the beginning of term and keep them till you've finished your exams. Find out what you can borrow and for how long, and what is available at other local libraries, the city or town library. If a library does not hold the article or book you want, you can borrow it from the British Library via the inter-library loan service. There is likely to be a charge for this service, so be sure it is a book or article you need. Many university libraries offer short loan arrangements for material that staff have indicated everyone will want to read. Check out the system, especially the time restrictions on a loan. Return your books on time. *Fines are serious,* especially for restricted loans, and a real waste of good drinking money. When you need to get your hands on texts that are out, RECALL them. It encourages other people, especially staff, to return them.

On-line searches

On-line searches can be made using the title, author or keywords. Before searching make a list of keywords, sort out your Boolean operators and decide which language(s) to search. This may mean three when you add English and American spellings. Boolean operators? These make web searches saner. There are 3 main Boolean operators used either in words or symbol form: **AND OR NOT** or +, –. Searching for 'Green Party' yielded 2,226,765 hits. But searching for 'Green+Party' yielded 1,119,973 hits – a big improvement! This is much too broad a term. What do you really want to explore? 'Green+Party+traffic+Germany' hits 3305 sites whereas 'Green+Party+traffic+Deutschland' hits 87 sites. Here is a classic case for using the ',' or OR term as in 'Green+Party+traffic+Deutschland,Germany' or 'Green AND Party AND traffic AND Deutschland OR Germany' giving a more manageable, though still too long, research list with 187 hits. Searching for sites where the language is German cuts the list to 56 (Figure 5.1).

Think hard about what you want to include, and what needs excluding: 'policy, policies' should pick up entries for both. 'Perestroika **OR** glasnost **AND** Yeltsin **OR** Putin **NOT** Gorba*' should locate material on perestroika and glasnost but not in relation to Gorbachev. Use **OR** when there are synonyms, and **NOT** to exclude topics. The introduction or Help information for each electronic database should explain which symbols can be used for searches. Gorba* is a root word, like euro*, which will find all the words that have euro as the first 4 letters, like Europe, European and Eurotunnel. In the example here it should let you pick up variant spellings such as Danish 'Gorbatjov', German 'Gorbatschow', Spanish 'Gorbachov', Estonian 'Gorbatdðov', Norwegian 'Gorbatsjov', and so on. Beware using root* too liberally. Poli* will get politics, policy, politician, political which you might want, and policeman, polite, polish and Polish, which you might not.

You also have to decide which language(s) to search in, and whether to use key words in each language. American and English spellings of place names can add to your problems, as can different anglicized and American spellings. Here is a starter table for English, American and some French, German and English

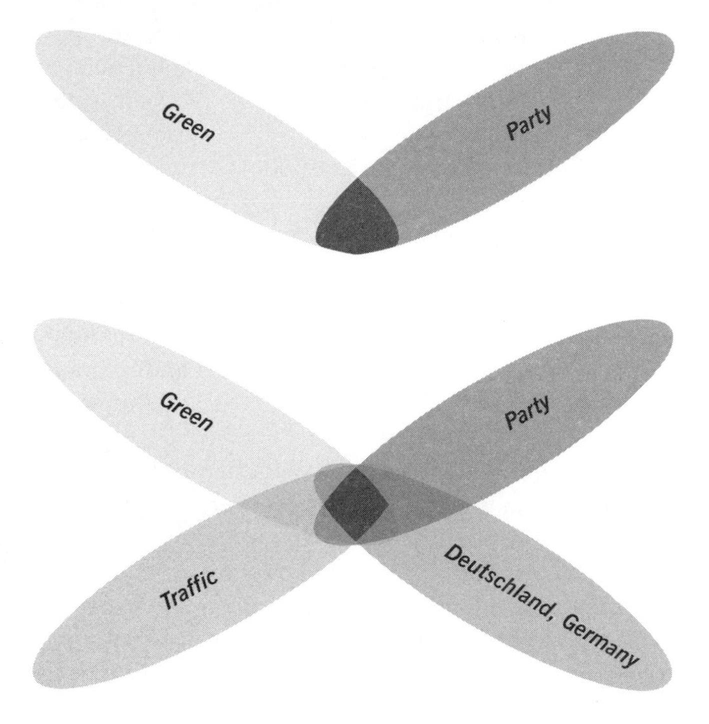

Figure 5.1 Refining searches with Boolean operators.

technical terms, but you could create your own language list to save time. Gender differences may also be relevant.

English	American	English	American	English	American
artefact	artifact	defence	defense	labour	labor
behaviour	behavior	dialogue	dialog	metre	meter
catalogue	catalog	draught	draft	mould	mold
centre	center	enclose	inclose	neighbour	neighbor
cheque	check	favourites	favorites	racquet	racket
colour	color	foetus	fetus	traveller	traveler
counsellor	counselor				

English	French	German
behaviour patterns	habitus	Verhaltensmuster
bilingualism	bilinguisme	Bilingualismus, Zweisprachigkeit
boundaries	frontières	Grenzen
coherence	cohérence	Kohärenz, Zusammenhang
cultural identity	identité culturelle kulturelle Identität	Kulturidentität,
dialect	dialecte	Dialekt, Mundart

English	French	German
discourse analysis	analyse de discours	Diskursanalyse
ethnic group	groupe ethnique/ ethniebout	Volksgruppe, ethnische Gruppe
functional linguistics	linguistique fonctionnelle	funktionale Linguistik
nation-state	état-nation	Nationalstaat
onomatopoeia	onomatopée	Lautmalerei, Onomatopöie
periphery	périphérie	Peripherie
slang	argot	Slang, Umgangssprache
vernacular language	langue vernaculaire	Landessprache, Volkssprache, Mundart

There is also the problem of place names. Internet searches for Lisboa or Köln will get you a great deal further than looking for Lisbon or Cologne, but logically use Lisboa **OR** Lisbon to cover the possibilities. There are many European examples to confuse and the problems increase when you tackle former countries of the Soviet Union, or the Far East. Some which are in common use include: Peking and Beijing, Ceylon and Sri Lanka, Burma and Myanmar, Canton and Guangzhou. You may need to cross-check through atlases, with map curators or *The Statesman's Year-Book* (Turner 2000).

5.2 Electronic resources

Databases

Databases contain information about journal publications and some include book details. There are usually author, title and source details and, in some cases, an abstract or short summary. Databases may be networked, held in a library CD-ROM collection, or accessed via the Internet. At best, only a few CD-ROMs will be available to you, because of the expense. Don't give your librarians a hard time if you cannot access them.

For UK students, the **Web of Science** is a goldmine and user-friendly. It holds details of academic papers in many journals. Check whether your library or local PC is networked to Web of Science, obtain a login name, password, and get on-line. You can search by authors and keywords. Explore the different options and menus to become familiar with what is on offer. Mark items of interest as you search, to download via e-mail to your own filespace.

Here is a selected list of databases that are of interest to linguists. BUT what sources can YOU access through your library? Your library catalogue should tell you.

Chicano Database (Latin American Studies) Bibliographic database for Mexican-American topics.

FRANCIS (International Humanities and Social Sciences publications). Bibliographic database indexing articles and books in many languages relating to the humanities and social sciences.

Goethes Werke im WWW. Full-text database of Goethe's complete written works.

Great Britain China Committee. Hyperlinked information on the People's Republic of China.

Handbook of Latin American Studies. Bibliographic database for Latin American Studies.

Hispanic American Periodicals Index. Bibliographic database for Hispanic America from 1970 to present.

MLA International Bibliography (Modern Languages Association). Bibliography of modern languages and literatures.

International Medieval Bibliography (IMB). Bibliography of medieval studies worldwide.

Online UK Chinese and Japanese library catalogues. Online Chinese and Japanese library catalogues.

Politique et Societé database. 300,000 references relating to France 1981–1995.

Russian Academy of Sciences Bibliographies. Bibliographic database derived from the Russian Academy of Sciences from 1992 to present.

SOCIOFILE. Citations and abstracts from journals in Sociology.

Teatro Español del Siglo de Oro (Spanish theatre). Full text database for Spanish Literature.

Voltaire éléctronique. Full text of the works of Voltaire.

World Wide Web (www)

The Web promises to be the most time wasting, but fun, element of a degree, while giving the comforting feeling of being busy on the computer all day. If you have no idea about the Internet and no option of doing a course at your university, do an online course – try Tonic (The Online Netskills Interactive Course) at http://www.netskills.ac.uk/TonicNG/cgi/sesame?tng

Use a keyword list as described above for library searches, (Mesopotamia, cultural change, Uruk, politics, archaeology) and Boolean logic to be precise in searches. Moving the cursor over highlighted text (usually blue) and double clicking the mouse will link to other documents. This is known as a *hypertext link*. Book marking 'favorite' pages will save you having to search from scratch for pages you use regularly. You should be able to e-mail documents to your own filespace, or save to floppy disc. On some computers you can open www and word processing packages simultaneously, and cut and paste between the two (but be aware of plagiarism issues).

Major problems can arise if you print files with pictures or graphics. Make sure the printer will handle graphics, or you will clog printer queues and run up an enormous printing bill. The www response rate is slow at some times of day. Be patient. Look around campus for the faster, newer machines. Check out some sites. **Try this 5.1:**

TRY THIS 5.1 WWW – Resources for linguists

Explore the resources available for your language and current lecture topics. All accessed 30 July 2000.

Do a web search with key words that include Linguistics, Language, Resources, ...

Starter sites might include:

BBC news on-line at http://news.bbc.co.uk/hi/english/uk/

Internet Resources for Language Teachers and Learners at http://www.hull.ac.uk/cti/langsite.htm

Languages, Linguistics, and Area Studies at http://www.lang.ltsn.ac.uk/

Linguistics Association of Great Britain at http://clwww.essex.ac.uk/LAGB/

Lingu@net Europa at http://www.linguanet-europa.org/y2/

US Census Bureau at http://www.census.gov/

The (London) Times at http://www.the-times.co.uk/news/pages/home.html

The Japan Times Online at http://www.japantimes.co.jp/

Virtual Library: Linguistics at http://www.emich.edu/~linguist/www-vl.html

WELL (Web Enhanced Language Learning) at http://www.well.ac.uk/menu.html (a site for modern language teachers, but with useful items).

Warning! Try This 5.2 could be totally useful or utterly frustrating. It is included because it will be useful to some people, but it may be obsolete before this book is published as everything changes so fast in this area. Some were accessed with an authorized login and password. Ask your librarian what is available to you. Do not get frustrated, libraries and departments cannot possibly afford to pay for access to all these sites. Not being able to access a specific item will not cause you to fail your degree.

Warning! The fact that a database exists is no guarantee that it holds the information you need.

Warning! www documents may be of limited quality, full of sloppy thinking and short of valid evidence. Be critical. Anyone can set up a www site. Look for reputable sites, especially if you intend to quote statistics and rely heavily on site information. Government and academic sites should be OK. Political party sites are potentially much less reliable, and may be positively misleading.

Warning! Think about information decay. Which time period does the content relate to? If you have economic or social data from the 1980s for Italy, or the former USSR, it will be fine for a study of that period in those regions, but of negligible value for a current day report. Check dates.

TRY THIS 5.2 – WWW

Develop your familiarity with www and library resources by accessing the following databases. Look at the page that describes the contents of the database – is it worth bookmarking for future use? Can you add other databases to this list? The addresses are given on p. 272, but find them yourself before looking.

Arnold Publishers home page.

Chicano Database (Mexican–American topics).

Consortium of University Research Libraries (CURL) Union Catalogue.

Deutsche Bibliothek Database.

Linguistics Abstracts Online.

Periodicals Content Index (PCI).

Russian Academy of Sciences Bibiography.

ITAR/TASS – News from the official state news agency for Russia, 1996+.

Reuters worldwide newswire – information for the last year.

E-journals

Electronic journals. Some journals of interest to language students are available on-line and the numbers will expand. Can you link to any of these, and how many more?

Europe-Asia Studies, German Life and Letters, Journal of Iberian and Latin American Studies, Journal of Linguistics, Journal of Phonetics, Language in Society, Language and Education (Accessed 30 July 2000).

5.3 Film, video and audio

Language courses with current affairs, sociological or historical elements often incorporate film and video material. This may include newsreel footage, interviews and programmes on specific topics specially produced for the educational market, and vast stocks of materials covering art, music and literature including interviews and videos of play performances. Entire modules are built around the study and analysis of a series of videos. Elsewhere, films or videos may appear on a 'reading list' as valuable additional sources of information. Either way, you need strategies for retrieving and managing the information efficiently.

Colleges store and catalogue video and audio material in various ways. It often depends on whether it was recorded off-air by the language centre or media services, or was bought commercially. Ready-made videos are treated like a book or CD-ROM and catalogued in the usual way (see p. 169). With off-air items, news broadcasts for instance, things get more tricky. They are often quite short and for practical reasons are stored on video cassettes along with other items, which may or may not be on related topics. But there will be a cataloguing system, so spend an hour finding out how the video and audio catalogues work. Do a few trial searches to really understand them, and try the machinery, including the index search facilities on the cassette players. If in doubt, get a member of staff to show you. A few leisurely minutes learning how to get the best out of the system saves hours of frustration when deadlines loom.

5.4 Research strategies

There are oodles of background research documents for just about every language topic, usually far too many. The trick in the library is to be efficient in sorting and evaluating what is available, relevant, timely and interesting. A library search strategy is outlined in Figure 5.2. Look at it carefully, especially the recommendations about balancing time between searching and reading. Library work is iterative. Remember that on-line searches can be done when the library is closed but computer laboratories are open. Become familiar with your local system. Use **Try This 5.3** and **Try This 5.4** as a starting point. Good library research skills include:

- Using exploration and retrieval tools efficiently.
- Reading and making notes.
- Evaluating the literature as you progress.
- Recording references and search citations systematically, so referencing or continuing the search at another time is straightforward.

TRY THIS 5.3 – Library search

Choose any topic from one of your modules. Make a list of three authors and six keywords. Do a search to explore the papers and texts available in your library. Compare the results with the reading list. Is there a paper that should be followed up which is not on the reading list?

TRY THIS 5.4 – Journal search

Use Web of Science and databases to check the authors and keywords used in Try This 5.3, but only note the journals in your library, those you can read later.

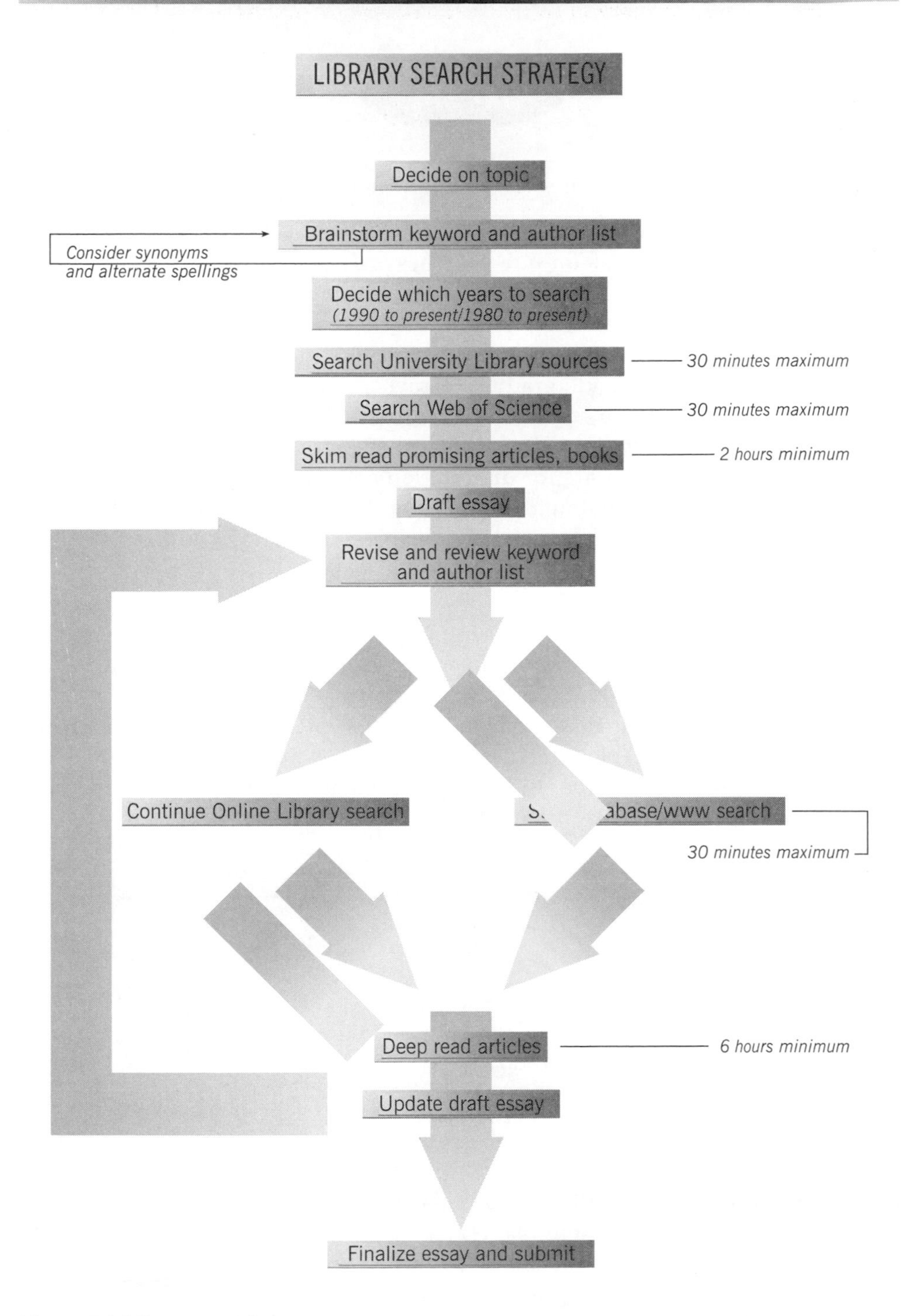

Figure 5.2 Library search strategy.

- Set a maximum of 30 minutes for on-line searching, then read for at least two hours.

Beware the enticements of on-line searches. It is possible to spend all day searching electronic sources. You will acquire searching skills and know that there is a paper with the ideal title in a library in Austria or in a language you can't read but you will have nothing for an essay. Ignore alluring www gateways during initial research. For most undergraduate essays and projects the resources in the library are adequate; search and read these articles first. Look at wider resources later, after the first draft is written, and only if there is bags of time. Internet searches are more appropriate for dissertation and extended project work. You cannot access and read everything. Essays have short deadlines, and reading time is limited. The trick is to find documents available locally and at no cost.

Reading lists

Some lecturers give long reading lists with lots of alternative reading. This is vital where members of large classes want to access documents simultaneously. Other lecturers give quite short reading lists, especially at levels 2 and 3. They may include essential reading items, and a list of authors and keywords. This approach allows each student to explore the available literature independently. Where the reading lists are of the first type, it is wise to view it as a big version of the second! Use **Try this 5.5** to explore an author's work.

TRY THIS 5.5 – Author search

Take one Languages author whose name appears on a reading list and design a library search to explore (a) what that author has written over a particular period, say 5 years; (b) what secondary literature has been published on these texts over the past 10 years. Then check the availability and locations of both (a) and (b) in your own library. (Hint: include databases, and the Arts and Humanities and Social Science indexes.)

Review articles

Review articles, especially those in a major journal such as *Modern Languages Review* or a specialist publication like *The Year's Work in Modern Languages*, record and evaluate all the leading scholarship published on a particular topic in a given year. These give illuminating syntheses of recent literature, and point you to other references. Some journals have themed issues. In 1999, the 250th anniversary of Goethe's birth, *German Life and Letters, Deutsche Vierteljahrsschrift* and others had themed issues on Germany's greatest writer and thinker. You may start out with one reference but in a themed volume there will be papers on interrelated topics that are, at the least, worth browsing.

Linked reading

If you happen to read Hyde (2010) you may realise you need to read Jekell (2005) in order to understand the later reference. It may seem obvious, but having read article A you may need to read article B to understand A. Cross-referencing is a normal process. Take accurate note of references to follow up.

Bias

Be particularly critical of sources which may have a bias or spin. Mass media materials and political web sites are particularly vulnerable to personal or biased reporting. They are not peer-reviewed. They can say anything. Think carefully about your information source and its quality before using it.

Which language?

You will get skilled in spotting the language articles written are in, which are available in translation, and which are worth chasing. Articles like Kawakami (1999) add interest by discussing in English Claudel writing in French about Japan including pictograms:

Kawakami, A. (1999) Claudel's Fragments of Japan: 'Co-naissance de l'autre' in Cent Phrases pour Évantails. *French Studies*, 53, 2, 176–188.

Use **Try This 5.6** to keep track of your reading, and a balance between electronic searching (30 minutes) and real reading (3++ hours.)

TRY THIS 5.6 – Self-assessment of a library search

Use this grid to keep a tally of sources and authorities when doing a library search or preparing a report or essay. Check for an advantageous balance of recent citations and that all the appropriate sources are used, in addition to those on the reading list.

Sources Used in Search for........................				
Books	Journal Articles	Government Reports	www Sites	Other

Number of papers NOT ON and ON the reading list:					
None	1	2–4	5–7	7–10	11+
/	/	/	/	/	

Number of papers from each time period:					
Pre-1980s	1980–1984	1985–1989	1990–1994	1995–1999	2000–date

5.5 Why am I searching?

Library searches are never done in isolation. Before starting, review your reasons for searching, and focus your keyword search. Limit your searching time and the types of document to search for. Suggestions include:

- *Module essay:* start with the reading list, and only explore further when you have an initial draft. Look critically at the gaps in your support material and use **Try This 5.6**.
- *'State of the art studies'*: explore the current state of knowledge on a topic. Limit searches to the last 2–5 years.
- *An historical investigation* of the development of an idea. Consider how knowledge has changed over 10, 20, or more years; aim for a balance between the older and newer references.
- *Literature review:* give the reader an outline of the 'state' of the topic. It may have a brief historical element, mapping the development of the subject knowledge, leading into a more detailed resumé of research from the past 5–10 years.

Do not forget international dimensions. The topic might be theoretical (cultural change, linguistic diversity, social influences, dialect) but there may be regional examples that are worth considering, so check out the journals of other countries. *Australian Journal of French Studies, Canadian Journal of Linguistics, Journal of Iberian and Latin American Studies, New Zealand Slavonic Journal* and *Yale French Studies* are international journals which also contain articles reflecting national and regional concerns.

WRITE UP AS YOU GO. Keep noting and drafting, and keep a record of references in full. Remember to add the reference, dates and pages on photocopies.

5.6 References and Further Reading

Battye, A. and Hintze, M.-A. (1992) *The French Language Today.* London: Routledge.

Tonic (n.d.) *The Online Netskills Interactive Course.* http://www.netskills.ac.uk/TonicNG/cgi/sesame?tng

Turner, B. (ed.) (2000) *The Stateman's Yearbook 2001,* (137th edn.) London: Macmillan Reference.

There are hundreds of starter guides to the Internet, check your library for your local copies that were published in the last three years. For updates to www sites see http://www.german.leeds.ac.uk/skillsbook/index.htm

Tales of Ancient Greece
MINNA TAUR
C'igue O'lo
Common Grammatical Errors
O Lavache
FOWE PARS
The Pig and the Carriage
– A Novella
Coche y Coche
THE HISTORY OF
THE ITALIAN MOTOR INDUSTRY
AL FRESCO
Dusty Rhodes
LANGUAGE STUDENT'S BOOKSHELF

6 EFFECTIVE READING

Reading goes faster if you don't worry about comprehension

You are 'reading' for a language degree, so it is not surprising that most time at university should (!) be spent with a book. Everyone reads – the knack is to read and learn at the same time. Pressure on library resources often limits the time books are available to you, so it is vital to maximize your learning. This chapter discusses some reading techniques and asks you to reflect on and evaluate what you do now, and to consider what you might do in future. As with salsa dancing, practice is required. There is a vast amount of information to grapple with in a language degree. Reading, thinking and note making are totally interlinked activities, but this chapter concentrates on the reading element.

6.1 Reading lists

Inconveniently, most language lecturers give you reading lists alphabetically by module, but you need them sorted by library and library floor location. Either use highlighter pens to indicate what is in which library, and take advantage of the nearest library shelf when time is limited, or make a list of the articles/chapters/papers you want to read each week. Now code it by *library, floor* and *classmark* rather than by module (see Figure 6.1) This list needs to be twice as long as you can reasonably do in a week, so that if a book is missing there are alternatives.

Author	Journal/Title	Class mark	Reading List	Library/Floor
Kuleshov V. 1997	*A.S. Pushkin: nauchno-khudozhestvennaia biografiia*	123.456	*Pushkin*	*Floor 1* *Slavonic Lib.*

Figure 6.1 Library list sorter.

Top Tip

- Carry Reading Lists at all times.

Reading lists are often dauntingly long, but you are not, usually, expected to read everything. Long lists give you choice in research topics and lots of options. Serendipity cheers the brain. If a book is 'On Loan', don't give up. There are probably three equally good texts on the same topic on the same shelf. Reading something is more helpful than reading nothing. Use the recall system to get hold of essential texts.

Students tend to request a module text and feel uncomfortable when a tutor says 'there is no set text'. Even where there is one, it may not be followed in detail. Reading recommended books is good, but watch out for those points where a lecturer disagrees with the text. Perhaps the author got it wrong, or our understanding of a topic has moved forward, or ideas have changed. Or perhaps your lecturer wants you to be aware of the extent of an ongoing debate in the area.

Language students tend to be avid readers and enjoy buying and owning books. There is always the temptation to snap books up on impulse, so include a realistic figure for books in your annual budget, and prioritize your purchases along the lines of essential (dictionaries and other reference works, set texts, and any others for daily or weekly use); important/useful (collections of essays, background material and reference works for less frequent use); supplementary/fun books you will read for pleasure and relaxation, maybe only once. Browsing in a bookshop leads to unexpected finds and gives maximum pleasure, but if you are after something in particular, check the retailers' websites for online savings before you buy. Can you buy some texts as a group and share? Watch the noticeboards for second-hand sales and check out second-hand bookshops and charity shops.

Reading in support of lecture modules is the obvious thing to do, and reading material in L2 simultaneously boosts your knowledge of language and content. Certainly the volume of reading expected for language modules is less than for content modules, but zero reading for language is not right either. Class activities tend to stress the hands on (vocal) elements, BUT you should still allocate plenty of time for reading, to understand more about the art and science of language.

- READ FOR ALL MODULES!

6.2 Reading Techniques

For most people there is a mega temptation to sit down in a comfy chair with a coffee and to start reading a book at page 1. **THIS IS A VERY BAD IDEA**. With many academic texts, by page 4, you will have cleaned the microwave, fixed a motorbike, sorted your CDs alphabetically and fallen asleep – or all four and more. This is great for the state of the house but a learning disaster.

Everyone uses a range of reading techniques – speed reading of novels, skip-reading headlines etc – the style depending on purpose. As you look through this section reflect on where you use each technique already. For effective study adopt the 'deep study' approach.

Deep study reading

Deep study reading is vital when you want to make connections, understand meanings, consider implications, and evaluate arguments. Reading deeply needs a strategic approach and time to cogitate.

Rowntree (1988) describes an active reading method known as SQ3R, which promotes deeper, more thoughtful reading. It is summarized in **Try This 6.1**. SQ3R is an acronym for Survey–Question–Read–Recall–Review. Give **Try This 6.1** a go; it may seem long-winded at first, but is worth pursuing because it links thinking with reading in a flexible manner. It stops you rushing into unproductive note making. You can use SQ3R with books and articles, and for summarizing notes during revision. You are likely to recall more by using this questioning and 'mental discussion' approach to reading. Having thought about SQ3R with books use **Try This 6.2.**

Browsing

Browsing is an important research activity used to search for information which is related and tangential, to widen your knowledge. In essence, it involves taking a broader view of the subject, which in turn provides you with a stronger base to add to with directed or specific reading. Browsing might involve checking out current affairs, history and introductory texts. Good sources of general and topical information include national newspapers and magazines. Browsing enables you to build up a sense of how languages as a whole, or particular parts of the subject, fit together. Becoming immersed in the language and experience of the topic encourages you to think about social, cultural and political issues in context.

Scanning

Scan when you want a specific item of information. Scan the contents page or index, letting your eyes rove around to spot key words and phrases. Chase up the references and then, carefully, (deep) read the points that are relevant for you.

TRY THIS 6.1 – SQ3R

SQ3R is a template for reading and thinking. Try it on the next book you pick up.

Survey: Look at the whole text before you get into parts in detail. Start with the cover, is this a respected author? When was it written? Is it dated?

Use the Contents and Chapter headings and subheadings to get an idea of the whole book and to locate the sections that are of interest to you. First and last paragraphs should highlight arguments and key points.

Question: You will recall more if you know why you are reading, so ask yourself some questions. Review your present knowledge, and then ask what else you want/need to know. Questions like: What is new in this reading? What can I learn from this book? Where does it fit in this course, other modules? Is this a supporting/refuting/contradictory piece of information?

Having previewed the book and developed your reasons for reading, you can also decide whether deep reading and note making is required, or whether scanning and some additions to previous notes, will suffice.

Read: This is the stage to start reading, but not necessarily from page 1; read the sections that are relevant for you and your present assignment. Read attentively but also critically. The first time you read you cannot get hold of all points and ideas.

On first reading: locate the main ideas. Get the general structure and subject content in your head. *Do not make notes during this first reading*, the detail gets in the way.

On second reading: chase up the detailed bits that you need for essays. Highlight or make notes of all essential points.

Recall: Do you understand what you have read? Give yourself a break, and then have a think about what you remember, and what you understand. This process makes you an active, learning reader. Ask yourself questions like: Can I explain this idea in my own words? Can I recall the key points without re-reading the original text?

Review: Now go back to the text and check the accuracy of your recall. Reviewing should tell you how much you have really absorbed. Review your steps and check main points: Are the headings and summaries first noted the right ones or do they need revising? Do new questions about the material arise now that you have gone through in detail? Have you missed anything important? Do you need more detail or examples? Fill in gaps and correct errors in your notes. Ask where your views fit with those of the authors. Do you agree/disagree?

The last question is 'Am I happy to give this book back to the library?'

TRY THIS 6.2 – SQ3R for papers

How do you adapt SQ3R to read a journal article? Work out a five point plan and try it on the next article you read.

Skimming

Skim read to get a quick impression or general overview of a book or article. Look for 'signposts': chapter headings, sub-headings, lists, figures, read first and last paragraphs/first and last sentences of a paragraph. Make a note of key words, phrases and points to summarize the main themes. Note, this is still not the same as detailed, deep reading.

Photoreading

Scheele (1993) describes a 'photoreading' method, one of many scanning techniques, that again requires you to identify your aims before scan reading and mentally and physically filing the contents.

When reading ask yourself:

? 'Is this making me think?'

? 'Am I getting a better grasp of the subject material?'

If the answer is no then try reading something else or using a different technique. Reading is about being selective. Cross-checking between articles, notes and more articles, looking back to be sure you understand the point and chasing up other points of view are all parts of the process. Breaking for coffee is OK and necessary! Talking to friends will help to put reading in perspective. Have a go at **Try This 6.3**.

TRY THIS 6.3 – Where do you read?

Where do you do different types of reading? 'I need pen and paper in hand to read and learn effectively?' How true is this for you? Three student responses to the first question are on p. 272. Have a quick look if you find reflecting on this difficult.

Academic journal articles and books are not racy thrillers. There should be a rational, logical argument, but there is rarely an exciting narrative. Usually, authors state their case and then explain the idea, position or argument, using careful reasoning. The writer should persuade the reader (you) of the merit of the case in an unemotional and independent manner. Academic writing is rarely overtly friendly or jolly in tone. You may well feel that the writer is completely wrong. You may disagree with the case presented. If so, do not 'bin the book'. Instead, make a list of your disagreements and build up your case for the opposition. If you agree, list supporting evidence and case examples. It keeps your brain in gear.

Organize your notes regularly

Get used to spotting cues or signposts to guide you to important points and the structure; phrases like 'The background indicates...', 'the results show ...', 'to summarize ...' or see **Try this 6.4** to find further examples.

TRY THIS 6.4 – Spotting reading cues

Look through one of the text books or articles you are reading at present, and pick out the cue words and phrases which identify key points and structure. There are some examples on p. 272.

6.3 How do you know what to read?

What do I know already?

Reading and note-making will be more focused if you first consider what you already know, and use this information to decide where reading can effectively fill the gaps. Use a flow or spider diagram (Figure 10.1) and mind maps (Try This 2.5, p. 24) to sort ideas. Put boxes around information you have already, circle areas which will benefit from more detail, check the reference list for documents to fill the gaps, and add them to the diagram. Then prioritize the information and references, making sure that you have an even spread of support material for the different issues. Coding and questioning encourage critical assessments and assist in 'what to do next' decisions.

Be critical of the literature

Before starting, make a list of main ideas or theories. While searching, mark the ideas that are new to you, tick those that reinforce lecture material, and highlight ideas to follow up in more detail. Questions to ask include:

- Is this idea up to date?
- Is the argument relevant/well argued?
- Are there more recent ideas?
- Are there better treatments/discussions of this subject?
- How does this paper or idea connect to the main thrust of the essay or argument?
- Is the evidence appropriate?
- Did the writer have a particular perspective that led to a bias in their interpretation/writing?
- Why did the authors research this area? Does their philosophy/methodology influence the results in a manner that might affect the interpretation?

Library, author and journal searches start the process, and practice allows you to judge the relative value of different documents. After reading, look at your author and keyword list again. Do you need to change it? Exploring diverse sources develops your research skills. Reading and quoting sources in addition to those on the reading list may seriously impress an examiner.

Narrow reading → predictable essays and reports → middling marks.

Wide reading → more creative, less predictable responses → higher marks (usually).

It doesn't normally matter what you read, or in what order. Read something.

How long to read for?

For most people two hours is long enough to concentrate on one topic. A short article should take much less. Longer documents need a reading strategy, and you need to take breaks. Use breaks to look at the SQ elements of SQ3R and decide whether your reading plan needs amending. If you cannot get involved maybe it's because you haven't found the point of the article or don't know why you should be interested. So STOP READING and skim the chapter and section headings, skim your notes, refresh your brain on WHY you are reading and what you want to get out of it.

6.4 Styles of writing

There are differences in writing styles across the literature, and some people have difficulty with reading and learning from certain kinds of writing. Styles range from the very direct through to the very discursive. Recognize that this variety leads to different reading, note-making and discussion styles matched to the different styles of writing and the kind of learning you need. Some social science, political and economic literature is technical in tone, characterized by short sentences and an information-rich content. Most of the language used in literary criticism is less direct and more discursive. Look for the broad themes rather than the detail. Writing styles reflect the discourse and approach adopted in particular areas of the discipline, and becoming familiar with the diversity of language is part of your training. The trick is to adapt your reading and note-making style to maximize your learning from different types of material.

For a very brief, factual style with diagrams see:

Batchelor, R.E. and Offord, M.H. (1993) *Using French: A Guide to Contemporary Usage*, Cambridge: Cambridge University Press, and compare that with the factual short sentence style adopted by Battye, A. and Hintze, M.-A. (1992) *The French Language Today*, London: Routledge. Take a look at Palmer, D. (1995) *Sartre for Beginners*, New York: Writers and Readers Pub., a book that reduces Sartre to a cartoon and key points (and is fun and useful) and compare that with the more discursive style of Hayman, R. (1986) *Writing Against: A Biography of Sartre*,

London: Weidenfeld and Nicolson. Can you use the approaches that Batchelor and Offord (1993) and Palmer (1995) offer to make (almost) waffle-free notes?

The paragraph above is a fine example of HOW NOT TO CITE REFERENCES. It should read:

For a very brief, factual style with diagrams see Batchelor and Offord (1993) and compare that with the factual short sentence style adopted by Battye and Hintze (1992). Take a look at Palmer (1995), a book that reduces Sartre to a cartoon and key points (and is fun and useful) and compare that with the more discursive style of Hayman (1986). Can you use the approaches that Batchelor and Offord (1993) and Palmer (1995) offer to make (almost) waffle free notes? (See Try This 8.1, pp. 88–89.)

Top Tips

- If you find certain articles difficult to read, it may be due to unfamiliarity with the topic, its setting and related information, rather than the written style. If an article seems difficult, try looking at some related, scene-setting materials and then re-read the paper.
- Ask yourself: 'Do I understand this?' Ask it at the end of a page, chapter, paper, tutorial, lecture … and not just at the end!

6.5 References and Further Reading

Using on-line searching to locate reading skills texts in your library may produce a long list. Refine the search by excluding TEFL (Teaching English as a Foreign Language) and school level texts.

Batchelor, R.E. and Offord, M.H. (1993) *Using French : A Guide to Contemporary Usage*. Cambridge: Cambridge University Press.
Battye, A. and Hintze, M.-A. (1992) *The French Language Today*. London: Routledge.
Buzan, T. (1971) *Speed Reading*. Devon: David and Charles.
Chambers E. and Northedge, A. (1997) *The Arts Good Study Guide*. Buckingham: Open University Press.
Girden, E.R. (1996). *Evaluating Research Articles from Start to Finish*. London: Sage.
Hayman, R. (1986) *Writing Against: A Biography of Sartre*. London: Weidenfeld and Nicolson.
Palmer, D. (1995) *Sartre for Beginners*. New York: Writers and Readers Pub.
Reynolds, M.C. (1992) *Reading for Understanding*. California: Wadsworth Publishing Company.

Rowntree, D. (1988) *Learn How to Study: A Guide for Students of All Ages* (3rd edn). London: Warner Books.

Scheele, P.R. (1993) *The PhotoReading Whole Mind System.* Minnesota: Learning Strategies Corporation.

Book Link

Add 2 letters in the middle squares to complete the 5-letter words to left and right. When complete the title of a book (8 letters) can be read. Answer p. 273.

G	A	N			P	A	N
C	L	O			X	U	S
D	I	C			R	I	E
C	A	D			M	I	T

7 TOOLS OF THE TRADE: DICTIONARIES, GRAMMARS AND OTHER REFERENCE MATERIALS

Leichtgläubig (Ger), Credulo (It), Facile à Duper (Fr), Crédulo (Sp), Hiszékeny (Hung), Dum (Da) – all words you won't find in dictionaries (Check it out).

All plumbers need wrenches, all linguists need the calorie shifting benefits of hefting weighty dictionaries. Why go weight training when you can swing the *OED*. This is a brief foray into resources to make your studies more successful. These tools are the vital crutches, zimmers, braces and struts that support a language degree. Modules like 'ARAB1003 Grammar 1' and 'RUSS3003 More Grammar' will take you into the idiosyncrasies of language, but try these apéritifs.

7.1 Dictionaries

Quelle différence y-a-t'il entre un dictionaire et un veau noyé?

L'un, c'est un vocabulaire, et l'autre c'est un veau qu'a bu l'eau.

Dictionaries come in two flavours, monolingual and bilingual; move something to get both on your bookshelf. The more proficient you become, the less you will need bilingual dictionaries but *everybody* (because learning a language is lifelong learning *par excellence*) needs them sometimes. Dictionaries also come in, literally, all shapes and sizes:

- Tiny pocket dictionaries, faithfully carried, but little used, on school exchanges.
- The great multi-volume dictionaries of the world. Body-builders may heft the *Deutsches Wörterbuch*, 32-volumes begun in 1854 by the Brothers Grimm of fairy-tale fame, and completed (by others!) in 1971, the *sept-tome, Grand*

Larousse de la langue française (1971) or the 20-volume Oxford English Dictionary (*OED*, 1989), now much lighter on CD-ROM (OED Online, 2000).

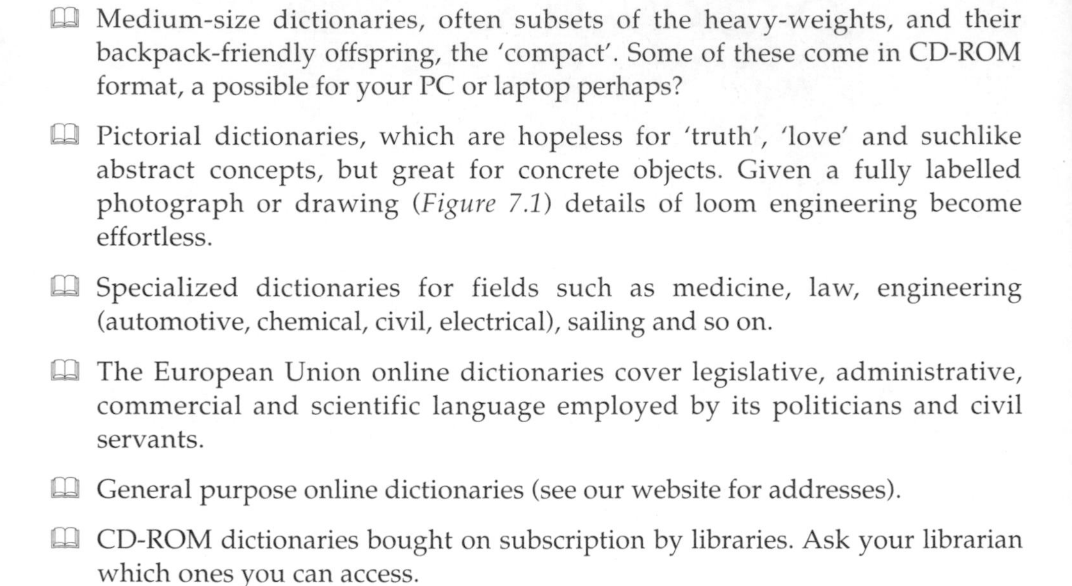

- Medium-size dictionaries, often subsets of the heavy-weights, and their backpack-friendly offspring, the 'compact'. Some of these come in CD-ROM format, a possible for your PC or laptop perhaps?
- Pictorial dictionaries, which are hopeless for 'truth', 'love' and suchlike abstract concepts, but great for concrete objects. Given a fully labelled photograph or drawing (*Figure 7.1*) details of loom engineering become effortless.
- Specialized dictionaries for fields such as medicine, law, engineering (automotive, chemical, civil, electrical), sailing and so on.
- The European Union online dictionaries cover legislative, administrative, commercial and scientific language employed by its politicians and civil servants.
- General purpose online dictionaries (see our website for addresses).
- CD-ROM dictionaries bought on subscription by libraries. Ask your librarian which ones you can access.

So which dictionary should you buy?

In the early stages of learning a language a pocket dictionary is *de rigueur*. Later on, you might like to have one in class despite the weight penalty! Go for a compact but don't expect it to provide much more than a basic look-up facility. For serious language assignments use the library reference materials, including the electronic dictionaries and grammars.

Back at base you need at least one good, medium-size dictionary. Your tutor may recommend one, but serious linguists can never have too many dictionaries, so if there are others you like the style of or are accustomed to, use them too. Sound out your fellow-students about *their* dictionary preferences, and when you are ready to go shopping, allow plenty of time to browse around to test out all the alternatives before you buy. Try looking up a few entries where you already know what to expect, including some idiomatic phrases which are difficult or complicated to translate, one or two grammatically tricky words, and a couple of technical terms. Note such things as:

- ✔ *Ease of use:* Are the headwords clearly identified? Are the entries clearly and logically ordered? Is there a coherent cross-referencing system? How would you rate the typography (choice of font, size, use of emphasis) for legibility?
- ✔ *Pronunciation guide:* Essential. See below.
- ✔ *Grammatical aids:* Look for a dictionary with concise grammatical data for each entry, linked to a succinct grammar section.

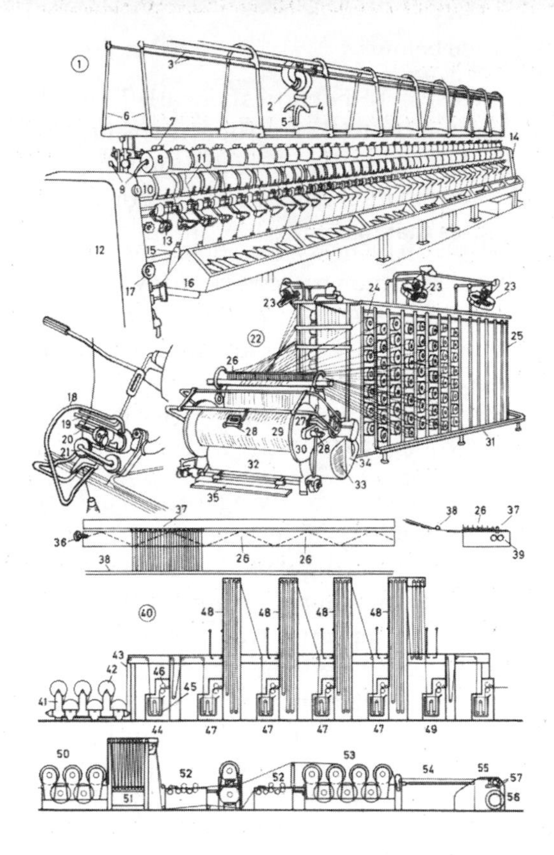

1.57 die Webereivorhereitung
- ***Processes preparatory to weaving***

1 die Kreuzspulmaschine
- *cone-winding frame*

2 das Wandergebläse
- traveling (Am. traveling) blower

3 die Lauftchiene, für das Wandergebläse
- *guide rail, for the traveling (Am. traveling) blower*

4 das Ventilatorgebläse
- *blowing assembly*

5 die Ausblasöffnung
- *blower aperture*

6 das Haltegestänge, für die Ventilatorschiene
- *superstructure for the blower rail*

7 die Anzeigevorrichtung, für den Kreuzspulendurchmesser
- *full-cone indicator*

8 die Kreuzspule, mit kreuzgeführten Fäden *m*
- *cross-wound cone*

9 der Spulenrahmen
- *cone creel*

10 der Nutenzylinder (die Schlitztrommel)
- *grooved cylinder*

11 der Zickzackschlitz, zur Fadenverkreuzung
- *guiding slot for cross-winding the threads*

12 der Seitentragrahmen, mit Motor *m*
- *side frame, housing the motor*

13 der Stellhebel, zum Abrücken *n* der Kreuzspule
- *tension and slub-catching device*

14 das Endgestell, mit Filtereinrichtung *f*
- *off–end framing with filter*

15 der Trosselkops
- *yarn package, a ring tube or mule cop*

16 der Kopsbehälter
- *yarn package container*

17 der Ein–und Ausrücker
- *starting and stopping lever*

18 der Bügel, zur Selbsteinfädlung
- *self-threading guide*

19 die automat. Abstellvorrichtung, bei Fadenburch *m*
- *broken thread stop motion*

20 der Schlitzfadenreiniger
- *thread cleorer*

21 die Belastungsscheibe, zur Fadenspannung
- *weighting disc (disk)for tensioning the thread*

22 die Zettelmaschine
- *warping machine*

23 der Ventilator
- *fan*

24 die Kreuzspule
- *cross-wound cone*

25 das Spulengatter
- *creel*

26 der verstellbare Kamm (Expansionskamm)
- *adjustable comb*

27 das Zettelmaschinengestell
- *warping machine frame*

28 der Garnmeterzähler
- *yarn length recorder*

29 der Zettel (Zettelbaum)
- *warp beam*

30 die Baumscheibe (Fadenscheibe)
- *beam flange*

31 die Schutzleiste
- *guard rail*

32 die Anlegewalze (Antriebswalze)
- *driving drum (driving cylinder)*

33 der Riemenantrieb
- *belt drive*

34 der Motor
- *motor*

35 das Einschaltfußbrett
- *release for starting the driving drum*

36 die Schraube, zur Kammbreiteveränderung
- *screw for adjusring the comb setting*

37 die Nadeln *f*, zur Abstellung bei Fadenbruch *m*
- *drop pins, for stopping the machine when a thread breaks*

38 die Streifstange
- *guide bar*

39 das Klemmwalzenpaar
- *drop pin rollers*

40 die Indigofärbeschlichtmaschine
- *Indigo dying and sizing machine*

41 das Ablaufgestell
- *take-off stand*

42 der Zettelbaum
- *warp beam*

43 die Zettelkette
- *warp*

44 der Netztrog
- *wetting trough*

45 die Tauchwalze
- *immersion roller*

46 die Quetschwalze
- *squeeze roller (mangle)*

47 der Färbetrog
- *dye liquor padding trough*

48 der Luftgang
- *air oxidation passage*

49 der Spültrog
- *washing trough*

50 der Zylindertrockner für die Vortrocknung
- *drying cylinders for pre-drying*

51 der Speicherkompensator
- *tension compensator (tension equalizer)*

52 die Schlichtmaschine
- *sizing machine*

53 der Zylindertrockner
- *drying cylinders*

54 das Trockenteilfeld
- *for cotton: stenter; for wool: tenter*

55 die Bäummaschine
- *beaming machine*

56 der geschlichete Kettbaum
- *sized warp beam*

57 die Preßrollen *f*
- *rollers*

Figure 7.1 The fun of a pictorial dictionary. (From: Oxford-Duden Pictorial German & English Dictionary, 1979, pp. 288–9).

- ✔ *Register and usage*: See below.
- ✔ *Vocabulary:* How extensive are the entries beneath the headword? It doesn't much matter if a dictionary for day-to-day use doesn't include archaisms, esoteric constructions or highly technical terms (which would make it too unwieldy in any case), but a good, up-to-date medium-size dictionary should contain most of the words and phrases that make up the contemporary language.
- ✔ *Size:* A reasonably sized dictionary for everyday use will have a similar number of entries and weight as: *Duden Deutsches Universalwörterbuch* (1996) – 120,000 headwords, of which 70,000 make up the central word-stock of the German language, or the bilingual *Oxford-Duden German Dictionary* (1997) – 260,000 words and phrases, and 450,000 translations, or the *Collins German–English, English–German Dictionary* (1997) – 280,000 headwords and 460,000 translations.
- ✔ *Information decay:* Languages are living organisms, they respond to their environment, new technology demands new terminology, obsolete items wither and die. Dictionaries struggle to keep up with the evolving language so check the publication date (on the reverse of the title page) before you buy. And distinguish between reprints (which means that the book sold well), revisions (varying degrees of updating) and completely new editions (major updating). We are great champions of second-hand and remaindered bookshops, and it is always worth picking up bargain older dictionaries, because one day you might need to know the meaning or translation of words like 'hansom cab' or 'whittling'. However, purchasing a discontinued edition as your *first* dictionary is a false economy.

What can you do with your dictionary?

Consulting a dictionary just for basic translations is merely scraping the surface. A good dictionary also tells you about:

- ☺ *Pronunciation and intonation:* This information usually appears immediately after the headword, in square brackets using phonetic symbols and stress marks to show emphasis. Even if your course doesn't include any training in phonetics, you should learn the International Phonetic Alphabet (IPA), at least as it applies to English and the language(s) you are studying. It won't take long, and you need ['nəvər mɪsprə'naʊns 'enɪθɪŋ 'evər ə'geɪ]!! http://www.sil.org/computing/catalog/ipahelp.html has some shareware software that may help you get into IPA. Do a www search using International Phonetic Alphabet.

- ☺ *Grammatical information:* Many dictionaries have separate sections on grammar, including basic information on verb conjugations, declensions and other essentials. Have a go at **Try This 7.1** and check out the grammar section of your dictionary.

TRY THIS 7.1 – Grammatical abbreviations

Take 5 minutes to remind yourself/learn the main abbreviations:

Abbreviation	Meaning	Abbreviation	Meaning	Abbreviation	Meaning
abs.	absolute	imper.	imperative	pluperf.	pluperfect
acc.	accusative	imperf.	imperfect	pos.	positive
adj.	adjective	impers.	impersonal	poss.	possessive
adv.	adverb	ind., indir.	indirect	pr.n.	proper noun
art.	article	indef.	indefinite	pred.	predicative
attrib.	attributive	int.	interjection	pref.	prefix
aux.	auxiliary	m., masc.	masculine	prep.	preposition
collect.	collective	n.	noun *or* neuter	pres.	present
comp.	comparative	neg.	negative	pret.	preterite
cond., condit.	conditional	neut.	neuter	pron.	pronoun
conj.	conjunction	nom.	nominative	rel.	relative
constr.	construed, construction	ns	nouns	suf.	suffix
dat.	dative	obj.	object	superl.	superlative
def.	definite	p.p.	past participle	s.v. v.aux.	strong verb auxiliary verb
dir.	direct	part.	participle	v., vb.	verb
f., fem.	feminine	pass.	passive	v.i.	intransitive verb
fut.	future	perf.	perfect	v.refl.	reflexive verb
gen.	gender *or* genitive	pl.	plural	v.t.	transitive verb

☺ *Register:* Some words carry labels to indicate when and where they are customarily used or not used (Figure 7.2). Watch out for derog, or sl./vulg. words that may be inappropriate in some contexts and you may need to check whether regional terms have widespread currency. Use **Try This 7.2** to get to grips with the conventions. Always respect distinctions of usage and style in your own writing and conversation.

TRY THIS 7.2 – Usage and style

Grab your foreign language dictionary and check out the usage and style conventions. Write all over Figure 7.2 (if it is your copy!) so that you have a useful parallel list in your foreign language.

Abbreviation	Meaning	Abbreviation	Meaning	Abbreviation	Meaning
aero., aeronaut.	aeronautics	comm., commerc.	commerce, commercial	joc.	jocular
agr., agric.	agriculture	derog.	derogatory	jur.	jurisprudence
Am., Amer.	American	dial.	dialect	lit.	*either* literal *or* literary
anat.	anatomy	eccl.	ecclesiastical	mar.	marine
arch.	archaic (but beware: can also	ecol.	ecology	mil.	military
	mean 'architecture')	econ.	economics	min.	mining
arch., archit.	architecture	euphem.	euphemism	obs.	obsolete
bibliog.	bibliography	fam.	familiar	pej.	pejorative
biol.	biology	fig.	figurative	prov.	proverbial
bot.	botany	hum.	humorous	rhet.	rhetorical
Br., Brit.	British	int.	interjection	sl.	slang
coll.	colloquial	iron.	ironical	typ.	typography, printing
				vulg.	vulgar

Figure 7.2 Register, usage and style.

- ☺ *Semantic groups and collocations:* Where a word has several different meanings or connotations in the source language, the dictionary will list and explain them one by one, giving examples of phrases or constructions with the word in context, showing how each one is handled in the foreign language. For example under 'pick up' there might be mention of a book, a sack of potatoes, the phone, a take-away, a scent, a virus, languages, the pieces, speed, someone from the station, someone at a party, etc. A good dictionary will show the foreign-language equivalents for each construction.

- ☺ *Compounds and phrases:* After the headword, you will usually find a list of compounds and phrases based on the root (which is normally indicated by a dash (-) or a tilde (~)), e.g. under 'garden' you might see 'kitchen ~, n.', 'market ~, n.', 'to ~, vb.' and 'to lead up the ~ path, fig.' The reward for paying close attention to these options is that you build up your vocabulary amazingly quickly, especially those colourful but more elusive turns of phrase. Noting how prefixes and suffixes act on the word-stem to modify meaning in compounds will give you a feel for word formation in the foreign language, and enable you to make educated guesses at compounds you're not sure about.

☺ *Synonyms:* Most dictionaries include synonyms and near-equivalents (often in brackets), along with cross-references to related entries. But this is where **monolingual dictionaries** really come into their own, and as a linguist you should own at least two of them, one for the foreign-language and the other for your native tongue. Get yourself a dictionary of synonyms (*Roget's Thesaurus* is the most famous, or its American counterpart, *Webster's New Dictionary of Synonyms*) and, if possible, one for your foreign language. Most word-processing packages offer a thesaurus, but this is severely limited compared to the wealth of ideas, associations and cross-references available in good printed versions. Use your thesaurus for all language work, especially for translations and essays. Keep it on top of the clutter!

☺ *Etymology:* A good monolingual dictionary indicates how a word and its uses have developed over time, and provides information about its etymology or derivation. Whole dictionaries are dedicated exclusively to this branch of linguistic science, but many general dictionaries include brief etymological notes, usually at the end of an entry. **Do not ignore this section!** It is fascinating in its own right, and of great practical use in helping you to connect what you know about the formation and meanings of words in your L2 with equivalent data in other languages, including your own.

Top Tips

- Get to know your dictionary, use it regularly.
- Don't rush. Using a dictionary effectively takes time! Some terms have exact word-for-word equivalences in two languages such as 'dishwasher' or 'golf course.' However, less tangible matters are much less clear-cut; explore and weigh up the alternatives.
- Always read (or at least skim) the whole dictionary entry, weigh up all the alternatives, it also widens your vocabulary. Jot down new related words, compounds or phrases to build up word clusters or families.
- Remember that dictionaries offer *equivalences* rather than *meanings*. Look for synonyms, related words, nuances and the figurative use of words, all of which are vitally important in language learning. Use more than one dictionary to explore the range of particular words and phrases.

- Languages use imagery. Look out for metaphors, similes and other figures of speech, and try to understand and assimilate the mental processes and the imagery that lie behind non-literal ways of expressing ideas in the foreign language.
- Memorize translation and grammatical information together. For a *noun* (depending on the language), this might mean *gender*, *declension* and *plural form*. For a verb, it might include *type* (weak, strong or irregular); which *auxiliary* is used; whether it is *transitive* or *intransitive*. Once you know the basic information and the corresponding grammatical rules, you can produce the correct forms in the foreign language effortlessly and accurately. Without these two sets of information, you are guessing.
- You recall new words more easily if you learn them in phrases or sentences. Make up and memorize (fun) phrases or sentences to remind you which verb is used with which noun in a particular construction, which preposition goes with which verb, and ...
- **Always** cross check words in both halves of a bilingual dictionary to ensure you pick an appropriate equivalent.

Thesaurus: an ancient dinosaur with excessive vocabular body-weight (Roget, coll.).

7.2 Grammar

Verbs has to agree with their subjects.

We all grasp grammar intuitively, but *understanding* grammar is an essential life skill for a linguist.

What is grammar, and where does it come from?

Grammar is the science which formulates rules to describe the workings of language, just like physics attempts to describe and codify the workings of the physical world. Physicists devise models and theories to help them make sense of their highly complex data, and similarly grammarians try to tease out the principles behind the multi-layered, multi-faceted entity that is language. The rules of grammar are, therefore, descriptive first and prescriptive second. Linguists distinguish between correct and incorrect usage. The rules of grammar are exemplified by the forms used by 'good' authors, the discourse of educated speakers and 'quality' newspapers and media. Correct usage is a much debated value judgement, but for present purposes we can assume that there is a broad consensus among grammarians as to what constitutes good French, Japanese, Hindi or Ket.

Grammar books draw on specialized terminology which you need to learn. It helps if you know the equivalent structures in your native tongue first. The

Make friends with your dictionary

structures and terminology of traditional English grammar, and all European languages, are derived from rules which describe the workings of Latin and Ancient Greek. This system assigns words to different classes, known as parts of speech, of which English has eight: nouns, pronouns, articles, verbs, adjectives, adverbs, prepositions and conjunctions. (For a reminder, with some amusing cartoons, see Gee and Watson 1990). Within each class, words are then further categorized according to a number of other features, e.g. a noun can have gender, number and case, a verb can have tense, voice and mood. Much of grammar is concerned with the relationships between words (e.g. *agreement*: Jane arrives at the party with her new Escort; Jane and Rachel leave the party with their new escorts). Syntax is the branch of grammar which analyses the structure of sentences and phrases and formulates rules accordingly.

But why do we have to learn grammar?

OK, OK, it is a pain. Many school students are taught languages by the 'direct method', where the first priority is communication, with grammatical accuracy coming a very poor second. This approach is great if you only want to acquire a general working knowledge of a foreign language. For 'dedicated' language students there eventually comes a time, irritatingly in the first year at university, when the necessity of producing accurate language and of following what your tutor is talking about means your grammar needs sorting.

You can live without grammar; most of the world does. But amid all the complexity of second language acquisition, it can be useful to have a framework and a set of guidelines, rather than just intuition, to fall back on. Native speakers and advanced learners refer to grammar books very occasionally to check a particular point. For the vast majority of language students, grammar books are invaluable tools, provided – as with chainsaws – they are handled sensibly and correctly. Grammar is a tool for the learner and language tutor who uses grammatical short-hand to avoid having to go through cumbersome circumlocutions. How much more convenient to say 'indirect object' rather than 'person or thing affected by occurrence of an action although not primarily acted on' (*OED*, 1989).

Children have oodles of time to absorb grammar and correct usage as they grow. They can experiment and get told off when they misuse words. You don't have that time and you need the short-hand methods. How do you learn?

? Complete immersion in an environment where the language is spoken is one option, but for most learners this is impractical. The year or term abroad serves as a valuable reinforcement rather than an initiation. And students report that even the year abroad tends to strengthen certain aspects of their language, notably colloquial dialogue, at the expense of others, notably formal writing. Alas! nothing is perfect, not even a year in Provence.

? Do you slot whatever you have learned into a logical or conceptual framework, like chemistry students learning the periodic table for elements? If so, you may well enjoy reading grammar books for their own sake, coming to grips with all the rules and exceptions to the rules, memorizing them and then relating them to authentic examples in the foreign language. And even if you aren't this type, there may be someone in your class who is, and the chances are that they enjoy explaining the rules and their application to other people. Cultivate them!

? Do you prefer to work from known expressions and examples rather than from theory? If so, you are probably good at storing patterns of words, phrases, sentences, or even whole passages in your head, and recalling them as and when the occasion demands. Are you like a good mimic, or an actor, who picks up and uses expressions almost unconsciously just from taking part in conversations? If you have this type of mind-set, you may come to grammar at a comparatively late stage in your language learning.

? Or what? – you have to find a learning style that works for you and works with your modules and assignments. Look at the reflection skills (Chapter 4) and see if you can see ways to help your own study patterns.

Most final year students agree that it is worth getting the recommended grammar reference book, but we also suggest that you look at others to see if they suit your style better. Many grammar books have built-in exercises; go for those with the answers at the back! These encourage autonomous learning and allow you to work on the exercises whenever you like (coach, sauna, cinema queue??) and to build up your command of grammar at your own pace.

We can't attempt to deal with the specifics of all the languages studied by readers of this book. Even a discussion of the major European languages is far beyond its scope and purpose. But the next section has some general study tips and advice about how to master grammar. Try them to find those that suit your learning style. We hope they help dispel the mystique, leaving grammar revealed as just another item in the toolkit of language acquisition.

Don't use long words where minuscule words will do.

Where should you start?

If you don't know the first thing about grammar, don't panic! There's quite a lot to be said for starting with something you do know quite a lot about – your native tongue. This may not work for the more 'exotic' languages, but those of Indo-European origin, which today means most European and Slavonic languages, have a broad family resemblance as far as grammar is concerned. For a real minimum see Figure 7.3.

Anglophones considering learning about English grammar might use Gee and Watson (1990) or try one of the websites devoted to English grammar like *The Internet Grammar of English* (1998). A www search using English+grammar will get you started (see p. 50).

Students of French, German, Italian, Latin, Russian or Spanish can have the best of both worlds by using one of the excellent *English Grammar for Students of [French, etc.]* series (Morton 1999, Zorach and Melin 1999, Adorni and Primorac

parts of speech	The term used to describe grammatical classes of words: noun, pronoun, adjective, verb, adverb, preposition, conjunction.
parse	To dismantle a sentence and assign a grammatical label to each word.
principal parts	'Those parts of a verb from which all others can be deduced' (*OED*, 1989). This is the whole point of learning the paradigm forms of classes of verbs. If you know the principal parts (the paradigms), you can apply the principles (!) to conjugate virtually any verb.
conjugate	'Applied to words which are directly derived from the same root or stem, and therefore usually of a kindred meaning; as wise, wisely, wisdom' (*OED*, 1989). Generally used with reference to verbs (see 'inflection' below).
decline	'To inflect (a noun, adjective, or pronoun) through its different cases; to go through or recite in order the cases of.' (*OED*, 1989).
declension	'a) The variation of the form of a noun, adjective, or pronoun, constituting its different cases; case inflexion. b) Each of the classes into which nouns of any language are grouped according to their inflexions. c) The act of declining i.e. setting forth in order the different cases of, a noun, adjective, or pronoun.' (*OED*, 1989).
indirect object	'Person (or thing) affected by the occurrence of an action, although not directly or primarily acted on ... Give *him* a book.' (*OED*, 1989).
inflect	'To vary the termination (of a word) in order to express different grammatical relations.' (*OED*, 1989).
inflection, inflexion	'The modification of the form of a word to express the different grammatical relations into which it may enter; including the declension of substantives [nouns], adjectives, and pronouns, the conjugation [number, tense] of verbs, the composition of adjectives and adverbs.' (*OED*, 1989).

Figure 7.3 Some common grammatical terms that tutors always expect students to know!

1999, Goldman and Szymanski 2000, Cruise 2000, Spinelli 1999). These books aim to explain grammatical points in the foreign language by reference to examples in English, that is, they work by analogy, from the known to the unknown, and the formula is a very successful one.

Horses for courses: grammar books for your L2

Grammar books vary. There is in practice a broad distinction between grammar books intended to cover the range from beginners to intermediate learners, and the very advanced reference grammars which attempt to provide a definitive coverage of every topic, every rule and every exception to every rule. Mostly you need the former, dip into the others only when life gets really serious. It's a bit like the difference between a JCB and a trowel. If you only want to plant a few daffodil bulbs, all you need is a trowel. If you want to dig a hole in the back garden a metre across and a metre deep, a spade is still more use to you than a mechanical digger. Only big tasks need big diggers. Similarly, there are levels and degrees of grammatical knowledge. Bear in mind that 'grammar' can be split up into many small portions of varying complexity – remembering this may help to make the apparently undo-able appear to be do-able after all.

The secret is to understand the difference between things you really must know about and be sure of getting right every time (the 'basics') and things you can be excused for getting wrong. Use **Try This 7.3**. and **Try This 7.4** to get into the groove. No one claiming to be even half-educated could get away with saying something like, 'He were right tired Saturday so he just stopped in bed and done nowt.' However, even educated people can get muddled about more obscure points of grammar (the difference between 'may' and 'might' for instance) without too much fire and brimstone raining down on their heads. In the same way, if you can consistently get the basics right in the foreign language, errors at a more sophisticated level stand a better chance of being condoned. This is NOT to be taken as an excuse for not bothering to master the more complex details of grammar but simply an acknowledgement that, depending on the level you have reached, some things are more urgent than others – some really obscure points can safely be left to the reference grammar, to be looked up as and when they are required.

TRY THIS 7.3 – Mastering the grammar basics in five easy steps

Tackling the basics – after all, it is basic mistakes such as endings and genders that most irritate red-pen-wielding tutors!

Step 1: With your marked written language exercises alongside you, go through the Contents page of your grammar book and note down the topics that most frequently cost you marks. (These will almost certainly be 'simple' things like genders and adjectival endings.)

Step 2: Create a study plan to cover, within one semester, all the grammar topics you consistently get wrong.

Step 3: Make a 20-minute slot for grammar study in your daily study plan and use it (Chapter 3 and **Try This 23.1**).

Step 4 *(optional but highly recommended):* Persuade a friend to do the same, with a different list of topics or in a different order.

Step 5: Set aside half-an-hour each week for revision. Use the time to: go back over a difficult section; try some test exercises on the topic(s) you covered that week; recite newly-learned verbs or whatever to a friend, listen to same; or – possibly best of all – explain a grammatical point to your friend until you have both got the hang of it.

That's it. Easy! Like all things connected with language, repetition and a regular routine are the keys to progress.

TRY THIS 7.4 – CALL Practice

Your Language Centre has sets of CALL (Computer-Assisted Language-Learning) grammar drills for all the languages taught in your college. Put time in your diary, ideally half an hour, twice a week, to do CALL grammar practice. Find the package that meets your needs, and stick with it. Using 30 minutes at the start of the day is a good tip – before your first lecture perhaps? You can download some CALL materials to your own machines from The Virtual CALL Library at http://www.sussex.ac.uk/langc/CALL.html

Top Tips

- Half-digested morsels of grammar can be highly toxic! Try to ensure you understand one topic before moving on to the next; ask a fellow-student or your tutor. This is what independent, autonomous university learning means (Chapter 4), working out what you need; and it won't be the same as what the guy along the corridor wants.
- Devise learning methods that work for *you*. For some, this means reading and listening to a large volume of authentic material in the foreign language, to help assimilate patterns and rhythms at first hand. Others find that rote learning suits them best, especially for the type of item that can be tabulated, such as adjectival endings or verb tenses. Either way, learning by combining the rules with examples, rather than just the rules on their own, helps glue them to the brain.
- There are many situations in grammar where logic is unable to come to your rescue. Remember, mind maps and mnemonics (pp. 24–6) may help. Eventually, you won't need to recite the mnemonic, because it will just 'sound' right or wrong. Often 'sounding right' is the only way a native speaker of English knows what is and what is not correct.

My Grammars not bad, she went to Cleethorpes last year wiv Grampar!

7.3 Specialist translating tools

Professional translators, and those training for a career as translators, have access to a comprehensive range of specialized reference works and translation aids. As well as conventional printed material such as dictionaries dedicated to specific subjects, there is a growing amount of software, some of it freely available, but most of it very expensive and aimed at the professional market. At their simplest level, the machine translation tools on the www are essentially databanks; you enter a word or phrase in the source language and it whizzes back the corresponding expression in the L2. Better packages offer several alternative translations, with examples in context, which illustrate how each term is used. One level up, there is translation software on the internet which can translate whole sentences more or less intelligibly. These websites can be very handy for a 'rough and ready' translation, especially of syntactically simple passages. If you need the gist of something of a technical nature, fine, but don't expect them to rise to either Shakespeare or the aerodynamics of the Space Shuttle! If your department has access to any of the software targeted at professional translators, try it. Commercial packages are very sophisticated. You can customize settings to suit needs and styles, build and maintain special vocabulary banks, and automatically deliver a draft translation. But material of any complexity still requires human intervention, post-editing, because no machine can match the human brain when it comes to that vital ingredient in translating – an understanding of the subject-matter.

And finally

Keep up the good work! The first trick is to get the 'basics'. But having got them and into the habit of working regularly on grammar, sort out a list of (more advanced) grammatical topics and incorporate them into your weekly work-plan. Remember to build in revision elements and to re-visit topics you learned earlier.

7.4 References and Further Reading

Adorni, S. and Primorac, K. (1999) *English Grammar for Students of Italian*. London: Arnold.

Collins German-English, English-German Dictionary (1997) (3rd edn). Glasgow: HarperCollins.

Cruise, E.J. (2000) *English Grammar for Students of Russian*. London: Arnold.

Crystal, D. (1997) *The Cambridge Encyclopedia of Language*. Cambridge: Cambridge University Press. [Excellent reference work on all aspects of language].

Duden Deutsches Universalwörterbuch (1996) (3rd edn). Mannheim: Dudenverlag.

Dupré, L. (1998) *Bugs in Writing, A Guide to Debugging your Prose*. Reading, MA: Addison-Wesley Longman Inc. [Fun].

Gee, R. and Watson, C. (1990) *The Usborne Book of Better English: Punctuation, Spelling, Grammar*. London: Usborne.

Goldman, N. and Szymanski, L. (2000) *English Grammar for Students of Latin*. London: Arnold.

Grande Larousse de la Langue Française (1971) Paris: Librairie Larousse.

Greenbaum, S. (1996) *The Oxford English Grammar*. Oxford: Oxford University Press.

Morton, J. (1999) *English Grammar for Students of French*. London: Arnold.
OED (1989) *Oxford English Dictionary* (2nd edn.). Oxford: Clarendon Press.
OED Online, Oxford English Dictionary Online (2000) CD-ROM. Oxford: Oxford University Press.
Oxford–Duden Pictorial German and English Dictionary German–English/English–German. (1979) (rev. edn.) Oxford: Clarendon.
Spinelli, E. (1999) *English Grammar for Students of Spanish*. London: Arnold.
Tallerman, M. (1998) *Understanding Syntax* London: Arnold. [Excellent introduction to the fundamentals of syntax. Draws on examples from over 80 languages, including English].
The Internet Grammar of English (1998) Survey of English Usage, Department of English Language and Literature at University College, London. [online] http://www.ucl.ac.uk/internet-grammar Accessed 30 July 2000.
The Virtual CALL Library. (2000) University of Sussex, Brighton [on-line] http://www.sussex.ac.uk/langc/CALL.html
Wardhaugh, R. (1995) *Understanding English Grammar*. Oxford: Blackwell.
Zorach, C. and Melin, C. (1999) *English Grammar for Students of German*. London: Arnold.

Links to a range of online dictionaries can be found on our web site or use the hotlinks from:

http://www.dis.strath.ac.uk/people/hendrik/Reference.html Accessed 30 July 2000.
http://www.lib.ed.ac.uk/lib/resources/collections/elrefcol/index.shtml#Dictionaries Accessed 30 July 2000.
Logos Multilingual Portal (2000) [online] http://www.logos.it/query/query.html Accessed 30 July 2000. [This is one example of translation software].

If your college library has a Linguistics section, look at the entries on grammatical terms in any of the encyclopedias of linguistics.

Authors, Poets and Philosophers Wordsearch

30 to find Answers p. 273.

S	O	L	Z	H	E	N	I	T	S	Y	N	N	O	R	M
I	A	P	T	R	E	B	U	A	L	F	W	S	M	E	A
L	T	R	T	A	C	R	O	L	A	I	C	R	A	G	I
N	W	O	T	A	N	I	A	W	T	H	C	E	R	N	S
E	O	U	C	R	F	L	E	T	I	R	M	H	K	I	N
S	O	S	S	Q	E	P	G	L	F	E	A	C	H	L	I
R	D	T	T	R	U	E	L	E	R	P	C	S	A	A	L
E	B	A	R	O	N	E	S	S	O	R	C	Z	Y	S	L
D	U	M	E	S	R	E	V	P	S	O	H	T	Y	E	O
N	E	D	T	R	O	Y	E	I	T	M	I	E	A	S	C
A	A	E	E	Z	T	E	O	C	L	E	A	I	M	P	E
S	I	S	R	K	C	O	C	A	E	L	V	N	A	I	I
N	S	I	A	H	C	R	A	M	U	A	E	B	N	N	K
A	N	G	O	G	O	L	E	R	E	I	L	O	M	O	L
H	O	U	S	E	M	A	N	S	Z	O	L	A	T	Z	I
G	N	I	V	R	I	N	O	T	G	N	I	H	S	A	W

8 MAKING EFFECTIVE NOTES

I made a mental note, but I've forgotten where I put it.

There is a mass of language information whizzing around in radio, video and TV reports, specialist documentaries, lectures, tutorials, discussion groups and all that written material including books, journals and newspapers. BUT, just because an article is in an academic journal, in the library, or on a reading list, does not make it a 'Note-Worthy' event. Making notes is time consuming, and ineffective if done on auto-pilot with the brain half-engaged. Note-making which lets you learn, requires your brain to be fully involved in asking questions and commenting on the ideas. Noting is not just about getting the facts down, it is also about identifying links between different pieces of information, contradictions and examples. Notes should record information in your own words, evaluate different points of view, and encourage the development of your own ideas and opinions. Note-taking is a multi-purpose activity, like ski-jumping, it gets easier with practice. Good questions to ask when making notes include: 'Is this making me think?' or 'Am I getting a clearer understanding of the topic?'

Many people start reading and making notes without any sort of preview. **A BAD IDEA.** They make pages of notes from the opening section and few, if any, from later in the document. The first pages of a book usually set the scene. Notes may only be needed from conclusion and discussion sections. Sometimes detailed notes are required, but sometimes keywords, definitions and brief summaries are fine. Use **Try This 8.1** to evaluate how the style and length of your note-making should change given different types of information, and consider how the SQ3R method (p. 65) fits in your note-making process. Then look at **Try This 8.2**, and reflect on what you do already. What could you do in future?

8.1 Making notes from presentations

Modern Languages lectures and seminars are awash with information so memory meltdown syndrome will loom. Make notes of important points – you cannot hope to note everything. Listen to the presenter's analysis of the topic and make connections. Highlight references mentioned by the lecturer, and keep a tally of new words. Your primary goal in presentations should be to participate actively, thinking around the subject material, not to record a perfect transcript of the proceedings. Get the gist and essentials down in your own words. Presenters that want you to concentrate on the presentation often give you handouts of the main

TRY THIS 8.1 – Styles of note-making

What styles of notes are needed for these different types of information? There are a few answers to kick start ideas (after Kneale 1998).

Academic content	Style of notes
Significant article but it repeats the content of the lecture.	*None, it is in the lecture notes, BUT check your notes and diagrams are accurate. Did you note relevant sources, authors?*
Fundamental background theory, partly covered in the lecture.	
An argument in favour of point x.	
An argument that contradicts the main point.	
An example from an odd situation where the general theory breaks down.	
A critically important case study.	
Just another case study.	
Interesting but off the point article.	*A sentence at most! HOWEVER, add a cross-reference in case it might be useful elsewhere.*
An unexpected insight from a different angle.	
An example/argument you agree with.	
An argument you think is unsound.	1. *Brief notes of the alternative line of argument, refs. and case examples.* 2. *Comment on why it does not work so the argument makes sense to you at revision.*
A superficial consideration of a big topic.	
A very detailed insight into a problem.	

TRY THIS 8.2 – How do you make notes?

Look at this jumble of note-making activities and ✔ those likely to assist learning, and put a ✘ against those likely to slow up learning.

What do you do already? Are there some ideas here that are worth adopting in the future?

	Leave wide margins		Ignore handouts
	Identify what is not said		Code references to follow up
	Compare and revise notes with friends		Store notes under washing
	Do loads of photocopying		Copy big chunks from books
	Underline main points		Always note references in full
	Use the library for socialising		Make notes from current affairs programmes
	Doodle lots		Make short notes of main points and headings
	Turn complex ideas into flow charts		Use cards for notes
	Ask lecturers about points that make no sense		Order and file notes weekly
	Ask questions		Jot down personal ideas
	Highlight main points		Share notes with friends
	Natter in lectures		Write illegibly
	Copy all OHTs		Use coloured pens for different points
	Scribble extra questions in margins		Write shopping lists in lectures
	Write down everything said in lectures		Annotate handouts
	Take notes from TV documentaries		Revise notes within three days of lectures

points; use these to jot occasional notes in the margin, and concentrate on the aural experience.

Lecture notes made at speed, in the darkness of a lecture theatre, are often scrappy, illegible and usually have something missing. If you put notes away at once, you may not be able to make sense of them later. Try to summarize and clarify notes within a day of the lecture. This reinforces ideas in your memory, stimulates further thoughts, and suggests reading priorities.

8.2 Making notes from documents

Noting from documents is easier than from lectures, because there is time to think about the issues, identify links to other material and write legibly the first time. You can read awkward passages again, but risk writing too much. Copying whole passages postpones the hard work of thinking through the material and thereby wastes time and paper. Summarizing is a skill that develops with practice. Give **Try This 8.3** a go next time you read a journal article – it won't work for all articles but is a start to structuring note-making.

TRY THIS 8.3 – Tackling journal articles

Use this as a guide when reading a journal article or chapter (from Kneale 1998).

1.	**First read the article**
2.	Write down the reference in full and the library location so you can find it again.
3.	Summarize the contents in two sentences.
4.	Summarize in one sentence the main conclusion.
5.	What are the strong points of the article?
6.	Do I agree/disagree with the argument, and why?
7.	How does this information fit with my current knowledge?
8.	What should I read to develop my understanding of this topic?

Think about where you will use your information. Scanning can save time if it avoids you making notes on an irrelevant article or one that repeats information you have already. In the latter case, a two line note may be enough, e.g.

Whydiffer (2010) supports O'Hackney's (2005) hypothesis of the causes of working-class prostitution around 1900 in his study of a comparable group of Argentinian women.

or

Dissenting arguments are presented by Dontlikeit (2010) and Notonyournellie (2010) who each undertook independent, detailed analyses of movements in electronics stocks and shares to define the extent of non-EU penetration of the market. Dontlikeit's main points are ...

or

> *Listenin (2010) studying 27 secondary schools in Norway and Sweden, showed cheating in phonetics exams to be widespread. Her results contrast with those of Whawastha's (2008) report on similar malpractices in Finland, because ...*

The fuller note may attract additional marks in an essay or exam. You do not have long to impress an examiner. An essay which draws on one case study as evidence is likely to do less well than one which covers a range of examples or cases albeit more briefly, PROVIDED THEY ARE RELEVANT. Make notes accordingly.

Top Tips

- **New words.** Almost every Modern Languages module has its specialist vocabulary. Keep a record of new words and check the spelling! The trick is to practise using the 'jargon of the subject' or 'languages-speak'. Get familiar with the use of words like mimesis, intertexuality historicism, catharsis, and oxymoron. If you are happy with language terminology, you will use it effectively.
- **How long?** 'How long should my notes be?' is a regular student query, and the answer relates to lengths of string. It depends on your purpose. Generally, if notes occupy more than one side of A4, or 1–5% of the text length, the topic must be of crucial importance. Some tutors will have apoplexy over the last statement. Of course there are cases where notes will be longer, but aiming for brevity is a good notion. **Try This 8.1** gave some guidelines.
- **Sources.** Keep an accurate record of all research sources and see Chapter 15 for advice on how to cite references.
- **Quotations.** A direct quotation can add substance and impact in writing, but must be timely, relevant and fully integrated. Always ensure quotations are properly referenced (Chapter 15). Reproducing pictures, diagrams or maps is also a form of quotation and again the source must be acknowledged. The amount of quotation that is tolerated, or encouraged, in an essay varies with the culture of the discipline. Direct quotations are comparatively rare in subjects that verge on the social sciences, but frequent in literary analysis, where they may be essential for the discussion of a text. A quote (but many tutors **loathe** the word 'quote'!) should be the only time when your notes exactly copy the text. Be careful not to distort the sense of the original when quoting out of context.
- **Plagiarism.** If you do not fully acknowledge your sources then the university may impose penalties, which can range from loss of marks to dismissal from a course. The regulations and penalties for plagiarism will be somewhere in your

University Handbook; something like: 'Any work submitted as part of any university assessment must be the student's own work. Any material quoted from other authors must be placed in quotation marks and full reference made to the original authors.' If you copy directly during note making, you run the risk of memorizing and repeating the material in an essay. It is therefore vital to adopt good note-making habits to avoid plagiarism. Read and think about ideas and main points, then make notes from your head, using your own language. Find new ways to express ideas. This is not as difficult as it seems, but practice helps. The original author wrote for a specific reason, but your reason and context for making notes is different. Keep asking questions and look for links to other references and modules. Notes should grab your attention, and make sense to you 10 weeks later. They may be shorter (or, exceptionally, longer) than the original but paraphrased in your language. Just swapping a couple of words is not enough. Using mind maps or flow and spider diagrams as a first step in note-making reduces the possibility of plagiarism. The style and language of the original author disappears behind a web of keywords and connecting arrows.

- **Check and share notes with friends.** Everyone has different ideas about what is important, so comparing summary notes with someone else will expand your understanding.

8.3 Techniques

Note-making is an activity where everyone has his or her own style. Aim to keep things simple, or you will take more time remembering your system than studying languages.

Which language?

As a general rule it's easier and more efficient to take notes in the language of the original, but see below. Trying to follow a lecture or read a book in Russian whilst translating the ideas into English in your head and then writing down coherent notes, is multi-tasking with a vengeance. Make life simpler:

- Write down only key words.
- Use your own words as far as possible.
- Use L1 or L2, whichever comes to hand.
- Don't worry about grammar or full sentences.
- Spider diagrams (Figure 10.1) or mind maps (Try This 2.5) can help.

Which medium?

Hang on while I staple this note to my floppy disk.

Cards encourage you to condense material, or use small writing. Shuffle and re-sort them for essays, presentations and revision.

Loose-leaf paper lets you file pages at the relevant point and move pages around, which is especially useful when you find inter-module connections.

Notebooks keep everything together, but leave spaces to add new information, comments and make links. Index the pages so you can find bits!

PCs and electronic organizers allow notes to be typed straight to disk. This saves time later, especially with cutting and pasting references. Keep information about different modules on separate floppies or in separate file folders on your hard disk.

Multi-coloured highlighting. Saunders (1994) suggests a colour code to highlight different types of information on *your own* notes, books and photocopies. He suggests: '*yellow* for key information and definitions; *green* for facts and figures worth learning; *pink* for principal ideas and links between things; *blue* for things you want to find out more about'. This approach requires lots of highlighter pens and consistency in their use, but it can be particularly useful when scanning your own documents. If this looks too complicated, use one highlighter pen – sparingly. On a P.C., changing the font colour or shading will do the same job.

Coding notes assists in dissecting structure, and picking out essential points. During revision, the act of classifying your notes stimulates thoughts about the types and relative importance of information. At its simplest, use a system of asterisks in the margin:

****	Vital	**	Useful
?*	Possible	↓	A good idea but not for this, cross-reference to ...

A more complex margin system distinguishes different types of information:

II	Main argument	B	Background or Introduction
I	Secondary argument	S	Summary
e.g.	Example	I	Irrelevant
[	Methodology, techniques	!!	Brilliant, must remember
R	Reservations – the 'Yes But' thoughts		
Π....	I agree	O	I disagree
?	Not sure about this, need to look at		to check it out.

Opinions. Note your own thoughts and opinions as you work. These are vital, BUT make sure you know which are notes from sources, and which your own opinions and comments. You could use two pens, one for text notes and the other for personal comments. Ask yourself questions like: 'What does this mean?' 'Is this conclusion fully justified?' 'Do I agree with the inferences drawn?' 'What has the researcher proved?' 'What is s/he guessing?' 'How do these results fit with what we knew before?' 'What are the implications for where we go next?'

Space. Leave spaces in notes, a wide margin or gaps, so you can add comments and opinions later. There is no time in lectures to pursue personal questions to a logical conclusion – do it when reviewing to re-focus your thoughts.

Abbreviations. Use abbreviations in notes **but not essays** – intro. for introduction; omitting vowels, 20c. for twentieth-century, histl for historical, Aufkl for Aufklärung or use symbols. You probably have a system already. Figure 8.1 has some suggestions.

+,&	and	?	question
=	is the same as	↑	is not the same as
→,>	leads to	←,<	is a result of, is derived from
xxx^n	diss^n as in dissertation	xxx^g	hear^g as in hearing
//	parallel to	Xpt	except
∴	therefore	∵	because
♂	male	♀	female
w/	with	w/o	without

Figure 8.1 Sample abbreviations for faster writing.

Millions of unordered notes will take hours to create but not necessarily promote learning. Aim for notes which:

- ☺ Are clear, lively, and limited in length.
- ☺ Add knowledge and make connections to other material.
- ☺ Include your own opinions and comments.
- ☺ Are searching and questioning.
- ☺ Guide or remind you what to do next.

Discuss everything

Finally, feeling guilty because you haven't made some, or any, notes is a waste of time and energy.

8.4 References and Further Reading

Kneale, P.E. (1998) Notes for Geography Students. *Journal of Geography in Higher Education*, Directions, 22, 3, 427–33.

Rowntree, D. (1988) *Learn How to Study: A Guide for Students of All Ages.* (3rd edn). London: Warner Books.

Saunders, D. (ed.) (1994) *The Complete Student Handbook.* Oxford: Blackwell.

Author Anagrams 2

Try these anagrams, answers p. 273.

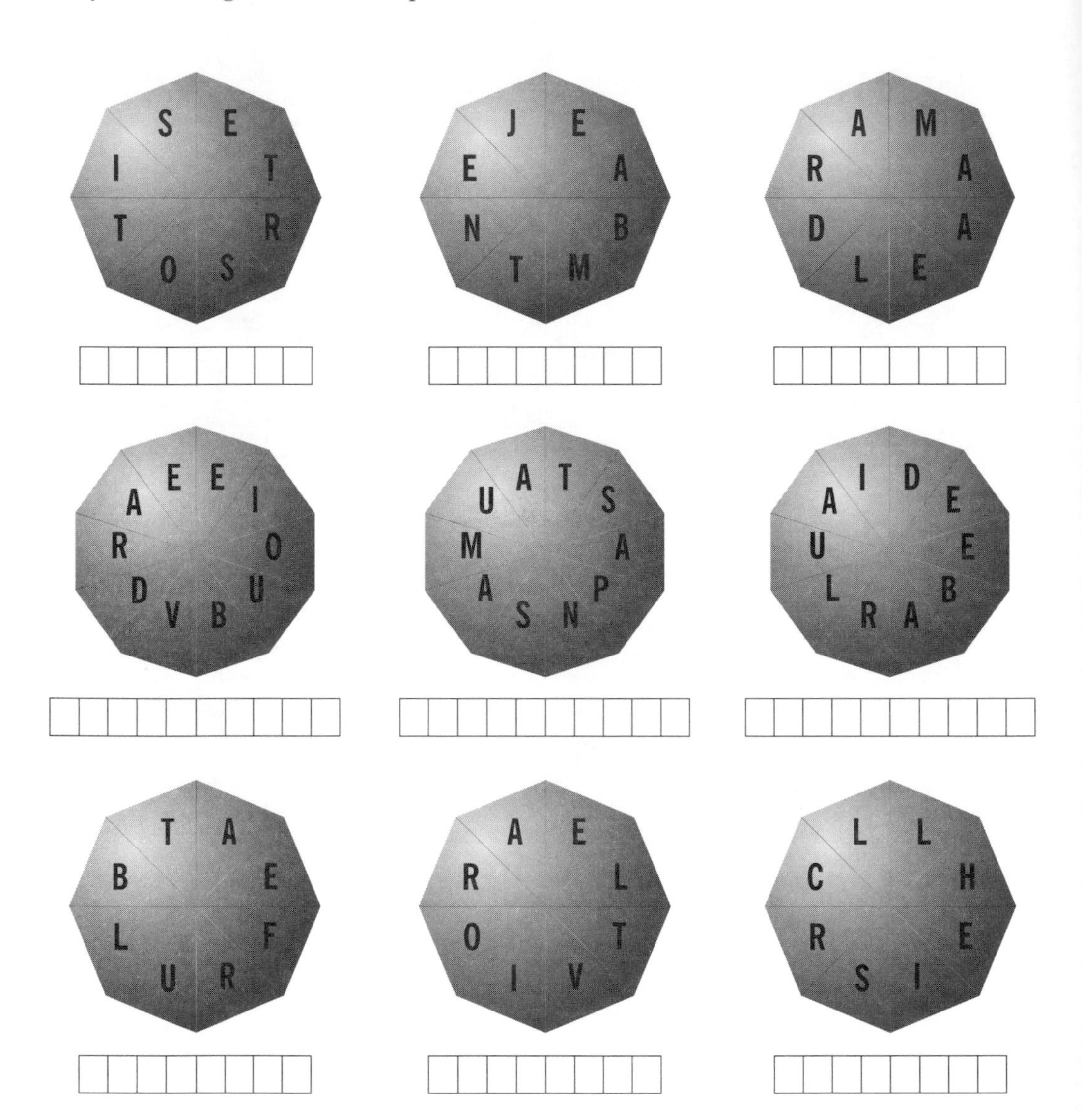

9 THINKING

"I don't think I understood what I said either"

Few people set aside 'time to think'. Indeed, refusing to go out on the grounds that 'I have to stay in and think about some really difficult grammar,' will not assist your street cred. Stick with 'washing my hair' or 'I want a quiet night in with a video'. For most people the effective stimulus to thinking is conversation and discussion. Being asked: 'What is your position on semiotics?' or 'How do you view St-Exupéry's use of the machine metaphor?' can stimulate thoughts you didn't know you had.

Language students are expected to apply their already well-developed thinking skills to a series of academic tasks and activities, to make reasoned judgements and arrive at conclusions about language-related issues. It is possible to pursue a languages degree at a rather superficial level, learning and re-presenting information. This is called surface learning. The aim of a university education is to practise the skills that move beyond this level to deeper learning, to being active in questioning, relating ideas and opinions to other parts of your degree and to other subjects, and developing one's ability to inter-relate evidence and draw valid conclusions. This links to the ideas of deep reading (p. 64).

Your intellectual sophistication should mature during a degree course, but it is sometimes difficult to know what this might mean in practice. To convey some aspects of this development UTMU (1976) takes Bloom's (1958) list of cognitive skills for university students, and unpacks them by assigning a series of associated verbs (Figure 9.1). More detailed criteria are outlined in Figure 9.2. Most universities and many departments publish similar statements in university and department handbooks, start of year lectures and briefings. Think about

Knowledge	Write; state; recall; recognize; select; reproduce; measure.
Comprehension	Identify; illustrate; represent; formulate; explain; contrast.
Application	Predict; select; assess; find; show; use; construct; compute.
Analysis	Select; compare; separate; differentiate; contrast; break down.
Synthesis	Summarize; argue; relate; précis; organize; generalize; conclude.
Evaluation	Judge; evaluate; support; attack; avoid; select; recognize; criticize.

Figure 9.1 Bloom's (1958) skills (from UTMU, 1976).

Level or Year	**Knowledge** *Broad knowledge and understanding of language and related areas. Fluency in subject vocabulary.*	**Analysis** *Problem-solving ability. Evidence of understanding. Ability to apply concepts to novel situations.*	**Synthesis** *Ability to bring together different facets of material, and to draw appropriate conclusions.*
1	Demonstrate a basic understanding of core subject areas, happy with language terminology. Demonstrate a knowledge of appropriate supporting analytical techniques (use of primary and secondary literature, bibliography, PC).	Apply analytical techniques through class examples. Understand that there may be unique or multiple interpretations of any issue. Appreciate the relative validity of results.	Be able to handle material that presents contrasting views on a topic and develop personal conclusions.
2	Demonstrate a comprehensive knowledge of specific subject areas. Be able to question the accuracy and completeness of information. Appreciate how different parts of the subject inter-relate.	Apply language methodologies and theories to individual situations and critically examine the outcomes. Understand that it may be appropriate to draw on multi-disciplinary approaches to analyse and interpret individual problems.	Locate and comment on diverse material, add personal research observations and integrate literature based information with personal ideas and opinions.
3	Demonstrate a deep understanding of a number of specialist subject areas and methods. Appreciate the provisional state of knowledge in particular subject areas.	Understand how to solve problems or offer interpretations with incomplete information, how to make appropriate assumptions. Develop appropriate research hypotheses.	Appreciate the breadth of information and interpretations available. Identify and tap into key elements of the material. Produce coherent discussions and reports.
MA	Demonstrate a broad, deep understanding of specialized subject areas and methods. Understand where this dovetails with the subject in general. Understand the current limits of knowledge.	Demonstrate an ability to propose solutions to problems involving appreciation of different approaches, gaps and contradictions in knowledge or information.	Be able to collate materials from a wide range of language and non-language sources. Integrate personal research materials in a coherent, thoughtful and professionally manner. Be able to work to a specified brief.

Figure 9.2 Skills matrix for language students.

Evaluation *Ability to review, assess and criticize one's own work and that of others in a fair and professional manner.*	**Creativity** *Ability to make an original, independent, personal contribution to the understanding of the subject.*	**Professionalism** *Ability to act as a language practitioner and researcher, to present arguments in a skilled and convincing manner and to work alone or in teams.*
Draw conclusions from results and identify the relative significance of a series of results. Evaluate the accuracy and reliability of information, interpretations and conclusions.	Offer original comment on language-related material. Display or present information in different ways.	Be effective in planning and using time and language resources, including libraries and computer packages. Present information, written and orally, to a high standard.
Review existing literature and identify gaps, appraise the significance of results and conclusions.	Develop original, independent research skills, interpret information and offer comment. Be able to display information in a variety of ways.	Confident use of computer packages for analysis and presentation. Confident group worker and collaborator in research activities. Produce written work to a high professional standard.
Critically appraise information, evidence and conclusions from own and others' work.	Gather new information through personal research, draw personal conclusions and show where these insights link to the main subject areas.	Be able to set objectives, focus on priorities, plan and execute project work to deadlines. Produce well structured and well argued essays, dissertations and reports. Demonstrate fluency in oral and electronic communications.
Perform independent critical evaluation of information, evidence and conclusions, including reliability, validity and significance. Be able to form and defend judgements in the light of contradictory information.	Offer insights into the materials under discussion that are independent of information immediately available. Propose investigative approaches to language-related problems using various approaches as appropriate.	Make confident, effective and professional presentations, answer detailed questions thoughtfully and clearly. Produce substantive reports that are well structured, well reasoned, well presented and clear. Work effectively as a team member and team leader.

where these statements match your experience. You are expected to progress from knowledge-dominated activities, to those with increased emphasis on analysis, synthesis, evaluation and creativity.

This chapter is a very minimal excursion into 'thinking'-related activities. It is very brief and partial, ignoring most of philosophy and the cognitive sciences. It concentrates on three elements – critical thinking, reasoning, and questions to encourage and focus your thinking. If you feel your thinking activities could take a little more polishing, then think through the ideas here. Like bicycle stunt riding, thinking gets better with time, not overnight. Thinking is tough.

9.1 Why do you think?

Cogito ergo sum: I think, therefore I am (Descartes)

Thinking is used to acquire understanding and answers. Adjectives used to describe quality thinking include reasoned, clear, logical, precise, relevant, broad, rational, sound, sensible and creative. Steps in quality thinking involve:

- Deciding on the objective (understanding a concept, recognizing the issues).
- Defining the background assumptions.
- Acquiring information and evidence of a suitable standard to build up a reasoned argument.
- Reasoning or inferring from the available information to draw logical conclusions.
- Considering the consequences of the results.

How good you are at thinking is a matter for personal development and self-assessment. When tackling multi-dimensional language problems, make notes while thinking, plot your thoughts on spider diagrams, and record connections and links as they occur to you. Ideas float away all too easily.

9.2 Critical thinking

Critical thinking involves working through for oneself, afresh, a problem. This means starting by thinking about the nature of the problem, thinking through the issues and striving for a reasoned, logical outcome. During the process you need to be aware of other factors that impinge, where bias may be entering an argument, the evidence for and against the issues involved, and to search for links to other parts of your language course. Essentially, critically evaluating the material throughout the process. Mind maps can be a helpful way of putting ideas on paper and finding the links between them (Buzan and Buzan 1995, **Try This 2.5**).

Being critical entails making judgements on the information you have at the time. It is important to remember that being critical does not necessarily imply being negative and derogatory. It also means being positive and supportive, commenting in a thoughtful way. A balanced critique looks at the positive and negative aspects. Some students feel they cannot make such judgements because they are unqualified to do so. Recognize that neither you, nor your teachers, will ever know everything – you are making a judgement based on what you know now. In a year's time, with more information and experience, your views and values may alter, but that will be a subsequent judgement made in the light of different information.

Discussion is a major thinking aid, so talk about language and related issues. It can be provocative and stimulating!

Where does **intellectual curiosity** fit into this picture? Research in language studies is about being curious about concepts and ideas. You can be curious in a general way, essentially pursuing ideas at random as they grab your imagination. We all do this. More disciplined thinking aims to give a framework for pursuing ideas in a logical manner and to back up ideas and statements with solid evidence in every case.

What to avoid. Uncritical, surface learning involves listening and noting from lectures and documents, committing this information to memory and regurgitating it in essays and examinations. The 'understanding' step is missing, and the rewards will be missing too. Aim to be a deeper learner.

9.3 Reasoning

Strong essay and examination answers look at the issues, develop robust arguments, draw inferences and come to conclusions. Judgements need to be reasoned, balanced and supported. First think about the difference between **reasoned** and **subjective reactions,** and reflect on how you go about thinking. Subjective reaction is the process of asserting facts, of making unsupported statements, whereas reasoning involves working out, or reasoning out, on the basis of evidence, a logical argument to support or disprove one's case (Figure 9.3).

Subjective statement	Reasoned statement
'Max Frisch portrays the Swiss as xenophobic'	'In *Andorra* (1961), Frisch explores a community under threat. The inhabitants of his fictitious Andorra respond in a variety of ways – aggressive, protective, defensive – to invasion by a Nazi-style army in pursuit of a victim.'

Figure 9.3 Examples of subjective and reasoned statements.

Support arguments with evidence

Create examples of reasoned rather than subjective statements with **Try This 9.1**. In your academic thinking and communications, avoid making emotional responses or appeals, assertions without evidence, subjective statements, analogies that are not parallel cases, and inferences based on little information – unless you qualify the argument with caveats.

TRY THIS 9.1 – Reasoned statements

Either write a fuller, reasoned version of the four subjective statements below, OR pick a few sentences from a recent essay and rewrite them with more evidence, examples and references.

1. Camus is too depressing an author to be let loose on the young.
2. The cost of breaking up the USSR has crippled the new states over the past 10 years.
3. The Austrians have very right-wing tendencies.
4. The Chinese economy is booming at the expense of the West.

9.4 Thinking in a Foreign Language

Becoming confident enough to construct complex statements in your foreign language takes a lot of practice, but you can make a start and build on it whenever you like. The next time you go to the supermarket for the week's groceries, try talking to yourself (under your breath, unless you are an incorrigible exhibitionist) in your L2. If this works – i.e. you don't get any silly answers – extend the process until you are both thinking and responding mentally to what is going on around you in the foreign language. This works much better abroad, of course, but it *can* be done in the UK as well. The trick is to project yourself mentally into the foreign environment and to respond accordingly. When you get to the point where your first thought when you wake up is in the foreign tongue, you've cracked it!

Next, try it in lectures. The basic rule is, take notes in the language of delivery, L2 lecture = L2 notes. But practise making L2 notes in L1 classes occasionally. Don't worry, if this proves too hard or the material is too important to risk, you can always revert to English for a bit.

The important thing is to exercise the brain cells in the foreign language. Whether you do this by listening to the radio, watching TV or chatting up the waiter/waitress in your local restaurant, is immaterial. As we are forever saying, just keep practising!

9.5 Questions Worth Asking!

Being a critical thinker involves asking questions at all stages of every research activity. These questions could run in your head as you consider language issues:

Is this a definitive conclusion?

- What are the main ideas here?
- Are the questions being asked the right ones or are there more meaningful or more valid questions?
- What are the supporting ideas?
- What opposing evidence is available?
- Is the evidence strong enough to reach a conclusion?
- How do these ideas fit with those found elsewhere?
- What is assumed?
- Are the assumptions justified?
- What are the strengths and weaknesses of the arguments?
- Is a particular point of view or social or cultural perspective skewing the interpretation?
- Are these seemingly 'objective' definitions truly objective?
- Is the information of an appropriate quality?
- Are causes and effects clearly distinguished?
- Is this a personal opinion or an example of intuition?
- Have I really understood the evidence?
- Am I making woolly, over-general statements?
- Is the information relevant? Keep thinking back to the original aims and argument. You can make statements that are clear, accurate and precise but if they are irrelevant they do not help. Off the point arguments or examples distract and confuse the reader, and may lose you marks.
- Is the argument superficial? Have all the complexities of an issue been addressed?
- Is there a broad range of evidence? Does the answer take into account the range of possible perspectives?
- Are the arguments presented in a logical sequence? Check that thoughts and ideas are ordered into a sequence that tells the story in a logical and supported way.

- Which examples will reinforce the idea?
- Can this idea be expressed in another, better way?
- What has been left out? Looking for 'gaps' is an important skill.
- Is this a definitive/true conclusion OR a probable/'on the balance of evidence' conclusion?
- What are the exceptions?

Take a little time to think and reflect before jumping into a task with both feet. Having completed a task or activity, take a few minutes to reflect on the results or outcomes. **Try This 9.2** and **Try This 9.3** are two exercises which develop critical skills. Both provide frameworks for thinking, evaluating and synthesizing language material.

TRY THIS 9.2 – Gutting an article

Select one article from a reading list, any article, any list! Make notes on the:

Content:	What are the main points?
Evidence:	What is the support material? Is it valid?
Counter case:	What are the counter-arguments? Has the author considered the alternatives fully?
Summary:	Summarize relevant material from other sources that the author might have included but omitted.

How well did the author meet his stated objectives?

TRY THIS 9.3 – Comparing articles

Take three articles on the same or related topic from any module reading list. Write a 1000 word review that compares and contrasts the contributions of the three authors. (Use the guidelines from the previous exercise.) Write 250 words on where these three articles fit with material from the module.

This seems like a major effort, but it really will improve your comprehension of a topic, so treat it as a learning exercise rather than an isolated skills exercise. Pick three articles you are going to read anyway. It is another approach to reading and noting.

In practice, few lecturers would argue that a logical perspective is the only way to deal with questions. This leaves room for you to express your aesthetic opinions within an essay, if they are relevant and appropriate.

Can you improve the quality of your thinking alone?

Yes, but it takes practice. You will probably become more disciplined in your thinking by discussing issues regularly. This is because the act of talking around an idea sparks off other ideas in your own mind. When someone else voices their point of view, you get an insight into other aspects of the problem, whereas thinking of arguments that run against your own position is difficult. A discussion group might:

- Start by summarizing the problem.
- Sort out objectives to follow through.
- Share data and evidence – the knowledge element.
- Share views on the data, 'I think it means ... because ...'
- Work out and discuss the assumptions the data and evidence are making.
- Discuss possible implications; evaluate their strengths and weaknesses.
- Summarize the outcomes.

A good reasoner is like a good footballer; s/he becomes more adept by practising.

Where to think?

Thoughts and ideas arrive unexpectedly and drift off just as fast unless you note them. Take a minute to recall where you do *your* thinking. There are almost as many varied answers as people, but a non-random sample of individuals in a lecture (N=67) shows favoured locations include: in bed at 4am; while walking to work; jogging; swimming; working out in the gym; cleaning the house; and cutting grass! There is certainly a common element, in that thinking can be productive if you are otherwise engaged in an activity that allows the mind to wander in all sorts of directions without distractions such as telephones and conversations. The majority of students who offered 'walking' and 'the gym' as their best thinking opportunities are evidence of this. Writing down ideas is vitally important, but is incompatible with note-making. Recognize this problem by taking 10 minutes over a drink after exercise, or a couple of minutes at a bus stop, to jot down thoughts and plans. This turns aerobic exercise into an effective multi-tasking activity by incorporating a 'thinking' element.

Avoiding plagiarism

Good thinking habits can minimize your chance of inadvertently plagiarizing the work of others. Get into the habit of engaging and applying concepts and ideas, not just describing or reporting them. That means thinking around the ideas to find your own contexts and alternative examples. Make sure you include your own thoughts, opinions and reflections in your writing. Be prepared to draft and redraft so that the thoughts are in your own language – and acknowledge your sources. Leave time to link ideas coherently. Finally, put the full reference for your citations at the end of each piece of written work.

Thinking and understanding involve a commentary in your head. Writing a summary in your own words is a good way to check you understand complex ideas. Doing it in your foreign language is a linguistic reinforcement exercise as well. Ask: 'Do I understand this?' at the end of a page, chapter, paper, tutorial, lecture … and not just at the end.

9.6 References and Further Reading

Bloom, B.S. (ed.) (1956) *Taxonomy of Educational Objectives: 1 Cognitive Domain*. London: Longman.

Buzan, T. and Buzan, B. (1995) *The Mind Map Book*. (rev. edn.) London: BBC Books.

UTMU (1976) *Improving Teaching in Higher Education*. London: University Teaching Methods Unit.

Van den Brink-Budgen, R. (1996) *Critical Thinking for Students: How to Use Your Recommended Texts on a University or College Course*. Plymouth; How To Books.

To get started with mind mapping see also:

Mind Mapping FAQ (1999) [online] http://world.std.com/~emagic/mindmap.html

Russell, P. (1999) Advantages of Mind Maps [online] http://www.peterussell.com/Mindmaps/Advantages.html (This site tells you how to draw them.)

So Tom, why are you reading French at University?

Ah, that's because my girlfriend said she liked cunning linguists

10 CONSTRUCTING AN ARGUMENT

Look, this isn't an argument, it's just a contradiction!

At the centre of every quality language essay, report or presentation is a well-structured argument. This is an argument in the sense of a fully supported and referenced explanation or interpretation. In producing an argument you are not looking to provide a mathematical proof, or evidence that is strong enough to support a legal case. You are trying to integrate a series of facts, examples and the connections that link them, so that your deductions and conclusions appear probable. In different parts of your degree your arguments may follow different styles. In discussions of literature the evidence comes primarily from your close reading of the text, and is an interpretation and appreciation of the material, enhanced by your own ideas and those of other critics. In cultural, historical or linguistic studies you develop evidence from a range of sources and link these with methodological ideas and approaches. Whatever your context the crucial skill is to establish enough appropriate links and evidence or examples, such that your argument cannot be rejected as improbable or unsubstantiated.

At the start think about your motive for putting pen to paper; not just 'I want a 2.1'. What are you trying to say? Most linguistic, literary and cultural issues can be viewed from a number of aspects, and exemplified with a wide range of material. This means unpacking the elements of an argument and structuring them logically. Your aim might be:

- To develop a point of view as in a broadsheet newspaper-style editorial or a debate.
- To persuade the reader, possibly your languages examiner, that you know about 'the role of gender and politics in the development of industrial societies and political structures in eastern Europe between 1919 and 1939.'

You may be more specific, perhaps wanting to define:

- How one concept differs from previous concepts.
- The implications of using one theory or methodology rather than another one.
- Whether a decision is possible or 'are you sitting on the fence'?

Some arguments are linear, but most rely on an accumulation of diverse threads of evidence which, collectively, support a particular position. Recognize that different language experts will present equally valid but conflicting views and opinions. For example, in researching issues that encourage quality writing by higher education students there are advocates of numerous approaches: do nothing (students sink or swim); detailed tutor notes for students; personal assessment and feedback to staff; peer review; peer feedback; group assessment and feedback, and so on. The discussion concerning the relevant pros and cons of each approach might include: student–teacher power relations; ownership; analytical methodologies; the role of the reviewer; overdependence of the student on the tutor generating students who write to the tutor's desired pattern and learn nothing about their own style; effectiveness of revision; what was really learned? In formulating a statement about what encourages the development of quality thinking which leads to quality writing, you would need to present the different views and consider: What are the limitations of each view? What elements are entrenched? How might a consensus be formed? There is a vast amount of research literature to be read, evidence to be considered and then you need to develop your own ideas.

A literary research project can leave you overwhelmed with evidence. 'Thinking' is involved in designing an approach to maximize your understanding of influences and interactions between different facets and elements of the material and presenting these in a coherent argument. Points of view should be part of the chain in an argument, or arise from the argument. It is the weight of the evidence or ideas, plus the quality of your argument, which makes your point of view and conclusions acceptable.

10.1 Structuring arguments

Any argument needs to be structured (see Figure 10.1) with reasoned evidence supporting the statements. A stronger, more balanced argument is made when examples for and against the general tenet are quoted. Russell (1993) describes three classic structures that can be adopted in arguing a case (see Figure 10.2). We contend that at university level the third model should be used every time, and that in every discussion, oral presentation, essay, report and dissertation you should be able to point to each of the six sections and to the links between them.

10.2 Cultural approaches

It is essential to be aware of the range of ideas and perspectives which surround any political or cultural issue in your studies. You cannot read and consider everything but you need a balanced selection of evidence. You are faced with different points of view, a lack of absolutes, and ideological baggage which colours opinions and investigative approaches. If you research green issues you need some background in politics, economics and sociology. But these are areas where theories are always open to argument, persuasion and debate. Your reading becomes the evidence from which you can draw and discuss, compare and contrast.

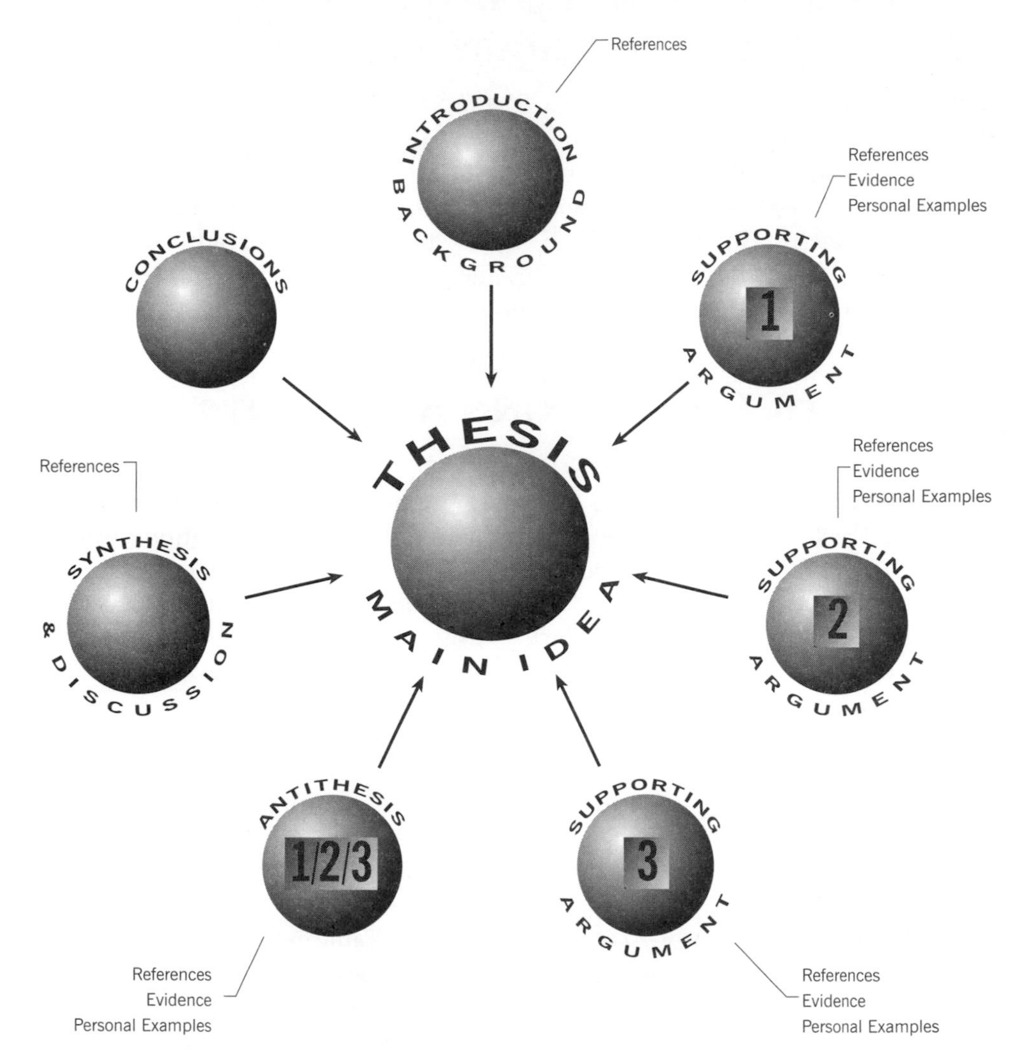

Figure 10.1 A spider diagram template for an argument.

1	Introduction	Thesis	Conclusion	References		
2	Introduction	Thesis	Antithesis	Conclusion	References	
3	Introduction	Thesis	Antithesis	Synthesis	Conclusion	References

Thesis	The argument under consideration
Antithesis	The counter-argument
Synthesis	The balancing of the different points of view made in the thesis and antithesis

Figure 10.2 Classic models for presenting argument (after Russell, 1993).

10.3 Literary studies

The text is at the centre of your argument, providing the basis for discussion and examples through quotations, but its place is complemented by your reading of the criticism and analyses which will help inform and develop your ideas and opinions. Breadth and narrow focus are both essential – breadth of reading around other works by the same author, and wider secondary (critical) sources; but above all, close reading of the primary text(s).

10.4 Unpacking arguments

It is all too easy when speaking and writing to put too much information into a sentence, or to make very general statements. One might say: 'In Reformation Germany a wedding provided a temporary break from everyday social constraints'. This is true but hides much information. A fuller statement like: 'The guilds, so influential in sixteenth-century German urban society, drew clear and sharp distinctions of status between the married master and his as yet unmarried journeymen, and determined how far each group could deviate from the behavioural norm on special occasions'. To further strengthen this assertion, add references or a supporting quotation, such as: 'In Augsburg the eve of the wedding was marked by a drinking party where master and journeymen rubbed shoulders, but at the wedding feast itself the masters sat separately and later only danced with their wives, while the young men processed separately and sat together and danced with as many young women as possible'. (Hufton, 1997).' (Plus ça change . . . .)

Another statement meriting some unpacking is 'Vampires cling tenaciously to life'. This is a straightforward sentence and might make a good essay title – just add *Discuss*. A more detailed version might read: 'Vampires exploit their victims by invading and "colonizing" their corpses, making them very difficult to destroy'. A fully developed statement, for top marks, might be: 'Every person killed by a *nosferatu* [vampire] becomes likewise a vampire after death, and will continue to suck the blood of other innocent people till the spirit has been exorcised, either by opening the grave of the person suspected and driving a stake through the corpse, or firing a pistol loaded with a bullet into the coffin. In very obstinate cases it is further recommended to cut off the head and replace it with the mouth filled with garlic, or to extract the heart and burn it, strewing the ashes over the grave'. (Frayling, 1991)

When reviewing your own writing, try to identify general sentences that could benefit from fuller explanation.

10.5 Rational and Non-Rational Arguments

Arguments are categorized as being rational and non-rational. The non-rational are to be avoided. Here are four examples:

1. 'The re-introduction of capital punishment would practically eliminate homicide in Great Britain.' Aside from being arguable, this is hyperbole. It might sell newspapers but it is not an argument unless supported by data.
2. 'People become obese primarily because they overeat. Students overeat when they are stressed, therefore they are more at risk of becoming obese around exam time'. This is a very poor argument and untrue in the majority of cases. Some students are obese, most are not, some overeat at stressful times, some forget to eat altogether. Everyone's weight fluctuates over time.
3. Going OTT with language or throwing in jargon to impress the reader is a typical journalistic device, involving an emotional rather than factual appeal to the reader. 'Politicians have been documented using styles of language that enable them to avoid giving direct answers to questions', is a more considered academic statement than 'All politicians excel in roundabout linguistic constructions that convey absolutely zero, because they are inherently incapable of giving straight answers to important questions'.
4. 'It is abundantly clear that de Gaulle's profound hatred of all things British set the economic evolution of Europe back by at least a decade'. Words which sound very strong like clearly, manifestly, undoubtedly, all, naturally, and obviously, are intended to influence the reader into thinking the rest of the statement must be true. Overuse of strong words is unprofessional and unhelpful, the written equivalent of browbeating or shouting; they should be used at best sparingly not least because university examiners are programmed to greet them with scepticism.

Inductive or deductive? Which approach?

In presenting an argument, orally or on paper, give some thought to the ordering of ideas. If you write deductively you begin with the general idea and then follow on with examples. Inductive writing starts with specific evidence and uses it to draw general conclusions and explanations. You must decide what suits your material. In general, use the inductive approach when you want to draw a conclusion. The deductive approach is useful when you want to understand cause and effect, test a hypothesis or solve a problem. The examples given here of an inductive (A) and deductive (B) approach are in paragraph form, but the same principles apply to essays and dissertations.

A. So far we have been discussing the two philosophical traditions which provided the background to Coleridge's interest in the philosophical status of poetry. The first was his native British tradition which had come to regard language in general, and poetry in particular, as being relevant to philosophy. The second was the German tradition. Coleridge's uses of both are far from straightforward. As regards the first, he had scarcely a good word to say about Kames, Reid and Beattie, but he had a lot to say for and against the notion of common sense. More importantly, his statements about common sense betray his habit of treating the phenomenon of language as evidence for a particular kind of philosophy. However, he moves beyond the conservatism of the common-sense philosophers to describe the development of knowledge as being analogous to the growth of a language. He thinks that language grows like an organic body, and that the principle explaining this growth is the progress of the human intellect. And, further, that language exemplifies the identity of the principles of natural growth and intellectual progress, and can be used as the model of this identity (Hamilton, 1983).

B. Coleridge's statements about common sense betray his habit of treating the phenomenon of language as evidence for a particular kind of philosophy, according to which: language grows like an organic body; the principle explaining this growth is the progress of the human intellect; language exemplifies the identity of the principles of natural growth and intellectual progress; and it can be used as the model of this identity. He makes use of both his native British philosophical tradition (which had come to regard language in general, and poetry in particular, as being relevant to philosophy) and that of the Germans, but in a far from straightforward manner. Although he had scarcely a good word to say about Kames, Reid and Beattie, he had a lot to say for and against the notion of common sense. But moving beyond the conservatism of the common-sense philosophers, he describes the development of knowledge as being analogous to the growth of a language.

10.6 Potential minefields

Watch out for bad arguments creeping into your work. The following examples are rather obvious but are there more subtle logic problems? Be critical in reviewing your own work. It is easy to spot logical errors when sentences are adjacent – they may be less easy to see if there are a thousand words in between.

✗ **Circular reasoning:** Check that conclusions are not just a restatement of your original premise. *The Russian Revolution brought the long rule of imperialism to a bloody end. It was the violent conclusion of an era of autocratic government that had gone unchallenged for centuries.*

✗ **Cause and effect:** Be certain that the cause really is driving the effect. *Students are forced to live in crime ridden areas, so crime becomes part of student life.*

✗ **Leaping to conclusions:** The conclusion may be right but steps in the argument are missed. (See Unpacking arguments, p. 110). Some arguments are simply wrong.

Levels of personal savings are higher in most countries which have adopted the Euro than in the United Kingdom. Britons will never be prosperous until Britain adopts the Euro.

Sons of alcoholic fathers are more likely than sons of non-alcoholic fathers to develop alcoholism. This tells us that alcoholism is hereditary.

Be clear about the difference between arguments where the supporting material provides clear, strong evidence, and those where there is textual or historical evidence supporting the case but uncertainty remains. In projects and dissertations dealing with very complex or ongoing issues, conclusions may have to be conjectural or provisional. Be clear about the limitations. Statements like 'On the basis of the information available at the time of writing, we can suggest that ...' or 'The most recent evidence suggests ...' or 'However the Hong Kong economy is still in a state of flux following the colony's return to China in 1997, and it would be rash to attempt to draw firm conclusions before 2007 at the earliest' are very acceptable. Qualifying statements of this type have the additional merit of implying that you have thought about the limits and drawbacks inherent in the research results.

Is this a good argument?

Watch out for arguments where the author gives a true premise, but the conclusion is dodgy. Just because you agree with the first part of a sentence does not mean that the second part is also right. Keep thinking right through to the end of the sentence. Having articulated an argument; do you buy it? Why? Why not? What is your view? Look at **Try This 10.1** as a starter:

TRY THIS 10.1 – Logical arguments?

Consider the following statements. What questions do they raise? Are they true and logical? What arguments could be amassed to support or refute them? See p. 273 for some responses.

1. It is evident from the fact that most university degrees in Britain take only three years to complete, compared to an average of six years in Italy, that Italian graduates are better educated.
2. Although his father eventually married his mother, August Strindberg was conceived out of wedlock, and the sense of moral stigma followed him through life (Bentley, 1969). This is why his attitude towards women always fluctuated between madonna worship and misogyny.
3. The outbreak of the First World War led to a severe shortage of men to do many essential jobs in the towns and on the land, resulting in greatly increased status and rapid emancipation for women.

TRY THIS 10.2 – Logical linking phrases

Identify words and phrases that authors use to link arguments by scanning through a couple of papers or chapters that you are going to read next. Examples on pp. 273–4.

Language that persuades

If you use strong statements like 'Clearly it has been demonstrated ...', 'This essay has proved ....' or 'The evidence has unquestionably shown ....', be sure that what you have written really justifies the hype. It is worth thinking about your stock of linking phrases. Use **Try This 10.2** to review what you currently use, and then look at the answers to see if there are others to add.

- When reviewing your work read the introduction and then the concluding paragraph. Are they logically linked?
- Keep all parts of your brain engaged.

10.7 Opinions and Facts

It is important in both reading and writing to make a clear distinction between facts supported by evidence, and opinions, that may or may not be supported. Telling them apart is a matter of practice in looking to see what evidence is offered and what else might have been said. Has the author omitted counter-arguments? In **Try This 10.3** there are some short extracts to practise your discrimination skills; which are facts, which opinions, and which have evidence offered in support?

TRY THIS 10.3 – Fact or opinion

Identify the steps in each argument, and try to decide whether they are factual or based on an opinion. It is not necessary to understand the details, just consider style and approach, e.g. reasoned, emotional, polemical. (All statements are taken *verbatim* from articles and reviews in *Second Language Research*, 15 (2), 1999, see page numbers to follow up.) Suggested answers are on p. 274.

1. 'It seems to me that Chomsky's MPLT [minimalist program in linguistic theory] reflects an acknowledgement that much of syntax reduces to the lexicon – it is not so much grammar that puts words in order as it is the words themselves' (Ellis, 1996a: 120). This interpretation of minimalism is

misconceived. In the MP, the grammar consists of a lexicon, which varies across languages and clearly must be learned, and a computational system, which mediates a perceptual system and a semantic interface. Constituents are not determined by pre-existing statements about phrasal structure, but by the combination of lexical items into larger categories by means of an operation called Merge (Abraham *et al.*, 1996; Chomsky, 1995). (Pérez-Leroux and Glass, 1999) (p. 224)

2. Given Grinstead's (1994; 1998) claim that there is a stage in L1 Catalan and L1 Spanish in which no overt subjects occur, it is surprising to find such a high percentage of overt subjects at the early stage. Thus, these data do not provide evidence for a stage without subjects. (Liceras *et al.*, 1999) (p. 174)
3. It has sometimes been claimed that second language (L2) researchers in the principles and parameters paradigm assume that linguistic competence can in fact be tapped directly, particularly through linguistic intuitions or grammaticality judgement (GJ) tasks (Carroll and Meisel, 1990; Ellis, 1990), or that they confuse competence and performance issues as far as judgements are concerned (Birdsong, 1990). This is a misconception. (Duffield and White, 1999) (p. 133)

A major problem with **Try This 10.3** is that only part of a paragraph is reproduced, and inevitably some opinions are based on limited information. As in life, if you start looking for arguments you will find them. **Try This 10.4** is a way of getting into analysing arguments. Use it as a framework next time you read .

TRY THIS 10.4 – Spot the argument

As you read any literature (or other) article: a) highlight the arguments; b) highlight the statements that support the argument; and c) highlight the statements that counter the main arguments. Is the information presented in a balanced manner?

10.8 Examples of arguments

It is impractical in this book to reproduce an essay and discuss the quality of the arguments. Rather, some students' answers, together with some examiners' comments, are used to make points about the adequacy of the arguments. This section could also be useful when revising for short answer examination questions.

As an exercise in exemplified brevity, expressing ideas or concepts in two or three sentences, or a maximum of 50 words, is a good game. Consider these four answers to the question:

Explain the place of the term *Aktie* in the development of the vocabulary of German.

A. *Aktie* was borrowed from Dutch and means 'shares'. It was originally borrowed from the English word 'action', but as is often the case when a receiving language misinterprets the original meaning, a new meaning is given. (36 words)

B. 'Eine Aktie' is a share, used in the business sense of stocks and shares. It came into the German language from Dutch. The Dutch however took the word from the English 'action'. This would have been in the 18th century when many trading words came from Dutch into German. This was a literal borrowing. (54 words)

C. This came into German from Dutch in the 19th century. The meaning used to be the same as English 'action', but now in German it is used in the term 'Deutsche Aktien Index', the equivalent of the English FT Index of Shares. Interestingly, the abbreviation 'DAX' sounds like the German word for badger ('Dachs'), so their emblem is this animal. (60 words)

D. 'Aktie' is a Latin borrowing. Many Latin words were borrowed between the fifteenth and seventeenth centuries. The majority of them had a legal, educational or religious context. This was because Latin was felt to be the language serious matters were conducted in. University lectures were conducted in Latin up until the eighteenth century. (53 words)

COMMENT: *Answer A* is not only well within the word limit, but is also 100 per cent correct – as far as it goes. There would still have been room to mention two other salient points: the first occurrence of the borrowing (1716, always of interest to etymologists), and the context – trading. (60%). *Answer B* overruns slightly, but is a better answer, because it covers all the aspects just mentioned. (66%). *Answer C* is considerably over length, gets the date wrong, doesn't mention the Dutch or merchants, but does supply a piece of information, more tangential than 'interesting' about the little logo of a badger used by the German Stock Exchange Index. (50%). Poor old *Answer D* is actually not quite as wrong as it looks, because some authorities would cite Lat. *actio*, a term in Roman law meaning 'claim', 'action' in that sense, as the true derivation of *Aktie* (Kluge 1963). Unfortunately, the second half of the answer is right off the point. (48%).

This question and the next one call for a supported factual response rather than an argument.

Write explanatory notes on denazification in Germany (max. 50 words):

A. Denazification was a process of screening for ex-Nazis. Minor members of the party, or anyone able to provide sufficient mitigating evidence, were declared 'denazified', but instead of being a process of weeding out offenders, it became a process of giving the majority a clean sheet, because their services were needed. (51 words)

COMMENT: Accurate as far as it goes, but leaves a lot unsaid, e.g. how the process was handled by the various Occupying Powers, what obstacles lay in their way. 58%.

B. Denazification is a term used to describe the removal of 'Nazis' from society. The word 'Nazi' denotes a strong nationalist who believes his race is the 'Master

Race' and as a result any other members of society who do not fit into this category – whether it be race, religion or nationality – are considered to be outcasts. (55 words).

COMMENT: This writer has already chalked up a full word quota whilst stating what can be taken as read, yet has barely begun to answer the question. Task not fulfilled, a clear fail. 27%.

C. Denazification was one of the 'Five Ds' imposed on Germany by the victors, the others being: democratization, decentralization, decartelization and demilitarization. Whereas the Soviets immediately removed anyone with Nazi links from positions of responsibility, the Western powers tried to distinguish between the most and least active and punish them accordingly. (51 words)

COMMENT: Useful additional contextual information, but it takes up valuable word-space. Doesn't have room to explain how the Soviets weeded out the Nazis in their zone, or mention that many ex-Nazis escaped punishment because records went went missing, but still a competent answer. 61%.

Top Tips

- Avoid 'cop out' statements like 'Others maintain that ...' – Who are these *others*? There are more marks for 'Knowitall (2010) and Jumptoit (2010) disagree, making the point that ...'
- No examiner will give marks for the use of '... etc.'.

Yes but ...

In addition to logical linking phrases keep a list of caveat or 'yes but' statements (in both languages) handy. There are alternatives to 'however': consequently; as a result; by contrast; thus; albeit; the lack of; therefore; so; hence; nonetheless; notwithstanding, admittedly, despite the fact that; although it has been shown that. Here are some more extended examples:

'A more systematic analysis of the text might have produced a less shaky framework on which to construct a working hypothesis, and indeed it has to be said that some structure would have helped the project enormously'; 'The author gives an interesting but superficial account of ...'; 'Another aspect that could/should be developed ...'; 'So far we have distinguished between'; 'More detailed scrutiny supports this criticism because ...'; 'On closer examination we find that ...'; 'The outcome may be influenced by ...'; 'Only a few of the conclusions are substantiated by the data'; 'Against all expectations ...'; 'The argument is stated but no supporting evidence is offered'; 'Authenticity may be buried beneath layers of unfocused ...'; 'Although this is an entirely reasonable exploratory approach it neglects ...'; 'and ... thereby weakening the conclusions that may be drawn'; 'Therefore the criticism should be directed at ... rather than at ...'; 'The inference, then, is that the writer has misunderstood the significance of the passages on which he bases his conclusions'.

Build on this list as you read. As you research use these 'yes but ...' phrases to help focus thinking and to draw valid and reasoned inferences.

Be critical (within reason) of your writing and thinking. This means allocating time to read critically, remove inappropriate clichés and jargon, and add caveats and additional evidence.

Top Tips

- Write in clear sentences, with relevant references to back up your statements.
- Give due weight to arguments that support and refute your main argument.
- Talk through your arguments with friends. Explaining and persuading someone of your case usually clarifies arguments.
- Ask 'Does this persuade me?'
- Use Figure 10.1 as a template to check that you have a balanced argument.

10.9 References and Further Reading

Bentley, E. (1969) *The Playwright as Thinker*. New York: Harvest.

Fairbairn, G.J. and Winch, C. (1996) *Reading, Writing and Reasoning: A Guide for Students* (2nd edn). Buckingham: Open University Press.

Frayling, C. (1991). *Vampyres. Lord Byron to Count Dracula*. London: Faber & Faber.

Hamilton, P. (1983). *Coleridge's Poetics*. Oxford: Blackwell.

Hufton, O. (1995). *The Prospect Before Her. A History of Women in Western Europe*. London: Fontana.

Kluge, F. (1963) *Etymologisches Wörterbuch der deutschen Sprache*. rev. Mitzka, W. (19th edn). Berlin: de Gruyter.

Russell, S. (1993) *Grammar, Structure and Style*. Oxford: Oxford University Press.

Toulmin, S., Rieke, R. and Janik, A. (1979) *An Introduction to Reasoning*. New York: Macmillan.

Language Cryptic Crossword 1

Answers p. 274.

Across

1 Borderline habits (7)
5 His optician would prescribe a monocle (7)
9 Play role, madam transposes with music (9)
10 Idol carved by very young Emily (5)
11 Chatty meetings in avionics zone, right? (13)
13 It's not necessary to select the timeless Otto Lapin (8)
15 Cut into zigzags between or behind entrance (6)
17 Roughly skinned the credits from a directionless church (6)
19 Papal round robin redrafted nicely by County Councillor (8)
22 Pervert clips intrigue from babbling and cooing (13)
25 Tuna I serve to eastern European Christians (5)
26 Wake up call (3,6)
27 Generously broad ship (7)
28 Homer's trip? (7)

Down

1 Highly affected pitch (4)
2 The way to encourage a business (7)
3 George I left golden times (5)
4 Required to delimit joined-up writing (5-3)
5 Sentence passed on oriental invader of chimneys (6)
6 Good manners for the barricades (9)
7 Match result (7)
8 Study of symbols has researchers confused in some cities(10)
12 Just an idea (10)
14 Top opening cell used in elite bout (9)
16 Main character misses the plaudits (4-4)
18 French workshop I relate to (7)
20 Gaps left in a cold sauna (7)
21 Serge's way out (6)
23 1/8, but not 12.5% (5)
24 Helen's weight (4)

11 ORAL PRESENTATIONS

Tension's what you pay when someone's talking.

Most Languages degrees are littered with speaking opportunities. This is a really good thing! Somewhere on your CV you can add a line like 'During my university career I have given 25 presentations to audiences ranging from 5–65, using OHTs, slides and inter-active computer displays'. This impresses employers, but many Languages graduates fail to mention that they have had these opportunities to hone this very saleable skill. Speaking lets you get used to managing nerves, dealing with the question and answer session that follows and become a very happy lapin. So grab all opportunities to practise your presentation skills. They all count, from 5-minute presentations in tutorials to seminars and mini-lectures.

You need a well argued and supported message, to enrapture (maybe) the audience. Other chapters explain how to get the information together, this one is about practical presentation skills. The four most important tips are:

1. Match the style and technical content of your talk to the skills and interests of the audience. Making the content accessible, so the audience wants to listen, will encourage a positive response.
2. Buzan and Buzan (1995) show that people are most likely to remember:
   - Items from the start of a learning activity.
   - Items from the end of a learning activity.
   - Items associated with things or patterns already learned.
   - Items that are emphasized or highlighted as unique or unusual.
   - Items of personal interest to the learner.

   Tailor your presentation accordingly. Help the audience to think and understand.
3. Get the message straight in your head, organized and ready to flow. Lack of confidence in the content ➔ insecure speaker ➔ inattentive audience = bad presentation.
4. Remember the audience only gets one chance to hear you, so pare down a short presentation to the essential points. Make clear links between points and add brief, but strong, supporting evidence.

You must have a plan, and stick to it on the day. Basically it is down to PBIGBEM (Put Brain In Gear Before Engaging Mouth).

11.1 Style

Can I read it? Reading a script will bore both you and the audience. Really useful tutors will remove detailed notes and ask you to 'tell the story in your own words'. You are allowed bullet points on cards, to remind you of the main points, but that is all. Where appropriate, illustrate your talk with pictures and diagrams on OHTs (overhead transparencies), but remember that reading OHTs aloud is another cop out.

Practise speaking aloud

Language. A formal presentation requires a formal speaking style. Try to minimize colloquial language, acronyms and paraphrasing, and limit verbal mannerisms like the excessive use of 'Hmm', 'Umm', 'err', and ' I mean'. Put new words or acronyms on a handout or OHT.

Look into their eyes! Look at the audience and smile at them. If they feel you are enthusiastic and involved with the material, they will be more involved and interested.

How fast? Not too fast, slower than normal speech, because people taking notes need time to absorb your ideas, to get them into their brains and on to paper. The ideas are new to the audience. Watch the audience to check if you are going too fast, or if they are falling asleep.

Stand or sit? Position is often dictated by the room layout and normal practice. Given the choice, remember that sitting will encourage the audience to feel it is a less formal situation and one where it is easier for the audience to chip in and comment.

How loud? Loud enough so that the audience can hear you, but do not feel you are shouting. Ask someone you trust to sit at the back and wave if you are too loud or too quiet – getting it right takes practice. Tape record yourself sometime. When you have finished laughing at the result, have a think about whether you speak at the same pace and pitch all the time. Changing pace and pitch, getting excited about the material and showing enthusiasm are all good techniques for keeping your audience attentive and involved.

What about repeating material? You can emphasize primary points by repetition, or by simultaneously putting them on an OHT or board, but only repeat the important points.

11.2 Crutches (OHTs, slides, flip charts)

Audiences need to understand your message. Visual assistance could include some or all of:

- A title slide that includes your name and (e-mail) address, so the audience knows who you are and where to reach you!
- A brief outline of the talk – bullet points are ideal. Adding pictures is fun and may act as a memorable substitute (See Figure 11.1).
- Colours on text and on complex diagrams help to disentangle the story. Diagrams and pictures.
- Finally, a summary sheet. This might be the second, outline, slide shown again at the end, or a list of the key points you want the audience to remember.

OHT

An OHT (overhead transparency) is shown on an OHP (overhead projector). Preparing good OHTs and managing OHPs takes practice.

What does not work: Small writing, too many colours, untidy handwriting, and writing from edge to edge – leave a 5 cm margin at least. Misuse of, or inconsistent Use of capitals Doesn't help Either.

Good practice includes:

OHTs must be visible from the back of the room

- OHTs prepared carefully in advance.
- SPELL CHECK EVERYTHING.
- Print in large font (18pt+) and then photocopy on to overhead film. (**Use the right film in both printers and photocopiers**. Putting overhead film through a computer printer will work with a few machines but it is more likely that you will bust the printer.)
- A cartoon, clipart item or picture will make a message more memorable, and lighten the atmosphere if part of the material is seriously technical or a tad dull.
- Keep writing VERY BIG and messages short!
- It is fine to use diagrams, pictures and maps, but usually you need to enlarge them and always cite their source.
- Some audience members will be colour blind so avoid green and red together, black with blue, and black on red. Yellow and orange do not show up well in large lecture theatres and orange and brown are not easy to distinguish from 30 rows back.
- Number your OHTs in case your 'friends' shuffle them or you drop them.
- Switch off the OHP when not in use. NEVER leave your audience staring at a brightly illuminated blank screen.
- If you have lots of information, and time is short, give the audience a handout with the detailed material and use the talk to summarize the main points.

Figure 11.1 Presentation outline.

Before giving a talk, investigate the projector, find the on/off switches, the plug and how to focus the transparency. 'Sod's law of talk-giving' says that the previous speaker will breeze in, move the OHP, give a brilliant talk and leave you to reset the stage while the audience watches you! KEEP COOL, and DON'T PANIC. Have a pen or pencil handy to act as a pointer. Pointing at the transparency on an OHP shows greater cool than throwing a pointer, javelin style, at a screen beyond your reach.

Slides

Make sure that the room has a projector, can be blacked out and that there is a carousel available. Run the slides through the projector in advance to ensure they are the right way round. Mixing overhead and slide projectors is a nightmare for novices and always wastes time in a talk. Try to use one medium or the other, so if you want to use slides put the title and talk outline slides on to film as well. Slides can be made from computer graphics package images. Just watch the cost and time for production. OHTs are fine for most purposes except very large audiences (over 300).

Flip charts

Again **Write Big** and make sure your pens are full of ink. Left- and right-handed persons need the chart in slightly different positions. Check beforehand what the audience can see, and adjust your position accordingly. If spelling is a problem, flip charts are a BAD IDEA. Irritatingly, the audience will remember your spelling error rather than your message.

11.3 What to avoid

☹ **Getting uptight.** All speakers are nervous. THIS IS NORMAL. Take deep breaths and relax beforehand. If you are well prepared there is time to walk slowly to the event and have a coffee first. Find the loos, lights and seats. Ensure that the projectors, computer display system, flip chart, handouts, notes and a pen are in the right place for you and the audience. Then take plenty of deep breaths. YOU WILL BE FINE.

☹ **Showing the audience you are nervous.** Ask your mates to tell you what you do when speaking. Everyone gets uptight, but fiddling with hair, pockets, clothes, keys, pencil, ears and fingers distracts the audience. They watch the mannerisms and remember very little of the talk. Practise speaking.

☹ **Overrunning.** As a rule of thumb, reckon you can speak at about 100–120 words per minute. Practise in advance with a stopwatch (there is one on most cookers), reducing the time by 10 per cent.

11.4 Handling sticky situations

☹ **Late arrivals** should be ignored, unless they apologize to you, in which case smile your thanks. Going back interrupts your flow and irritates the people who arrived on time.

☹ **Time is up and you have 20 more things to say.** This is bad planning and usually only happens when you have not practised the material aloud. You can read your material much, MUCH faster than you can speak it. However, if you do run over time then either skip straight to your concluding phrases OR list the headings you have yet to cover and do a one-line conclusion.

☹ **Good question, no idea of the answer.** Say so. A phrase like 'That's a brilliant thought, not occurred to me at all, does anyone else know?' will cheer up the questioner and hopefully get others talking. If you need time to think, offer variations on 'I am glad this has come up ...' , 'I wanted to follow up that idea but couldn't find anything in the library, can anyone help here?', 'Great question, no idea, how do we find out?'

Top Tips

- Self-assess your bathroom rehearsals against your department's criteria, or use the guidelines in Figure 11.2 to polish a performance.
- Use clear language! Try not to use colloquial speech or to substitute less than technical terms, *'The early Sicilian poets seem a bit iffy.' 'There was Dante and his mate Guido Cavalcanti'* or *'... drama, mmm, the Greeks had loads of it.'* Strive in presentations to use a formal, technically rich style.
- Practise your talk on the hamster, the bathroom wall and ... Speaking the words aloud will make you feel happier when doing it for real. It also gives you a chance to pronounce unfamiliar words like Occitan, Castiglione's Cortegiano ..., and get them wrong in the privacy of your own bus stop! If in doubt about pronunciation ask someone – the librarian, your mum, anyone.
- Most marks are given for content, so research the topic thoroughly.

Oral Presentation Criteria Name .... Title of Talk					
		Great	Middling	Oh Dear!	
Rendition					
Speed	Spot on				Too fast/slow
Audibility	Clear and distinct				Indistinct
Holding attention	Engaged audience				Sent them to sleep
Enthusiasm	Ebullient delivery				Boring delivery
Substance					
Organization	Organized, logical structure				Scrappy and disorganised
Pertinence	On the topic				Random and off the point
Academic accuracy	Factually spot on				Inaccurate
Support materials					
Suitability	Tailored to talk				None, or off the topic
Production quality	Clear				Unclear
Treatment	Professionally presented				Poorly integrated and presented
Question time					
Handling queries	Thoughtful answers				Limited ability to extend the discussion
Adaptability	Coped well				Limited, inflexible responses
Teamwork					
Co-ordination	Balanced, team response				Unequal, unbalanced response

Figure 11.2 Oral Presentation Assessment Criteria.

11.5 Further Reading

Buzan, T. and Buzan, B. (1995) *The Mind Map Book.* (rev. edn.), London: BBC Books.

Play Link

Add 2 letters in the middle squares to complete the 5-letter words to left and right. When complete a 10-letter play title can be read. Answer p. 274

D	I	S			L	O	N
K	U	K			V	A	L
C	A	R			I	V	E
T	I	T			G	E	R
F	O	C			A	G	E

Tie-breaker: Is Boccaccio
(a) an Italian bread; (b) an Italian writer; (c) vino rosso secco?

12 DISCUSSION

Great minds discuss ideas, small minds discuss people.

Language students develop their research abilities through discussion in workshops, tutorials and seminars. Talking through the details of a topic leads to a greater degree of understanding and learning. In most jobs being able to discuss topics calmly, fairly and professionally is essential, so discussions are valuable opportunities to practise.

To learn effectively from discussions there needs to be a relaxed atmosphere where you can think about the content, and note what others are saying. Ineffective discussions occur when people worry about what to say next, and run through it mentally, rather than listening to the person speaking. Some of this is nerves, which will calm down with practice, but in the meantime, preparing fully is the best way to lower your stress levels. You have plenty of background and specific information to share.

Be positive about seeking the views of others and value their contributions. Employ open-ended questions, those which encourage an elaborated, rather than a brief yes or no answer. 'What are the main features of the picaresque novel?' is an open ended question and more useful than 'Do you like the picaresque novel?' 'What do you think about Thomas Mann's use of the leitmotiv/song in Brecht/Spanish cuisine?' are good questions, but 'What do you think?' is a bit general. Use phrases like 'What are the main narrative conventions of the *Bildungsroman*?' or 'In what ways do you consider the critics influenced writing for the stage in the immediate post-war period in Italy?' or 'What is undervalued about Samuel Beckett's use of monologue?'

Keep up the quality of argument in discussion. For example, if discussing the musical properties of the sonnet you might make a general point like 'There is evidence that the more complex rhyme scheme of the Petrarchan sonnet allows for finer melodic differentiation than other varieties.' This is a general argument that would be strengthened, and get more marks, by adding references and examples as you speak. You might say 'Appiani and Grimaldi in their 1999 study of rhetorical structures in verse suggest that Petrarch's virtuoso command of rhyme pattern variations produces a markedly wider and more sophisticated range of melodic effects than either Shakespeare or Milton achieved'. By adding an example and citing the authors, the argument is stronger and more memorable. For top marks, take examples from more than one source.

12.1 Types of discussion

Brainstorming

Brainstorming is a great way of collecting a range of ideas and opinions and getting a group talking. The process involves everyone calling out points and ideas. Someone keeps a list, maybe on a flipchart so everyone can see. A typical list has no organization – there is overlap, repetition and a mix of facts and opinions. The art of brainstorming is to assemble ideas, including the wild and wacky, so that many avenues are explored. The points are reordered and arguments developed through discussion, so that by the end of a session they have been pooled, ordered and critically discussed. Have a go at **Try This 12.1** as an example of working with a brainstormed list , and use **Try This 12.2** with your next assignment

TRY THIS 12.1 – Working with a brainstormed list

Brainstorming produces a list of ideas with minimal detail and no evaluation. This list was created by a group in five minutes. Items overlap and repeat, facts and opinions are mixed, and there is no order. Take five minutes to categorize the items. A possible sort is given on pp. 274–5.

What factors brought about the fall of the German Chancellor, Helmut Kohl?

Kohl had Germany's long-term interests at heart.
Kohl was also a great achiever – re-united East and West Germany.
'All power corrupts, absolute power corrupts absolutely': Kohl was near-absolute ruler.
Secret donations to political parties are illegal in Germany.
Kohl's motive was retention of power at any price.
Sleaze endemic in government, all succumb in the end.
Kohl's split loyalties: to party, to 'benefactors', to nation.
Politics is about votes, not morals.
CDU too long in power.
Sleaze is a particular problem for a party that espouses 'traditional values'.
Kohl would never have had a problem if German economy hadn't slowed down.
All political parties are corrupt in one way or another.
General need to redefine values in German politics.
The SPD is cashing in on CDU's discomfort with a holier-than-thou stance.
Sleaze more than a German problem (Tories, Mitterand).
CDU brought down by unemployment, not sleaze.
New CDU leader, new hope: Angela Merkel female, young and squeaky-clean.
Leaders once in power are prone to arrogance vis-à-vis the electorate.

CDU needs new initiatives/programme.
Kohl's fall linked to Euro, demise of DM, loss of national pride.
SPD unpopular over its ecologically-driven policies – chance for CDU.
Kohl did everything for the best.
CDU needs new image.
Schröder charismatic, Kohl dull and unappealing.
CDU in crisis.
Kohl: age problem, perceived as past it.
CDU needs to atone for past mistakes.
Kohl a virtual dictator.
Re-unification an albatross around CDU's neck.

TRY THIS 12.2 – Brainstorm an essay plan

Using your next essay title or a revision essay or assignment, brainstorm a list of ideas using the blue/red pen technique (p. 148), alone or with friends, including references and authors, and use this as the basis for essay planning. Brainstorming 'what I know already' at the start of essay planning, can indicate where further research is required.

Role play exercises

These may involve the simulation of a meeting, as for example, where a committee discusses the progress of a project. You will prepare a role in advance, not necessarily a role you would agree with personally. Procedure depends on the type of topic. It may lead to a decision given by the Chairman, or a vote from observers.

Transactional discussion

This is the term for a dialogue centred around a real-life activity such as buying a rail ticket, ordering a meal, describing an aching tooth to the dentist or making a phone call. It is used regularly in the early stages of language learning, one you can practise with friends or alone.

What are the supporting ideas?

Debate

The normal format for a debate presupposes that there is a clear issue on which there are polarized opinions. A motion is put forward for discussion. It is traditionally put in the form 'This house believes that …'. One side proposes the motion, and the other side opposes it. The proposer gives a speech in favour, followed by the opposer speaking against the motion. These speeches are 'seconded' by two further speeches for and against, although for reasons of time these may be dispensed with in one-hour debates. The motion is then thrown open so everyone can contribute. The proposer and the opposer make closing speeches in which they can answer points made during the debate, followed by a vote. Issues in literature are rarely clear-cut and a vote may be inappropriate, but a formal debate on a current affairs topic is a useful way of exploring positions and opinions, and for eliciting reasoned responses.

Oppositional discussion

Oppositional discussion is a less formal version of debate, in which each side tries to persuade an audience that a particular case is right and the other is wrong. You may work in a small group, assembling information from one point of view, and then argue your case with another group that has tackled the same topic from another angle. Remember that all your arguments need supporting evidence, so keep case examples handy.

Consensual discussion

Consensual discussion involves a group of people with a common purpose, pooling their resources to reach an agreement. Demonstrations of good, co-operative, discussion skills are rare; most of the models of discussion on TV, radio, and in the press are set up as oppositional rather than consensual. Generally you achieve more through discussing topics in a co-operative spirit, and one of the abilities most sought after by employers of graduates is the ability to solve problems through teamwork.

Negotiation

Negotiation, coming to an agreement by mutual consent, is another useful business and professional skill. One practises and improves negotiation skills in everyday activities like persuading a tutor to extend an essay deadline, getting a landlord to do repairs or persuading someone else to clean the kitchen. In formal negotiations:

- ✔ Prepare by considering the issues in their widest context, in advance.
- ✔ List the strengths and weaknesses of your position. It reduces the chances of being caught out!
- ✔ Get all the options and alternatives outlined at the start. There are different routes to any solution and everyone needs to understand the choices available.
- ✔ Check that everyone agrees that no major issue is being overlooked, and that all the information is available to everyone.
- ✔ Appreciate that there will be more than one point of view, and let everyone have their say.

- ✔ Stick to the issues that are raised and avoid personality-based discussion; s/he may be an idiot BUT saying so will not promote agreement.
- ✔ If discussion gets over-heated, break for coffee, or agree to meet again later.
- ✔ At the end, ensure everyone understands what has been decided by circulating a summary note.

There are many books on discussion, assertiveness, and negotiation skills; see Drew and Bingham (1997) or Fisher *et al.* (1997), or do a library keyword search.

Top Tips

- Being asked to start a discussion is not like being asked to represent your country at football. You are simply 'kicking off'. Make your points clearly and 'pass the ball' promptly. Focus thoughts by putting the main points on a handout or OHT.
- Don't wait for a 'big moment' before contributing. Ask questions to get a topic going.
- Don't be anxious about the quality of your contributions. Get stuck in. Early in a discussion everyone is nervous and too concerned about his or her own contribution to be critical of others.
- Keep discussion points short and simple.
- Use examples to illustrate and strengthen your argument.
- Share the responsibility for keeping the group going.
- Have a short discussion before a tutorial to kick ideas about. Meet in the bar, over coffee or supper.

12.2 Electronic discussions

It is not always possible to get people together for a discussion. Electronic discussions can solve groupwork timetabling problems and are especially useful for part-timers and students off-campus, on years abroad or in work-placements. They are also good practice for business discussions. One advantage of electronic discussions is that you can build research activities into the process. Having started a discussion, you may realize that you need additional information. You can find it and feed it in as the discussion progresses. Electronic discussions use e-mail and bulletin boards, or computer conferencing. The methodology depends on the local technology (Aldred 1996; Bonk and King 1998).

Here are some suggested ground-rules to make electronic discussions successful, with possible times and numbers for an e-mail tutorial discussion in brackets.

- Agree a date to finish (2 weeks).
- Everyone must make a minimum number of contributions (three).
- Agree to read contributions every x days (two or three).
- Appoint someone to keep and collate all messages so there is a final record (Luigi).
- Appoint a 'devil's advocate' or 'pot stirrer' to ask awkward questions and chivvy activity (Santana).
- Ask someone to summarize and circulate an overview at the end (Gianni, the basis of a group report for everyone to amend if the discussion is assessed).
- Be polite. In a conversation you can see and hear when someone is making a joke or ironic comment. The effect is not always the same on the screen.
- Where further research is required, attempt to share tasks evenly (Maria, Francesca).
- Replying instantly is generally a good idea. That is what happens in face to face discussion, and first thoughts are often best.

Some people 'lurk' quietly, listening rather than commenting, which happens in all discussions. Point two, above, should overcome this issue to a certain extent. One of the more off-putting things that can happen is someone mailing a 3000 word essay to the group. This is the equivalent of one person talking continuously for an hour. It puts off the rest of the group as they feel there is little to add. Try to keep contributions short in the first stages. One good way to start is to ask everyone to brainstorm 4–6 points to one person by the end of Day 2. Someone collates, orders and mails a full list around the group as the starting point for discussion and research. (See **Try This 16.1 – E-mail in action**, p. 181).

12.3 Group management

The quality of discussion depends above all on the dynamics of each particular group. Some work spontaneously without any problems, others are very sticky. There are no hard and fast rules about behaviour in group discussions but here are some general points to consider. Meetings flow well when members:

- ☺ Steer the discussion to keep it to the point, sum up, shut up people who talk too much, and encourage and bring in people who talk too little.
- ☺ Keep track of the proceedings.
- ☺ Inject new ideas.
- ☺ Are constructively critical of ideas.
- ☺ Play devil's advocate.
- ☺ Calm tempers.
- ☺ Add humour.

Formal meetings have designated individuals for the first two tasks (Chair and Secretary), but in informal meetings **anyone** can take these roles at any time. Everyone is better at one or two particular roles in a discussion; think about the sorts of roles you play and also about developing other roles using **Try This 12.3**.

TRY THIS 12.3 – Discussant's role

Here is a list of the actions or roles people take in discussions (adapted from Rabow *et al.* 1994). Sort them into those which are positive and promote discussion, and those which are negative. How might you handle different approaches?

Asks for examples.	Seeks the sympathy vote.
Asks for opinions.	Keeps arguing for the same idea, although the discussion has moved on.
Encourages others to speak.	Asks for reactions.
Helps to summarize the discussion.	Is very defensive.
Ignores a member's contribution.	Gives examples.
Is very (aggressively) confrontational.	Offers opinions.
Is very competitive.	Summarizes and moves discussion to next point.
Keeps quiet.	Diverts the discussion to other topics.
Mucks about.	Supplies factual information.
Speaks aggressively.	Waffles.

12.4 ASSESSING DISCUSSIONS

At the end of each term or as part of a Learning Log (see Chapter 4) you may be asked to reflect on your contribution to discussion sessions, and in some cases to negotiate a mark for it with your tutor. The attributes an assessor might check for are included in **Try This 12.4**. Assess friends, seminar and TV discussants on this basis. What can you learn from those with high scores? Having analysed what makes a good discussant, have a look at **Try This 12.5.**

TRY THIS 12.4 – Assessment of discussion skills

Evaluate a discussant's performance on a 1–5 scale and note what they do well.

Assessment of discussion skills	1 (useless), 3 (average), 5 (brilliant) Comment on good points
Talks in full sentences.	
Asks clear, relevant questions.	
Describes an event clearly.	
Listens and responds to conversation.	
Discusses and debates constructively.	
Speaks clearly and with expression.	
Selects relevant information from listening.	
Responds to instructions.	
Contributes usefully to discussion.	
Reports events in sequence and detail.	
Is able to see both sides of the question.	
Finds alternative ways of saying the same thing.	
Listens to others, and appreciates their input, efforts and needs.	

Reflect on the tips you can pick up from 4–5 point performers.

TRY THIS 12.5 – Self-assessment of discussion skills

Level 1 students at Leeds brainstormed the following list of 'skills they needed to argue effectively'. Look down the list and select 3 items where you would like to be more effective. Do you have items to add to the list?

Having got your list, plot a strategy to work on each of these three issues at your next group discussion. (e.g. I will not butt in; I will ask at least one question; I will say something and then shut up until at least three other people have spoken).

Being open-minded.	Staying cool.
Listening to both sides of the argument.	Being tolerant.
Using opponents' words against them.	Using good evidence.
Playing devil's advocate.	Being willing to let others speak.
Summing up every so often.	Only one person talking at a time.
Thinking before speaking.	Being firm.

Some final points

Getting better at discussion and argument needs practice, and hearing one's own voice improves one's self-confidence. You can practise in private. Listen to a question on a TV or radio discussion programme. Then turn the sound down, take a deep breath to calm down, and use it as thinking time. What is the first point? Now say it out loud. Subject matter is not important, get in there and have a go. Respond with two points and then a question or observation that throws the topic back to the group or audience. That is a good technique because you share the discussion with the rest of the audience, who can contribute their views. You might want to tape a programme and compare your answer with the panellists' – remember to look at the style of the answers and their content.

Where points of view or judgements are needed, you may want to seek the opinions of people with different academic, social and cultural backgrounds and experience. Their views may be radically different from your own. Seminars, workshops and tutorial discussions in literature and language classes are explicitly designed to allow you to share these kinds of complementary views. To get the most out of a discussion or conversation:

- ✔ Be positive.
- ✔ Ask yourself questions, like 'How will this help me understand . . . *assonance*?'
- ✔ Make eye contact with the group.
- ✔ Give the speaker feedback and support.
- ✔ Aim to be accurate and on the point.
- ✔ Include examples and references as you speak.

12.5 REFERENCES AND FURTHER READING

Aldred, B.K. (1996) *Desktop Conferencing: A Complete Guide to its Applications and Technology*. London: McGraw-Hill Book Co.

Bonk, C.J. and King, K.S. (eds.) (1998) *Electronic Collaborators: Learner-centered Technologies for Literacy, Apprenticeship, and Discourse.* Mahwah, N.J. : Erlbaum Associates.

Drew, S. and Bingham, R. (1997) Negotiating and Assertiveness, In Drew, S. and Bingham, R. (eds.), *The Student Skills Guide.* Aldershot: Gower, 121–134 and 255–262.

Fisher, R., Ury, W. and Patton, B. (1997) *Getting to Yes: Negotiating an Agreement without Giving In* (2nd edn.) London: Arrow Business Books.

Rabow, J., Charness, M.A., Kipperman, J. and Radcliffe-Vasile, S. (1994) *William Fawcett Hill's Learning Through Discussion* (3rd edn.) California: Sage Publications Inc.

Tutorial conundrum

Work out who did what in the comparative literature tutorial, and what mark they got. ***Answers on page 275.***

The Flaubert researchers had an 8 in their mark.
Natasha and Tim didn't get 78% and the epistolary novel pair didn't get 72%.

13 LISTENING AND INTERVIEWING

Hearing is easy, listening is tough.

Language lectures, seminars and discussion groups can involve twelve or more hours of listening each week, so listening skills are important – for content and to hone your L2 accent. Listening is often considered an automatic activity, but is increasingly quoted by employers as a vital skill for effective business performance (Gushgari *et al.* 1997). In business, valuing the customer or client and taking the time to understand what the speaker is conveying, gives a better impression, not to mention a better outcome. Interviewing is a standard research methodology in market research, and a vital skill for managers of every sort. All in all, being good at listening has the potential to enhance the quality of your work in almost every walk of life

Listening is not the same as hearing, it is a more active and interactive process. Listening involves being ready to absorb information, paying attention to details, and the capacity to catalogue and interpret the information. In addition to the actual material and support cues like slides and OHTs, there is information in the speaker's tone of voice and body language. As with reading, the greater your language background, the more you are likely to understand. Which means that listening is a skill involving some preparation, a bit like parachuting.

13.1 LISTENING IN LECTURES

Arriving at a lecture with information about last night's activities or juicy scandal is normal, but the brain is not prepared for advanced information on the phonetics of Cantonese or Hegel's dialectics. Some lecturers understand that the average student audience needs 5 minutes background briefing to get the majority of brains engaged and on track. Others leap in with vital information in the first five minutes because 'everyone is fresh!' Whatever the lecture style, but especially with the latter, you will get more from the session having thought 'I know this will be an interesting lecture about ...' and scanned notes from the last session or library. Assuming from the start that a lecture will be dull usually ensures that it will seem dull.

✔ A lecturer's words, no matter how wise, enter your short-term memory, and unless you play around with them and process the information into ideas, making personal connections, the words will drop out of short-term memory into a black hole. Think about the content and implications as the lecture progresses.

- ✔ You may feel a lecturer is wildly off beam, making statements you disagree with, but do not decide he or she is automatically wrong, check it out. There might be dissertation possibilities.
- ✔ Keep a record of a speaker's main points.
- ✔ Be prepared for the unpredictable. Some speakers indicate what they intend to cover in a lecture, others whiz off in different directions. This unpredictability can keep you alert! But if you get thoroughly lost, then ask a clarifying question (mentally or physically), rather than 'dropping out' for the rest of the session.
- ✔ If you feel your brain drifting off ask yourself questions like – 'what is s/he trying to say?' and 'where does this fit with what I know?'
- ✔ Have another look at pp. 5–6, expectations of lectures.
- ✔ Treat listening as a challenging mental task.
- ✔ Don't imagine you can remember every point of a lecture in your head. Develop a technique of making notes whilst still following the lecture.

13.2 Listening in discussions and language classes

No one listens until you make a mistake.

Discussion is the time to harvest the ideas of others, improve your accent and build self-confidence. In most modules there is such a diversity of style, delivery, points of view and interpretation, of literature, that open discussion is vital. Endeavour to be open-minded in looking for and evaluating statements which may express very different views and beliefs from your own. Because ideas fly around fast, make sure you note the main points and supporting evidence (arguments) where possible. Post-discussion note collation is crucial, mostly involving ordering thoughts and checking arguments that support or confute the points. Have a look at **Try This 13.1** and think about how you score on effective listening.

TRY THIS 13.1 – Assess your listening effectiveness in discussions

Think back over a tutorial or a recent conversation and rate and comment on each of these points. Alternatively, score this for a friend or fellow tutee, and then think about your skills in listening, compared with theirs.

Score your effectiveness in discussion	**Yes ✔** **Sometimes ?** **No ✘**	**Comments**
Did you feel relaxed and comfortable?	Yes ✔ ? No ✘	
Did you make eye contact with speaker?	Yes ✔ ? No ✘	
Were you making notes of main points and personal thoughts during the discussion?	Yes ✔ ? No ✘	
Did you discuss the issues?	Yes ✔ ? No ✘	
Were you thinking about what to say next while the other person was still talking?	Yes ✘ ? No ✔	
Did you ask a question?	Yes ✔ ? No8	
Did you get a fair share of the speaking time?	Yes ✔ ? No ✘	
Did you empathize with the speaker?	Yes ✔ ? No ✘	
Did you accept what the others said without comment?	Yes ✔ ? No ✘	
Did you interrupt people before they had finished talking?	Yes ✔ ? No ✘	
Did you drift off into daydreams because you were sure you knew what the speaker was going to say?	Yes ✘ ? No ✔	
Did the speaker's mannerisms distract you?	Yes ✘ ? No ✔	
Were you distracted by what was going on around you?	Yes ✘ ? No ✔	

13.3 Telephone listening

Almost everyone agrees that listening and talking on the telephone is the scariest foreign-language activity! There are no facial and body language clues to help your comprehension. Scary – but you need to set up your overseas placement, get a job abroad or interview people as part of a research project. Get ready! Remember:

- Telephone talking improves dramatically with practice.
- Telephone conversations have a certain ritual. You use regular phrases, protocols, conventions and turns of phrase so transactional discussion and role play practice pays in spades (p. 130).

General conversations and research interviews:

- Find a quiet room to call from, and get rid of all distractions.
- Lay your notes out around you and have two pens ready.
- Plan the call in advance. Organize your questions and comments so you can really concentrate on the responses and implications.
- Make notes of main points rather than every word, and leave time after the call to annotate and order the responses while it is fresh in your brain.
- Query anything you are unsure about. Be certain you understand the caller's nuances.
- Show you are listening and interested without interrupting, using 'yes', 'mmm', 'OK' and 'great' (or their equivalents in L2).
- Search for verbal clues, like a changed tone of voice, to 'hear between the lines'.
- Don't think you know all the answers already. If you disengage, the other caller or interviewee will become less engaged, less enthused and be a less productive informant.
- Curb your desire to jump in and fill pauses, let the speaker do most of the talking. Silences are OK.

Listening is difficult, concentrate

Job interviews

- Prepare in advance as you would for a visit to a company, by researching the company background and position. Visit your Careers Centre library, try the www.

- Make notes of points as you speak, and query anything you don't understand.
- Be enthusiastic! All linguists have lots to offer.
- Be formal in your conversation, there is a job in prospect. It is easy to drop into a colloquial, conversational mode as if chatting to a friend, which you would not do in an office interview.
- Be careful to use polite forms like 'vous' and 'Sie' – don't lapse into the universal studenty 'tu' and 'du'.

13.4 One-to-one interviews

Most of the tips for telephone interviews apply equally to personal interviews. If you can, choose locations where you will not be interrupted. Take a coffee break in a long session to give both your own and your interviewee's brain a break. Remember people can speak at about 120 words a minute, but you can listen and process words at 375 to 500 words a minute so it is easy to find your brain ambling off in other directions. Don't daydream!

Jumping to conclusions in discussion is dangerous, it leads you to switch off. Possibly the speaker is going in a new direction, diverting to give additional insights. Watch out for those 'yes but ...' and 'except where ...' statements.

Got a difficult customer? Let them talk, they will feel in charge and get the idea you agree with their discourse, which you may or may not.

Top Tips

- Really good listeners encourage the speaker by taking notes, nodding, smiling and looking interested. Do the whole open, relaxed, friendly posture bit. Verbal feedback is often better as a statement that confirms what you have heard, rather than a question which will probably be answered by the speaker's next statement anyway. 'Did you mean ... ?' or 'Am I right in thinking you are saying ...?' Unhelpful responses include yawning, looking out of the window, checking your watch, writing shopping lists and going to sleep. Relating similar personal experiences or offering solutions does not always help as, although you think you are offering empathy or sympathy, it may appear that you just turn any conversation around to yourself.
- When you are listening, interruptions need sensitive management. If you answer the telephone or speak to the next person, the person you are speaking

to will feel they are less important than the person who interrupts. If you do this to someone in business, they are very likely to take their business elsewhere. So turn the telephone off and shut the door.

- If you are emotionally involved you tend to hear what you want to hear, not what is actually said. Remain objective and open-minded.
- Keep focused on what is said. Your mind does have the capacity to listen, think, write and ponder at the same time. There is time to summarize ideas and prepare questions, but it does take practice.
- Make a real attempt to understand what the other person is saying.
- Think about what is not being said. What are the implications? Do these gaps need exploration?

13.5 References and Further Reading

Bolton, R. (1979) *People Skills: How to Assert Yourself, Listen to Others and Resolve Conflicts*. New York: Simon and Schuster Ltd.

Brownell, J. (1986) *Building Active Listening Skills*. New Jersey: Prentice Hall.

Gushgari, S.K., Francis, P.A. and Saklou, J.H. (1997) Skills critical to long-term profitability of engineering firms. *Journal of Management in Engineering*, 13, 2, 46–56.

Word Ladder

Change one letter at a time to make a new word each time you move down the ladder. Answers on p. 275.

C	E	L	T		C	O	P	T		M	A	N	X		P	I	C	T
D	A	N	E		T	H	A	I		P	O	L	E		T	U	R	K

14 EFFECTIVE ESSAY SKILLS

I'm getting on with the essay. I started the page numbers yesterday morning, and they look really good.

Some of the chapters in this book start with reasons why acquiring a particular skill might be a moderately good idea, and an analogy involving practising playing musical instruments or sport. Now demonstrate your advanced creative skills by designing your own opening. Create two well-argued sentences using the following words or phrases: reports, communication, language, persuasion, cheerful examiners, life-long, clarity; and reorganize to make a coherent sentence: with needs . solos practise, bagpipe As writing

The paragraph above may give you an insight into how annoying examiners find disjointed, half-written paragraphs, with odd words and phrases rather than a structured argument. Such paragraphs have no place in essays. If this is the first chapter you have turned to, keep reading!

This chapter picks up some important points for the kind of essays language students write, but many texts discuss writing skills in more detail. Students who have 'not written an essay in years' should find Russell (1993) or Fitzgerald (1994) valuable. Many universities run essay skills classes. The fact that so much assessment in language degrees is still essay-based should encourage *everyone* to go along.

Tutors are often asked what a good answer looks like. The most helpful response involves comparing and evaluating different pieces of writing. This chapter includes some examples of student writing at different standards. Compare the extracts to get a feel for the type of writing you are expected to produce. Space restricts the selection but you can continue to develop this critical skill by comparing essays with friends and other members of your tutor group.

All essays need good starts and ends, lots of support material and a balance of personal research and lecture-based evidence. This usually requires an initial plan, some rethinking, writing, further research, and re-writing. This should be followed by a heavy editing session where the long sentences are ruthlessly pruned and paragraphs broken up, so that each paragraph makes or develops a separate point. The first version of anything you write is a draft, a rough and ready first attempt, requiring development and polish before it is a quality product. Most marks disappear because the first drafts are submitted as the final product.

14.1 What kinds of essays are there?

The 'what do you know about ...' style essay should be disappearing from your life. University questions usually require you to *think* about information that you have researched and to *weave* it into an argument. You are asked to analyse, criticize, examine, and debate ideas in a structured way, using apt examples to illustrate your arguments. Essays that get high marks interweave lecture material with personal research findings and ideas. Facts from lectures, by themselves, are not enough – painful but true! Reproducing the facts and arguments as presented in a lecture may get you a mark of 30–50 per cent. To get 50 per cent plus you need to show an examiner that you have thought about the issues. This involves adding other information gleaned through reading, sorting out what it all means for you, and re-stating the argument coherently in your own words (Figure 14.1). OK, that is our opinion. Ask your language tutors what they think about this – get your own department's view.

You will increasingly be asked for *discussion* rather than *descriptive* essays. Compare these questions:

1. *Descriptive:* Describe the main structural elements of classical tragedy, or;
2. *Discussion:* 'The *peripeteia* is far and away the most significant moment in classical tragedy'. Discuss.
3. *Descriptive:* Describe the impact of social change on Japanese daily life, or;
4. *Discussion:* 'The contradictions, complexity and stresses of modern living impacts on all aspects of Japanese life.' Discuss.

The descriptive essay title may have pointers to the structure, content and type of answer required. The discussion essay needs more thought and planning; you must establish your own structure, and write an introduction to signpost it to the reader. Follow this with linked arguments supported by evidence, leading to a conclusion justified by the points you have made. Including material that veers off at a tangent, or is irrelevant, or presenting evidence in ways that do not really support your case, loses marks.

Many essays in language studies involve a question with no right answer. You may be asked to consider the various dimensions of a problem, evaluate alternative interpretations, provide supporting evidence and reach a balanced conclusion. Questions like: 'The vocabulary of a language is often considered too unstructured to describe systematically. What concepts and categories can one nevertheless apply in describing Russian vocabulary?' or '"The Weimar Republic was doomed from the start." Discuss', and 'Consider the impact of the euro on foreign exchange mechanisms during the past three years.'

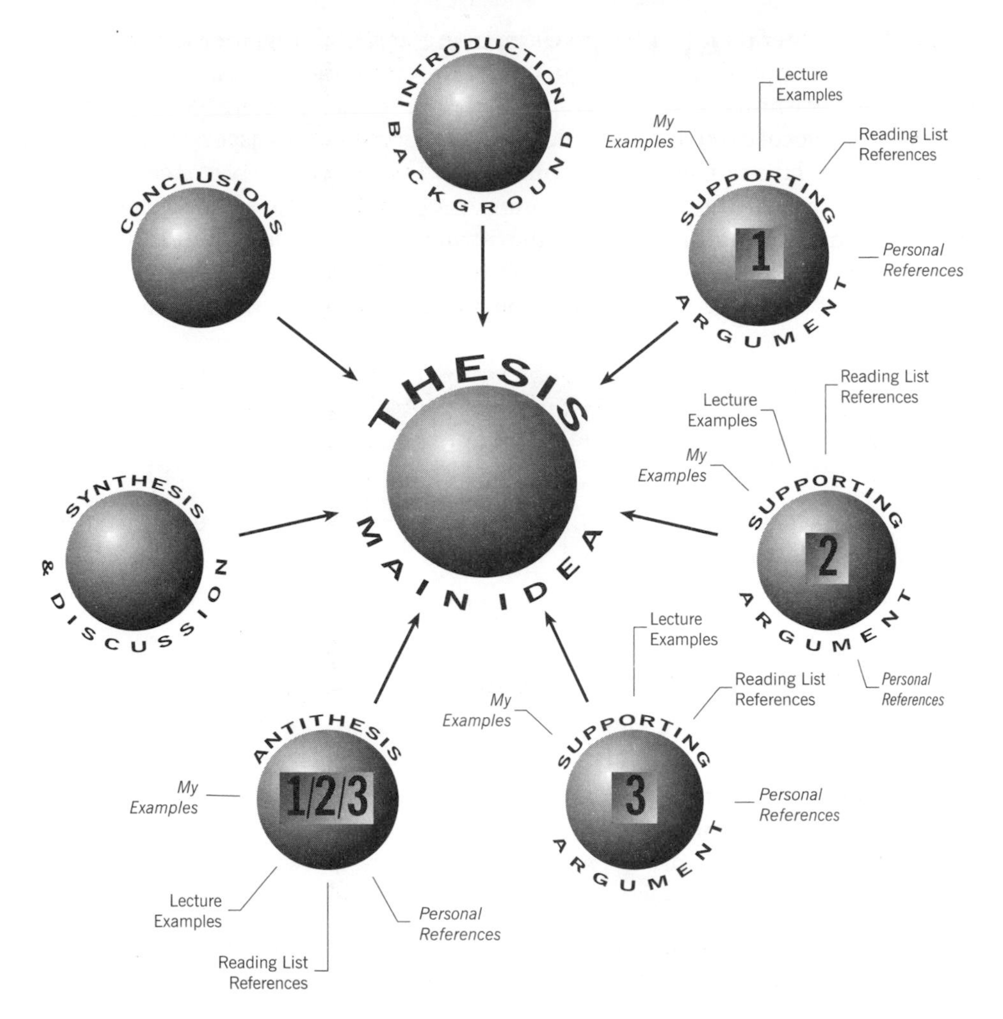

Figure 14.1 Structuring an essay, AND adding value with 'My examples' and 'Personal References'.

14.2 CAREFULLY ANALYSE ESSAY TITLES

The wording of a question can give you guidelines for your answer. Take time to analyse the question. For example:

Describe the main features and evaluate the significance of the Second Sound Shift.

What are the Keywords? The problem with this essay is that there is too much information. A *description* of the Second or High German Sound Shift calls for a solid grasp of the historical development of Indo-European and Germanic languages in general and Old High German in particular, together with a working knowledge of phonetics. The linguistic and etymological impact of the Second Sound Shift is immense, and *evaluating its significance* is a bit like gauging the length of a piece of string. Should you for instance be assessing its role in distinguishing High ('German') German from Low German, or concentrating on the lexical distinctions to which it gave rise, or looking at the relationships between German and English in particular, or ... ? There is an excess of Knowledge material. Most students attempt to include all the knowledge and thereby throw away the 50 per cent of the marks for the 'evaluate the significance' section.

- Assume all essay questions include the phrase 'with reference to specific examples relevant to the topic'.

Now apply your critical skills to **Try This 14.1**.

TRY THIS 14.1 – Keywords in essay questions

What are the keywords and pitfalls in these questions. Answers on pp. 275–6.

1. Political fragmentation, religious divisions, an inadequate transport system and the lack of a standard currency are generally cited as major factors in the Holy Roman Empire's failure to evolve economically in the eighteenth century. Explain the weaknesses in two of these sectors.
2. To what extent have economic growth and social change been accelerated by the advance of English as a lingua franca in Latin America?
3. Critically explain how Schwartz and Eubank (1994) arrive at their generative theory of transfer.
4. Account for the rapid growth in e-commerce since 2000, and assess its implications for graduates in languages other than English.
5. Evaluate the role of mass media reportage of environmental issues.

Getting started – 'red and blue pen modes'

Having analysed the essay title make a spider diagram or plan to get started. Think about using a particular colour (blue) to write down all the things that come to mind; let your ideas flow, don't get self-critical just yet. At this stage there is no need to look for the exact technical term, phrase or reference. When you have done the free and creative bit, take a different coloured (red) pen and annotate your work for structure, style, references, grammar and spelling. This approach can help take the 'fear' out of writing, and you don't waste time searching for references and digging out the thesaurus in mid flow. If you are working on a PC get typing, get the ideas down. You can go back later with the grammar and spell checkers and revise the manuscript

14.3 Effective introductions

A good introduction serves two purposes. It outlines the general background or position and signposts the structure and arguments that follow. It gives the reader confidence that you are in command of the topic. There is no reason for the introduction to be long, 100–200 words or half a side is usually plenty. If the introduction is longer, consider editing it and putting some of the material later on in the essay.

Introductions require a good deal of thought. **Planning is vital**. This is the place where you define the parameters of your essay. You need to tell the reader how you intend to answer the question – set out your stall. Copying out the essay title for your first paragraph counts as waffle or playing for time. Writing a crit of the title or indulging in verbal quibbles of the 'it is arguable that "grave" is a more apposite term than the word "serious" used in the essay title ...' variety serve merely to irritate the examiner. It *may* be appropriate to include a succinct historical or biographical resumé, but don't overdo it, don't state the obvious, and be mindful of your word-count. Lengthy quotations, references or examples are not usually good opening material. If you *must* have an example in the first paragraph, limit it to one sentence. Further details belong in the body of the essay. Here are three introductions to the same essay:

Compare the policies of literary exclusion in Nazi Germany and the GDR

Literary politics in Nazi Germany and the GDR can be seen as completely opposite in that the Nazi regime fought communist leanings in literature, whereas the politics of the GDR were anti-fascist.

True enough, but the style of the essay is not indicated. This all-too-brief opening is one-dimensional and gives the reader scarcely any clues about the writer's plans. AVOID THIS APPROACH please.

In both Nazi Germany and the GDR, a totalitarian regime ruled over politics, and both regimes showed similarly exclusive control over all aspects of cultural life. In both cases the importance of ideological incorporation amongst those working within the cultural sphere was paramount, and those who did not conform were subject to similar policies of exclusion.

Much better. The writer identifies similarities between the two regimes – their totalitarian nature and their determination to control cultural activities – and then goes on to flag a key factor in the process of literary exclusion, the need to ensure that all concerned conform to norms imposed by the state. The wording of the second sentence could be improved by changing it to 'In both cases, the incorporation of those working within the cultural sphere was of paramount importance . . .', but this is a minor stylistic detail. Far more important is the fact that the reader has clear pointers to the direction the essay is taking.

The practice of literary exclusion was an important political and ideological device in both Nazi Germany and the GDR. Although one might perhaps expect the methods and implementation of such a device to differ significantly between the two societies, there are in fact marked similarities in the way in which such methods were engineered and applied.

The best of the three. The opening paragraph makes it clear at the outset that literary exclusion was a *tool* favoured by both regimes, and reinforces the idea of something artificial and alien to literary creativity by repeating the word 'device', and by choosing significant words like 'methods', 'implementation', 'engineered' and 'applied'. The notion that despite superficial differences, totalitarian regimes have a great deal in common with one another, is subtly conveyed with the aid of feigned surprise (a handy ploy, but use it with caution!). The reader is left in no doubt that the essay will take due account of the political and ideological importance of literary exclusion and will deliver a comparative analysis of the how it operated under the two regimes.

Pretend to be an assessor and take a critical look at your own work with **Try This 14.2**.

TRY THIS 14.2 – Evaluate an introduction

Pretend to be an examiner looking at these four introductory paragraphs to the same essay. You need no knowledge of German linguistics; a small gap in your knowledge will let you concentrate on the main issues for good opening paragraphs. Questions to ask include:

- Is the general case outlined and explained?
- Does the introduction indicate how the author will tackle the essay?
- Is the language suitably technical (or 'grown up' as a tutor once described it)?

The essay title is horribly general, which makes a good opening particularly important. Some comments are on pp. 276–7.

Discuss the validity of the concept 'Standard German' in the description of the language.

Version 1

The task of identifying a standard and uniform form of German is a complex and challenging one. Standard forms of a language often develop as a media for newspapers, literature and education, and enjoy a much higher prestige than other dialects do. However it is extremely difficult to nominate one particular form of German as a standard form, particularly as different standards exist within the language, for example Austrian Standard German and Swiss Standard German.

Version 2
When we are chatting amongst friends we do not, as a rule, speak like a book, or as if we were addressing royalty. Spoken German, like spoken English, differs in many respects from its written counterpart. Written German itself will appear in numerous different forms, ranging from an informal letter to Oma to the style used by the *Frankfurter Allgemeine*. Stylistic variation is what I wish to discuss in this essay, making particular reference to the main differences between spoken and written German, before giving an outline of the significance and nature of technical language, and other stylistic aspects.

Version 3
It is a well known fact that no language is constant and static in all situations. Indeed, Standard German as described in Hammer and Duden, which foreigners learn, is just one of the linguistic varieties of German. Within any given area, speakers choose their speech from numerous varieties along a continuum. The German dialect continuum consists essentially of standard German, colloquial standard, colloquial non-standard, regional *Umgangssprache*, and traditional dialect otherwise known as 'Mundsprache'. In Germany, there is a lot of switching up and down the continuum. The point at which a speaker's language is located on such a continuum is influenced by a number of factors. One of the most obvious is region; however, social factors such as sex, age, profession, social class and educational background also play a highly significant role in determining the type of language chosen by a speaker.

Version 4
Language is never uniform – it will always be open to variation and will be constantly changing. Variation appears at a number of levels: language differs according to locality, social situation and the style or register needed for certain circumstances. I will be concentrating on social variation, although it must be noted that all three of these factors are often interchangeable and affect one another.

14.4 The middle bit!

This is where to put the knowledge and commentary, developed in a logical order, like a story. **You need a plan.** Sub-headings will make the plan clear to you and to the reader, but whether you use sub-headings mentally, or mentally and physically, is to some extent a matter of personal taste. It is worth asking your tutor if s/he minds. Some tutors will not, but some will be vitriolically against sub-headings in essays. Find out first.

Examples are the vital evidence that support the argument. In literature essays, these come in the form of quotations from the primary text(s) and references to, or quotations from, secondary literature. Use quotations sparingly but tellingly. If they are over three lines long, indent them in a paragraph of their own, otherwise run them into the body of your essay. Generally speaking, quotations are ignored for word count purposes, but check. In essays on historical/political/social/cultural/economic/linguistic subjects, evidence consists of citing specific events/legislation/sets of circumstances/movements/data, and references should be precise and concise.

Where you have a general question like 'Describe the impact of satellite TV on global foreign language acquisition,' aim to include a range of case examples. BUT, if the question is specific, such as: 'Comment on the impact of American films ...' then the essay needs to be mostly about American films and American English. In the 'foreign language acquisition' essay, remember to make the examples global. There is a temptation to answer questions like this with evidence from Europe, the USA and Japan, forgetting the developing world. Our advice is to use as many relevant examples as possible with appropriate citations. As a rule, for the general type of essay, many examples described briefly get more marks than one example retold in great depth. For the specific type, of course, an in-depth analysis will reap greater rewards. In either case, examples mentioned in lectures will be used by 80 per cent of your colleagues. Exhilarate an examiner with some new examples!

Reference appropriately

All sources and quotations must be fully referenced (see p. 165) including the sources of diagrams and data. Avoid the over obvious: 'Read what you write, be critical of your own writing (Myteacher 2010), is one . . . .' OK it is true, and your tutor may have said it, but this is not really an appropriate example of referencing, whereas 'Read over your own compositions, and wherever you meet with a passage which you think is particularly fine, strike it out (Boswell 1953)' is a proper and highly desirable example of referencing. Quoting Dr Johnson from *Boswell's Life of Johnson – c'est encore mieux*. For real authenticity quote original documents – Boswell 1791.

14.5 Synthesis

The discussion or synthesis section allows you to demonstrate your skill in drawing together the threads of the essay. You might express the main points in single sentences with supporting references, but this is just one suggestion. The following paragraph, part of a response to an invitation to 'Outline briefly and evaluate the principal stages in the study of language from the beginnings down to 1916', illustrates how a essay can combine statement of fact with synthesis:

The ancient Greeks and Romans were the first cultures recorded as having attempted to describe and analyse the structure of language, and the categories and terminology of traditional grammar are derived from theirs, in particular a work by a Greek grammarian, Dionysius Archilochos (c. 170–c. 120 BC), the Art of Grammar. Yet the Biblical story of the Tower of Babel suggests that there must have been an awareness of linguistic difference, and with it perhaps an interest in the nature of language, long before then. In the 18th century the German philosopher Friedrich Wilhelm Leipnitz speculated that most of the languages spoken in Europe and Asia must have had a common ancestor, which we now call Indo-European. In the 19th century, grammarians and lexicographers began to discover more about the essential links between language families and individual languages that enabled them to go beyond the theories of the classical grammarians and of Leipnitz, deep into the realm of language evolution. This province, which became the main focus of interest in the field of linguistic science throughout that century, was dominated by a handful of scholars, notably the Austrian Wilhelm Grimm, who formulated Grimm's Law in 1832. Grimm's Law, which stated that unvoiced p, d, *and* ch *in the hypothetical parent language, Proto-Indo-European, became voiceless* f, d, *and* h *in Old High German, and* v, th, *and* ch *in English, was augmented by the work of the Swedish philologist Karl August Werner (1846–1906). Werner's Law stated that whether or not the initial and final dentals were voiced in the Germanic languages depended on whether they came after an accented or an unaccented syllable in Indo-European. Since the beginning of the 20th century, the interest of linguists has shifted to new areas, among them that of deconstructive linguistics. This developed from theories first postulated by the Frenchman Ferdinand de Saussure (1857–1913). His work concentrated on the relationship between the surface level of language (the words we speak) and the structure that lies beneath it, or rather, above: a meta-hidden system of rules and syntax which we grasp intuitively.*

So what do you think? Maybe a little light on the 'evaluate' part, but lots of information, interwoven references, useful information – this should get high marks and is a style to aim for. The register and tone are scholarly, the overall impression is very good. If only the facts were right it *would* get high marks. BUT this particular paragraph will be lucky to score 40%. The Greek grammarian was called Dionysius Thrax, and his dates are wrong, as are numerous others. Several names are also wrong and/or misspelt (Gottfried Wilhelm Leibniz, not Wilhelm Grimm but his older brother Jacob, Verner); the Grimms were German, Verner was a Dane, and Saussure a Swiss, and his work was in the field of structural linguistics. Grimm, who formulated his Law in 1822, had rather different things to say about sound shifts in Indo-European – this author confuses voiced and unvoiced consonants, refers to them rather unhelpfully as 'unvoiced' one moment and 'voiceless' the next (they mean the same thing, but wealth of synonym is not a desirable stylistic feature in a technical explanation); and Verner's Law concerns medial and final fricatives, not initial and final dentals. Examiners are on the look-out for factual inaccuracies, they notice spoof and imaginary references.

With all the right facts, and a few linking sentences along the lines of: – 'Grimm's contribution to our knowledge of the evolution of language was immense. It remains even to this day a cornerstone in the edifice of classical philology, whilst Verner's observations, though modest by comparison, nicely complement our theoretical understanding of this branch of linguistics. It was not, however, until the early years of the 20th century that Saussure and others gave the subject a fresh impetus by proposing that the language we speak is underpinned by a distinct, abstract language' – this essay is destined for top marks.

14.6 Conclusions

A conclusion is the place you have reached when you are tired of thinking.

The conclusion should sum up the argument but without directly repeating statements from the introduction. Introducing new material can cause examiners to comment, 'The conclusions had little to do with the essay as a whole'. It is hard to judge the standard of conclusions in isolation, because the nature and style of a conclusion depends on the content of the essay, but it helps to look at other examples. Check out conclusions in any of the general language and linguistics periodicals. Now criticize the examples in **Try This 14.3**.

14.7 Assessment and plagiarism

TRY THIS 14.3 – Good concluding paragraphs

Read the following concluding paragraphs and consider their relative merits. Comments on p. 277.

Version 1

Unlike the bourgeois women's movement, who sought to improve their lot by campaigning (with their louder voices than working-class women) in the same capitalist, split-class society in which they lived, the working-class women sought to gain gender equality via the wider and (for them) more important method of gaining social equality. They wanted to do this via socialism. They must have looked at the bourgeois women's movement's demands and thought: 'What? Why do you want to work?' They hated the bourgeois movement.

Version 2

Therefore, the situation of working-class women was poor in the nineteenth century but gradually through the strategies they employed it began to improve. The most significant achievement being the acquisition of the vote in 1919. It is easy to underestimate the achievements made and also to forget that men totally dominated society. They worked with sensible realistic strategies, altering them as they saw fit. By 1909 the *Vereinsgesetz* had been repealed too.

Version 3

We have seen that certain strategies were employed by the working-class movement to improve the social position of women, although in general this must be seen as an essentially middle-class aim. The working-class women's movement was more concerned about seeing improvements in their everyday lives, for example working conditions. They were primarily interested in pursuing their own practical concerns, and could not see much reason for the complaints of many middle-class campaigners. The working-class women were accustomed to being powerless within the state, they were crushed by the anti-*Frauenfrage* laws such as no female editors (1852), as well as the anti-socialist laws 1875–90, which stifled what little hope they had had of gaining a political voice.

Assessment

Either use you department's assessment criteria or Table 14.1 and Figure 14.2 to critically review your writing. In Figure 14.2 the percentage equivalents are given for guidance, but these values vary. Self-assessing a first draft can indicate where to focus your next research and writing effort.

Another way of developing your evaluation skills is to use **Try This 14.4** which builds on an idea from note-making by using codes to locate the different sections of an essay and to compare their relative weights. **Try This 14.5** presents another way of creating essay structures by posing questions about the mark distribution. If the balance of the reward changes then so does the content.

TRY THIS 14.4 – Analysing essay structures

Look at any essay you have written. With 5 coloured pens, or a code system, mark in the margin the sections which show Knowledge, Analysis, Synthesis, Evaluation, and Creative Abilities. Now think about the relative structure and content.

- Is there a good opening paragraph?
- Does the argument flow logically?
- Are the arguments summarized effectively?
- Are the conclusions justified?
- How would you re-write this essay to strengthen the analysis section?
- How would you redesign to improve the evaluation content?
- Are the examples relevant?
- Where could the balance of the essay be altered to improve it?

Criterion	First 70–100%	2(i) 60–69%	2(ii) 50–59%	Third 40–49%	Ordinary 37–39%	Fail 0–36%
Structure: Organization, logical order of material, aims, conclusion	Well organized throughout. Good structure. Appropriate aims stated and conclusion argued clearly.	Mostly well organized, appropriate structure. Aims and conclusion stated and argued clearly.	Structure attempted. Evidence of organization. Sound aims and conclusion.	Some attempt at structure or organization but weak or inappropriate.	Little attempt at organization.	Disorganized. No structure, aims or conclusion.
Accuracy and understanding of material, focusing on the question	Accurate and thorough understanding. Focused on the question throughout.	Good understanding of the subject. Mostly focused on the question.	Sound understanding of the subject but not effectively focused on the question. Some inaccuracies or misunderstandings.	Inaccuracies evident. Some limited understanding of the subject, not applied to the question.	Some glimpses of understanding but much work inaccurate or unfocused.	Totally fails to address the question posed. Fails to demonstrate understanding of the subject.
Coverage: Comprehensive-ness, relevance, evidence of reading, research, use of examples	Developed own ideas based on thorough understanding of the relevant literature. Comprehensive coverage of material. Excellent use of illustrative examples.	Demonstrates evidence of reading well beyond lecture material. References are relevant. Good use of illustrative examples.	Covers lecture material reasonably well. Mostly accurate and comprehensive. Some evidence of further reading. Some relevant examples provided.	Lecture material only, but not comprehensive. Little evidence of further reading. Some examples given but not all relevant.	Much irrelevant or missing material. Too brief but some knowledge of the general topic. Little attempt to exemplify.	Lack of relevant material. No use of examples.
Clarity of argumence: Coherence fluency, criticality, innovation	Excellent coherence and clarity of expression. Demonstrates application of critical thought. Shows originality in handling arguments.	Mostly coherent. Some attempt at critical analysis and original argument.	Generally coherent but some lack of clarity of thought or expression.	Some clarity but too simplistic.	Somewhat disjointed and lacking in development.	Incoherent. Disjointed.
Presentation: Grammar, spelling, legibility, referencing system	No errors. Clear, relevant and consistently accurate referencing.	Few errors. Referencing relevant and mostly accurate.	Occasional errors. Minor inaccuracies or inconsistencies in referencing.	Frequent errors. Referencing with some inaccuracies or inconsistencies.	Very frequent errors. Referencing inaccurate or inconsistent.	Riddled with errors. Referencing absent.

Table 14.1 Essay assessment criteria.

Name .... Essay Title...						
	I	2.1	2.2	3	Fail	
Knowledge 30%						
Topics covered in depth						Superficial responses
Appropriate subject content						Limited/no subject content
Good use of primary sources						Poor/no use of primary sources
Good use of secondary literature						Poor/no use of secondary literature
Structure and argument 40%						
Logical presentation						Disorganized
Good synthesis and evaluation						No synthesis and evaluation
Clear, succinct writing style						Rambling and/or repetitive
Creativity 20%						
Includes new ideas						No new ideas
Innovative presentation						Incoherent presentation
Presentation 10%						
Fully and correctly referenced						No references
Correct spelling and grammar						Poor spelling and grammar
Good use of illustrative materials						Poor/no use of illustrative materials

Figure 14.2 Essay self-assessment form.

TRY THIS 14.5 – Marks for what?

Take any essay title (the last or next) and work out a plan for researching and answering the question when the mark distribution is:

1. Knowledge 20%; Analysis 20%; Synthesis 20%; Evaluation 20%; Professionalism 20%,

AND

2. Knowledge 10%; Analysis 50%; Synthesis 20%; Evaluation 10%; Creativity 10%,

AND

3. Knowledge 30%; Evaluation 70%

Consider how the plans change as the mark distributions alter.

Avoiding plagiarism

Academic staff are good at noticing words copied from texts and papers without acknowledgement. They spot changes in the style of writing, use of tenses, changes in formats and page sizes, the sudden appearance of very technical words or sentences that the writer doesn't seem happy with, and quotations without citations. The advice is 'never cut and paste any document', whether from the www or friends. Think through the point you want to make, express it in your own way and cite sources as you write. Put quotations in quotation marks and cite the source.

Getting advice

Showing a draft essay, or any document, to someone else for comment is not cheating. It is normal practice in business and academic publishing, as shown by the acknowledgements at the end of many published papers. For example, in *The Modern Language Journal* 84, 1,2000 there are thanks for reviewer's comments and suggestions on pages 24, 66, 82 and 100. You do not have to take note of the comments, but having an independent check on grammar and spelling and someone asking awkward questions about content does no harm.

14.8 GETTING THE ENGLISH ~~RIGHT~~ BETTER

Try ~~NEVER to cross anything out~~!

Keep sentences short wherever possible. See **Try This 14.6** for starters!

TRY THIS 14.6 – Shorten/tighten up these sentences

Answers on p. 278.

Wordy	Better
In a great many instances, the authorities were powerless to act.	
The use of case is an important factor in many inflected languages.	
In much of eighteenth-century Europe, the law of primogeniture applied and daughters and younger sons had no inheritance to look forward to.	
Moving to another phase of the project ...	
Dialect variations were studied in Provence and the Dordogne region respectively.	
Iambic pentameter is a kind of metre. (Should read 'Iambic pentameter is a type of metre.')	
One of the best ways of investigating the women's movement in its early phases is ...	

The process of integrating genuine asylum-seekers into mainstream society continues along the lines outlined.	
The nature of the problem ...	
Childbirth is an important, perhaps *the* most important, factor of life.	
One prominent feature of blank verse is the absence of rhymes.	
It is sort of understood that ...	
It is difficult enough to explore gender issues in the media without time constraints adding to the pressure.	
The body of evidence is in favour of ...	

Technical terms

Good professional writing in any subject uses technical language, defining technical terms when necessary. Definitions can be very important – 'romantic' in colloquial usage is far removed from its meaning in literary criticism; 'state security' means one thing in Berne, but something rather different in Beijing; and the connotation of terms like 'socialist' or 'conservative' varies from one regime to another. There is no need to define technical terms that are in everyday use and where you are using words in their normal sense; assume the reader is intelligent and well educated. In a student's essay on the aftermath of German re-unification, the second paragraph started with: 'The GDR came to an end with the fall of the Berlin Wall on 9 November 1989. At last East Germans were able to cross to the West without let or hindrance, for the first time in 28 years.' In our view this student wasted time and space on the second sentence as an examiner already knows about the Berlin Wall, and it was not appropriate to do more than mention its collapse in the context of that essay. Keep the language suitably technical and the sentences simple. Use the correct technical terms wherever possible and avoid being unnecessarily long-winded.

Startling imagery

'It is a truth, universally acknowledged, that a man in possession of a large screen satellite TV on Cup Final Day, must be in want of a six pack'. The impact is greater for being a parody of Jane Austen. However this comment, while arresting, is also dangerously stereotypical, far from being 'politically correct' and generally genderist. Creative use of language is great, but avoid the temptation to bowdlerize or tabloidize in an inappropriate manner.

One idea per paragraph

In a lengthy essay, restricting paragraphs to one idea plus its supporting argument should make your message clearer. Use **Try This 14.7** to analyse one of your own essays.

TRY THIS 14.7 – One idea per paragraph

Look back through your last essay and underline the ideas and supporting statements. If each paragraph has a separate idea and evidence, award yourself a chocolate bar and a cheer. If not, redesign a couple of paragraphs to disentangle the arguments and evidence. The challenge is to make the evidence clear to the reader by separating out the different strands of the argument.

N.B. This is a good exercise to do at the end of the first draft of every essay.

Synonyms

Part of the richness of English comes from the many synonyms that add variety, depth and readability to writing. Make sure you write what you mean to write! A common error is to confuse 'infer' and 'imply' – they are not synonyms; 'infer' is used when drawing a conclusion from data or other information, 'imply' means to suggest or indicate. We might infer from a study of *Antigone* that Jean Anouilh was a misogynist, or a lecturer might imply during a discussion that Jean Anouilh was a misogynist. Have a practice with **Try This 14.8** and **Try This 14.9**. Look at any sentence you have written, and play around with a thesaurus (book or electronic) and find synonyms you might use. If you tend to overuse certain words, make a list of synonyms and substitute some of them, WHERE RELEVANT.

TRY THIS 14.8 – Synonyms, homonyms and look-alikes

Which of the paired words makes sense? Answers on p. 279.

1. Womens' sexuality is a remarkably *pernicious/persistent* theme of the *Roman de la Rose* as a whole
2. In the 19th century, many Scots and Irish decided that although they could *better/improve* themselves through education, the only real way to *better/improve* themselves was by emigrating.
3. Having hoped for *disinterested/uninterested* advice, she was deeply shocked by her teacher's apparently *disinterested/uninterested* response to her predicament.
4. Anna was mildly surprised that Sue had been so deeply *affected/effected* by the incident.

5. Unlike certain other countries, Britain's National Health Service does not provide *complimentary/complementary* medical treatment.
6. Heidi was flattered by her boss's *unwanted/unwonted* attention.
7. It is impossible to learn or write a language fluently without *practicing/practising* for many hours.
8. The author *hesitantly/tentatively* offers a feminist reading of this overtly homosexual novel.

TRY THIS 14.9 – Synonyms again

These two tables show a perfectly acceptable sentence and some of the synonyms that might be substituted. Some synonyms are acceptable, others make no sense at all. Which are useful substitutes?

Right									notice
Apt		special		allocates		lyrical	distinction		appeal
Decent		selected	three feet	accepts		elegiac	discrepancy	furthermore	attract
Fitting	*the*	*chosen*	*metre*	*allows*	*for*	*rhythmical*	*variation*	*and*	*interest*
Proper		elected	gauge	permits		flowing	difference	plus	attention
Fit		preferred		agrees		graceful	disparity	as well as	concern
Correct				consents to		prosaic	deviation		hobby
Appropriate				tolerates					advantage

							useful	handy	disapproval
		study		creative writing	change		customary	matter of fact	condemnation
May	fashionable	examination		novel	fluctuate		fixed	realistic	denigration
Does	*stylistic*	*analysis*	*of*	*literature*	*differ*	*from*	*traditional*	*practical*	*criticism?*
Can	trendy	investigation		narrative	vary	since	established	nifty	analysis
	smart	scrutiny		short story	diverge		accepted	sensible	censure
		breakdown		fiction	disagree		habitual	functional	disparagement

Argument by analogy can be very useful but, as this example shows, it can also get out of hand:

The vocabulary of English is legendary for its eclecticism. In fact, it is not unlike a linguistic garbage can when it comes to accumulating words from other languages. In this case the first sentence would be better standing alone.

I know what I meant! Trying to get students to re-read and correct written work is an uphill struggle for most tutors. Re-read to spot illogical statements or those where a crucial word was missed. Here, for your amusement, are some essay statements that do not exactly convey the writer's original intention: *'The former GDR has increasingly become a thing of the past.' 'Fathers and grandfathers were also entitled to take maternity leave.' 'There was a huge influx of Turks, usually young males, to help build the Berlin Wall.' 'Gregor Samsa seems to lack a distinctive personality. However he has a few traits.' 'According to Lessing, laughter helped one reflect far easier and this was the basis for the Age of Enlightenment.'*

Spelling

Spelling is a potential minefield – use a spell-checker but remember that it will not pick up the errors in the following sentences, caused by *homonyms* (words that sound the same but have different spellings and meanings): 'Archaeologists investigating the Bronze Age burial site in Brittany have discovered a large horde of gold coins.' 'Shogun warriors had to be skilled in the marshall arts.' 'The position of the tongue relative to the palette is highly significant in the pronunciation of certain sounds.' 'In speech, the tongue and the teeth compliment one another.' 'In business, appropriate stationary is an essential element in projecting the desired image.' 'Most academic books have a forward, but very few books have an epithet.'

Abbreviations and acronyms in text

Replacing long words or phrases with initials or abbreviations is regarded as lazy by some tutors. However, with well known and established acronyms (see p. 269) and phrases like WYSIWYG (What You See Is What You Get), it is reasonable to adopt this approach. Consider your response to abbreviations in **Try This 14.10**. When using abbreviations the full definition must be given the first time the phrase is used, with the abbreviation immediately afterwards in brackets.

NB: Linguists (especially philologists) conventionally adopt an abbreviation strategy when citing the names of languages: Fr., Gmc., IE, Jap., L., MHG, OE ... and so on (French, Germanic, Indo-European, Japanese, Latin, Middle High German, Old English).

TRY THIS 14.10 – Abbreviations

How do you feel about the use of ES in Chapter 17, and YAT in Chapter 24? Is it a procedure to adopt?

Colloquial usage

Regional or colloquial terms may not be universally understood so are best omitted. Writing as you speak can also be a trap, as in these examples from student essays:

'He therefore put to greater emphasis on .... ' It should read 'He therefore put too great an emphasis on ...'; 'The Central Bank will of always considered interest rates', should read 'The Central Bank will have always considered ...'.

Punctuation and style

The excessive use of **exclamation marks**!!!!!!!!!!, of which these authors are generally guilty, is also less than good practice! *And never* start a sentence with 'And', 'But' or 'BUT'. But having said that, there are plenty of examples of its incorrect usage in this book, where BUT and capitalization are used to emphasize points.

When editing, check that you do not over-use certain words. Find synonyms or restructure the paragraph if repetition is a problem! Keep sentences short and TO THE POINT. Ensure paragraphs address one point only. Be consistent in your use of fonts and font sizes, symbols, heading titles and position, bullet points and referencing. Decide on your style and stick to it. If you feel you have trouble with your writing, or you are unsure about the use of colons, semi-colons and apostrophes, see Kahn (1991) or Russell (1993).

Top Tips

- Read and revise everything you write. Make time at the end of an essay to re-read and re-draft, correct spelling, insert missing words, check grammar and insert references.
- Check that your arguments are logical.
- Read what is written, not what you meant to write.
- Work with a friend.

14.9 References and Further Reading

Some genuine references were embedded in some of the essay extracts, and the full citation would appear at the end of the essay. They are not included here. A BIDS search will find them, or see http://www.german.leeds.ac.uk/skillsbook/index.htm. Most study skills books discuss essay writing, but see also:

Barrass, R. (1982) *Students Must Write – A Guide to Better Writing in Course Work and Examinations*. London: Routledge.

Boswell, J. (1953) *Boswell's Life of Johnson.* (new edn.). London: Oxford University Press.

Dummett, M. (1993) *Grammar and Style for Examination Candidates and Others.* London: Duckworth.

Fairbairn, G.J. and Winch, C. (1996) *Reading, Writing and Reasoning: A Guide for Students.* (2nd edn). Milton Keynes: Open University Press.

Kahn, J.E. (ed.) (1991) *How to Write and Speak Better.* London: Reader's Digest.

Russell, S. (1993) *Grammar, Structure and Style.* Oxford: Oxford University Press.

Language Anagrams 3

Try These Language anagrams, answers p. 279.

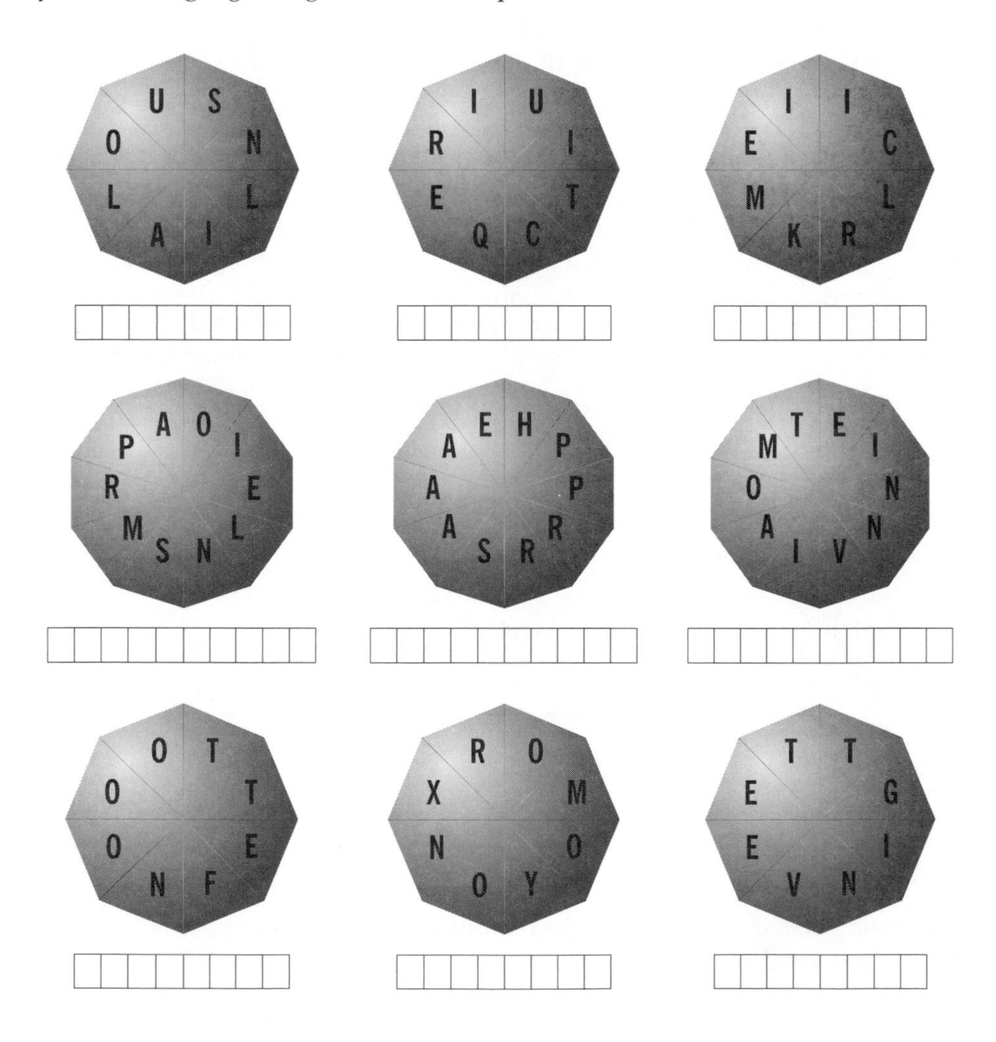

15 CITING REFERENCES AND OTHER SOURCES

Opere citae – *is not a post modern city opera.*

When Eric Morecombe played the Greig piano concerto with André Previn, and the notes were not as André expected, Eric explained that he was 'playing all the right notes, just in a different order'. Referencing is mostly about getting the right notes in the right order.

Advising you on citing references is a procedural minefield but you will be blown out of the water for any/every piece of academic writing that does not include references. **References** are the sources for material you cite in your document, whether you read them or not. References do not include 'other things I read but didn't mention in the text'. A **bibliography** is an alphabetical list of sources or references on a particular topic; a complete bibliography would aim to include every document relating to a topic. To create an 'annotated bibliography', sort the references into subsections with a brief statement or paragraph justifying your groupings and describing the contents.

There are a number of standard ways to acknowledge research sources and this is the problem. The standard reference for all language students is the *MHRA Style Book* (Modern Humanities Research Association, 1996) but this gives you twelve different ways to cite a book and no indication as to which you might use. The references in any good text or journal will show you their house style and these vary widely. Some use a footnotes pattern putting references at the foot of the page where they first appear, others place them in alphabetical order or order of occurrence at the end. Some systems cite authors' given and surnames, others cite surname and initials. **Given the variety it is important to get organized from the start of your degree,** because each time you read you need to note the reference, and depending on your citation system you record slightly different things. If your department has a preferred style for essays and dissertations, check the student handbook and **follow it exactly**. In the absence of departmental guidance, follow the advice here. We use the system, exemplified in this book, where materials are cited by author and date within the text, and all the references are listed alphabetically at the end of the document. The key skill with referencing is consistency. Decide on a style and stick to it.

15.1 CITING PAPER SOURCES IN TEXT

Within text, a book or article is cited by the author's family name and year of publication. When there are two authors both are quoted. Conventionally, when there are three or more authors the *et al.* convention is adopted. For example 'Discussing the superiority of argument over propaganda, Verrcalm (2010) suggested impartial evidence given by Blatant and Bitter (2007) undermines current thinking, whereas the effect of advertising as studied by Persuasivo *et al.* (2008) produced a series of new insights into . . . .' '

Where information in one text refers to another, quote both: 'As reported by El'vated (2010), Ground (2009) showed that . . . .' Both the El'vated (2010) and Ground (2009) references should appear in the reference list. Similarly: 'In an extensive discussion of homophony Singularus (2010) shows the approach taken by Dunlisnin (2005) was unreliable, and therefore the methodology adopted by Dunlisnin is not followed'. Again quote both sources, even though you have probably only read Singularus, so the reader can locate the original. If you want to make clear that you have acquired your information from a secondary source use a sentence like 'High frequencies are mediated nearest the oval window, and low frequencies at the farther end of the basilar membrane (Cochlear 2005, cited Implant *et al.* 2010)'. In this type of case it is important to give the two dates which indicate the age of the original data, 2005, rather than the 2010 date of the reference you read. You should quote both Cochlear and Implant *et al.* in the references. The Cochlear reference should be cited in the Implant *et al.* paper, so not including it would be lazy. If Implant *et al.* does not cite Cochlear, use a Web of Science search (see p. 52) to find the source.

Take care with oriental names where given names are second, the family name first. It is all too easy to reference by the given name by mistake.

Referring to government publications, where the author is awkward to trace, is also problematical. There are no absolute rules, use common sense or follow past practice. This example is a classic referencing nightmare:

CSICSC (1992). *China Statistical Yearbook 1992*. Fan Z., Fang J., Liu H., Wang Y. and Zhang J. (eds). Beijing: China Statistical Information and Consultancy Service Centre.

There is no single right way to cite this source – even librarians have different views on how to handle this one. Some would reference it by the editors as 'Fan *et al.* (1992)', others by the full title 'China Statistical Yearbook (1992)'. In a library search you might have to try a number of search options. Searching by title is likely to be the fastest successful route to locating this volume.

Referencing by initials can be convenient and time saving. You might refer in your document to *MBS* (2004) or UNESCO (1999), but you must use the full title in the reference list:

UNESCO (United Nations Educational, Scientific and Cultural Organization) (1999). *World Communication and Information Report 1999-2000.* Paris: UNESCO Publishing.

UNSD (United Nations Statistics Division) (2000) *Monthly Bulletin of Statistics (MBS)*, [online] http://www.un.org/Pubs/whatsnew/mbsonlin.htm Accessed 31 July 2000.

Finally, if there doesn't seem to be a rule, invent one and use it consistently.

Citing a reference – be consistent

15.2 CITING PAPER SOURCES IN REFERENCE LISTS

The key is consistency in format which includes a standard sequence of commas, stops, italics and underlining. Most journals which use reference lists cite each reference in full, but those which use a footnote scheme, citing references in passing, normally also employ three abbreviations to minimize repetition:

ibid. – *ibidem*, the same, used when a reference is the same as the previous one.

loc. cit. – *loco citato*, in the place cited.

op. cit. – *opere citato*, in the work cited.

Citing a book

Template:
Author(s) (Year) *Title* (edition). Place of publication: Publisher.

Example:
Ibsen, H. (1883) *Gildet på Solhaug: Skuespil i tre akter.* København: Hegel and Søn.

Citing a chapter in an edited volume

The author(s) of the chapter or paper in an edited text are cited first, followed by the book editors' details. Note that it is the title of the book that is placed in italics, not the chapter title.

Template:
Author(s) (Year) Chapter title. In Editors' name(s) (ed(s.)), *Book title* (edition). Place of publication: Publisher, page numbers.

Example:
Iwanga, K. (2000) Europe in Japan's Foreign Policy. In Edström, B. (ed.), *The Japanese and Europe: Images and Perceptions.* Richmond, Surrey: Japan Library, 208–235.

Citing an edited book

Template:
Editor(s) ed(s). (Year) *Title* (edition). Place of publication: Publisher.

Examples:
Kelly, C. and Lovell, S. eds., (2000) *Russian Literature, Modernism and the Visual Arts*. Cambridge: Cambridge University Press.

Citing a journal article

Template:
Author (Year) Article Title. *Journal Title*, volume number, issue number, page numbers.

Examples:
Jones, S.F. (2000) Democracy from below? Interest groups in Georgian society. *Slavic Review*, 59, 1, 42–73.

Laviosa, S. (1999) Come studiare e insegnare l'italiano attraverso i corpora. *Italica*, 76, 4, 443–453.

Citing a conference paper

Template:
Author. (Year) Article title. *Conference Title*. Location of conference, date (month).

Examples:
Milburn, D. (1997) 'Denn die Toten reiten schnell.' Anglo-German Cross-Currents in Bram Stoker's *Dracula*. *The Novel in Anglo-German Context Conference*, University of Leeds, Leeds, UK, September.

If the conference papers are written up in proceedings or a journal, cite the paper version rather than the oral presentation.

Citing a newspaper article

Most newspaper articles have an author attribution and should be referenced alphabetically by the author, for example Browaeys and Kaplan (2000). Where there is no author, use the first couple of words of the title as the cross-reference and the full title in the reference list, as in *French Face Welsh* (1699).

Template when an author is cited:
Author. Full Date. title. *Newspaper*, volume number if applicable, page number(s)

Example:
Browaeys, D.B. and Kaplan J.-C. May 2000. La tentation de l'apartheid génétique. *Le Monde Diplomatique*, 554, 1.

Template for an unattributed item:
Title, full date. *Newspaper*, volume number if applicable, page number(s).

Example:
French face Welsh racism inquiry, 16 March 1699. *The Daily Groat*, 3.

Citing unpublished theses

Thesis citations follow the general guidelines for a book; then add 'unpublished', and enough information for another researcher to locate the volume.

Ennis, J.S. (1993). *A comparison of Richard Wagner's 'Der Ring des Nibelungen' and William Morris's 'Sigurd the Volsung'*. University of Leeds: Unpublished PhD thesis, Department of German.

Careless, I.M. (2000) *The Elaboration of Parody by Baudelaire in 'Les Fleurs du Mal'*. University of Life: Unpublished BA thesis, School of French.

Citing dictionaries

Dictionaries are an oddity – they have editors or compilers who should be the cited individuals, but these noble people are rarely well known and where dictionaries are cited it is usually by title.

Collins Spanish–English, English–Spanish Dictionary (1997) (5th edn.) Glasgow: HarperCollins.

The Sansoni Dictionaries: English–Italian, Italian–English (1981) (2nd edn.) Firenze: Sansoni.

OED (1989) *Oxford English Dictionary* (2nd. edn.). Oxford: Clarendon Press.

OED Online (2000) *Oxford English Dictionary Online*, CD-ROM, Oxford: Oxford University Press.

But with more specialized texts we suggest you use the author:

Hérail, R.J. and Lovatt, E.A. (1984) *Dictionary of Modern Colloquial French*. London: Routledge.

Trask, R.L. (1997) *A Student's Dictionary of Language and Linguistics*. London: Arnold.

Citing video and audio material

Template when an author is cited:
Composer or Author (Date) Title. Publisher, tape section number/duration if applicable

Examples:
Citing an audio-tape:
Dyson, P. and Worth, V. (1987) *Actualités Radio-Presse*. London: Macmillan.

Video-tape:
Broady, E. and Meinhof, U. (1995) *Téletextes*, Oxford: OUP.

Video clip:
'Deutsche Einheit – Grenze: Minensuche' (25.6.91) *Tagesthemen*, 2′ 44″; ARD.

15.3 Citing electronic sources

A standard template for citing electronic sources of information is not yet agreed. These notes follow recommendations from various library sources. If you are writing for a publication, check whether an alternative method is used. **The crucial new element is adding the date when you accessed the information, because the contents of electronic sites change.** The next person to access the site may not see the same information.

Referencing within text.

Internet and other electronic sources should be treated in the same way as a book or journal reference. For example '... exploring party music options in Holland (Salsa Dancing in Amsterdam 2000) we estimate ...' or '... exploring party music options in Holland (Hautus 2000) we estimate ...'. The latter example is better provided the name of the author is clearly stated on the site. If there is no obvious author, use the title.

Citing individual Internet sites

To cite Internet sources use the document's URL (Internet) address. Addresses tend to be long, so typing needs careful checking. If the citation is longer than one line the URL should only be split after a forward slash / in the address. ThecaSe/ofchaRacters/inTheAddress/sHouldnOt/bealterEd.EVER. Avoid putting a full-stop after the URL, or if you must, leave a clear space before it, to indicate that it does not form part of the URL.

The safest way to cite correctly is to copy and paste www addresses to text or notepad files as you view them.

Template:

Author/editor. (Year) *Title* [on-line] (edition). Place of publication: Publisher (if ascertainable), URL, Accessed Date.

Example:

Hautus E. (2000) *Salsa Dancing in Amsterdam* [on-line] http://www.xs4all.nl/~ehautus/salsa-amsterdam.html Accessed 30 July 2000.

Salsa Dancing in Amsterdam (2000) [on-line] http://www.xs4all.nl/~ehautus/salsa-amsterdam.html Accessed 30 July 2000.

Donald, S. (1996) From Logs to Licentiateships: a case-study in natural progression [on-line].
http://www.lle.mdx.ac.uk/hec/journal/ccss/sdonald.htm Accessed 30 July 2000.

When the electronic publication date is not stated write 'no date' (or n.d.). The term [on-line] indicates the type of publication medium. Use it for all Internet and e-journal sources. The 'Accessed date' is the date on which *you viewed or downloaded* the document.

'Publisher' covers both the traditional idea of a publisher of printed sources, and organizations responsible for maintaining sites on the Internet. Many Internet sites show the organization maintaining the information, but not the text author. If in doubt, ascribe authorship to the smallest identifiable organizational unit.

Example:

Center for Advancement of Learning (1998). *Assessment – Learning and Study Strategies Inventory (LASSI), Learning Strategies Database* [on-line]. Center for Advancement of Learning, Muskingham College. http://muskingham.edu/~cal/DATABASE/lassi.html Accessed 12 April 2000.

Citing E-Journals (electronic journals)

Template:

Author. (Year) Title. *Journal Title* [on-line] *volume, issue,* page numbers or location within host. URL Accessed Date.

Example:

Gregory, A. (2000) Contemporary trends in women's employment in France. *Modern and Contemporary France* [on-line] 8, 2, 175–191.
http://pinkerton.bham.ac.uk/vl=85883676/cl=2/nw=1/rpsv/catchword/carfax/09639489/v8n2/contp1-1.htm Accessed 30 July 2000.

BUT if you try to access this URL direct you will get nowhere. Access to this journal is controlled by a password. Look up the journal title in your library catalogue to see whether you have access. In some electronic journals the 'page' location is replaced by screen, paragraph or line numbers.

Citing personal electronic communications (e-mail)

For reference to personal e-mail messages use the 'subject line' of the message as a title and include the full date. Remember to keep copies of e-mails you reference.

Template:

Sender. (Sender's e-mail address), Day Month Year. *Subject of Message*. E-mail to Recipient (Recipient's e-mail address.)

Example:

Swotoff, I. (1234slav@leeds.ac.uk), 21 October 2000. *Essay for Second Tutorial*. E-mail to Dodge, R. (8901slav@leeds.ac.uk)

Top Tips

- **Authors**. Generally an author's name can be found at the foot of an electronic document. Authors of journal articles are usually stated at the beginning of the article as in hard copy. Where the identity of the author is unclear the URL should indicate the name of the institution responsible for the document. However, this organization may only be maintaining the document, not producing it, so take care to assign the right authorship.
- **Date of publication.** This is often at the foot of the page with the author's name, and sometimes with 'last updated' information. In newer versions of Netscape you can select *Document Info* on the *View* menu. This shows the 'last modified date' of the document. Other browsers have similar ways of viewing this information.
- You must keep accurate records of the material you access. Using an on-line database bibliographic package such as Idealist or End Note can help to keep track of research resources.

Producing correct reference lists is an important skill, demonstrating your attention to detail and professionalism. Correct **Try This 15.1** to develop this skill. The ultimate test of a reference list is that someone else can use it to locate the documents. Make sure your citation lists meet this standard.

TRY THIS 15.1 – The nightmare reference list

There are many deliberate errors here. If a reference list like this appears at the end of an essay or dissertation the marks will drift away. How many errors can you spot in 5 minutes? (There are about 25.) PLEASE DO NOT USE THIS LIST AS AN EXAMPLE OF GOOD PRACTICE, use the corrected version on p. 279.

Ince, K 1996 *L'Amour la Mort: the eroticism of Marguerite Duras*. In Hughes, A. and Ince, K. (Eds.) French erotic fiction: women's desiring writing, 1880–1990. Oxford: Berg 147–181

Xiguang, Y. and McFadden, S. (1997) *Captive spirits: prisoners of the Cultural Revolution.*

Katherine Kelly, Editor, (1996) *Modern Drama by Women 1880s-1930s: An international anthology*. Routledge, London.

King C (1999) Michael Davitt and Lev Nikolaevich Tolstoy: Meetings 1904, 1905. *Irish Slavonic Studies*

Kubicek, P. (2000) Regional Polarisation in Ukraine: Public Opinion, Voting and Legislative Behaviour. Europe-Asia Studies, 52, 2,

Muñoz Molina, A. (1997) Escrito en un instante. Palma Mallorca: Calima

Air pollution index of major Chinese cities. *China Daily*, 19, 6047, 2, 23 October 1999.

Bourges 1987 Le crépuscule des dieux

Polizzotto, L. 1998 *Patronage and Charity in Savonarola's Reform. Patronage, Piety, Prophecy: Savonarola and After, The Savonarola Quincentenary Conference*, Trinity College Dublin, November 1998.

Roskies, G., Ed., (1989) *The Literature of Destruction: Jewish responses to catastrophe*. Jewish Publication Society, Philadelphia .

Walter 1997 Web of shudders: sublimity in kierkegaard's fear and trembling, *MLN*, 112, 753–785.

Neilan, E. *The siren song of 'the China market'*. The Japan Times. http: / /www. japantimes. co. jp/ June, 3 2000.

15.4 Sources and Further Reading

BUBL (Bulletin Board for Libraries) (1998) *Bibliography* [on-line]. BUBL Information Service, Strathclyde University, http://link.bubl.ac.uk/bibliography Accessed 30 July 2000.

ISO (1998) *Bibliographic References to Electronic Documents* [on-line]. International Organization for Standardization, National Library of Canada, http://www.nlc-bnc.ca/iso/tc46sc9/standard/690-2e.htm Accessed 30 July 2000.

Modern Humanities Research Association (1996) *MHRA Style Book: Notes for Authors, Editors and Writers of Theses* (5th edn.) London: Modern Humanities Research Association.

TAFIS Reference Collections (2000) *Writing References and Bibliographies: Guides Available on the Web, Guides to Citing Printed Sources* [on-line] http://www.tay.ac.uk/tafis/references/other-citations.html Accessed 30 July 2000.

Xia, L. and Crane, N.B. (1996) *Electronic Styles: A Handbook for Citing Electronic Information* (2nd. edn.). Medford, New Jersey: Information Today Inc.

Language Link

Add 2 letters in the middle squares to complete the 5-letter words to left and right. When complete an 8 letter word can be read. Answer p. 280.

A	L	I	A	S	I	D	E
T	R	I	T	E	R	S	E
M	A	O	R	I	G	H	T
W	H	I	S	K	I	L	L

16 RESEARCHING AND WRITING IN TEAMS: IT'S FUN AND EFFICIENT

My team will beam down, read the runes, create a report and return alive and unhurt

Employers want people who work happily in teams. A soloist may be useful, but if s/he cannot get on with colleagues, explain and relax in management situations, that person may impede progress. More importantly, teamwork allows the exploration of more material than is possible for an individual. Team members can bounce ideas around. Where resources are limited, getting involved in co-operative activities and sharing has benefits for everyone. The skill benefits include teamwork, developing professional standards in presentation, problem solving, negotiation and responsibility.

A bunch of linguists having supper together may talk about Prof. Fettucini's lecture on *The impact of vested interests in durum wheat futures*. Everyone has different ideas. If some people decide to chase up further information and pool it, they are beginning to operate as a team. In some modules you will be called on to research and write as a team, but remember you can use team skills and approaches to tackle other parts of your course as well. Two to five people in the same flat, hall of residence or tutor group can team up to extend and optimize research activities, and talking together about literature or social history or the slump in the Yen will develop your discussion skills and broaden your views.

This chapter raises some of the issues associated with group work and suggests some ways of tackling group tasks. There are pitfalls. Not everyone likes teamwork and sharing. Some people feel they may be led down blind alleys by their team-mates. We think the advantages of team research outweigh the disadvantages, but if this is an issue that bothers you, try to analyse why some members might be a handicap. Possibly:

☹ Those who do not pull their weight.

☹ The perennially absent.

☹ Those who do not deliver on time.

☹ The over critical who put others down, suppressing the flow of ideas.

☹ Anyone who gets touchy and sulks if their ideas are ignored.

If you are aiming to benefit from team activities, these are some characteristics to suppress! You may not like working in teams, but when you do, it is in everybody's interests for the team to pull together and reap the benefits. Having identified unhelpful teamwork characteristics, consider what good team qualities might include:

- ☺ Making people laugh.
- ☺ Getting stuff finished.
- ☺ Communicating well.
- ☺ Being reliable.
- ☺ Making friends.
- ☺ Keeping calm in arguments.
- ☺ Speaking your mind.
- ☺ Resolving disputes.

Reducing tension in a group promotes cohesion and encourages learning.

There is a natural pattern in life that is also seen in the normal reaction of people to teamwork and life in general (Figure 16.1). Map these natural reactions to an event in your life, or to an assignment as in Figure 16.1. Each time you are given an assignment you are likely to experience all these reactions. The people who realize 'where' they are in the sequence, and push on to the Recovery and Getting on track stages, give themselves more time to do the task well.

	Natural reactions	Reactions mapped to an essay	Reactions mapped to a team project
↓	**Shock**	I know nothing about . . .	We know nothing about . . .
	Recrimination	I didn't want to do this module, who made it compulsory?	I don't want to work in groups/with them.
	Disagreement	No motivation, nothing done.	Everyone does their own thing, or nothing.
	Reorganization	2 weeks to go, do a plan.	There are 2 weeks to go, we have to get it together! Make a plan.
	Recovery	Parts of this are quite interesting.	Everyone knows which bits to do. Some people start to enjoy it.
	Getting on track	Got parts of two sections sorted and found some more references.	It is coming together, disks are swapped and ideas evaluated.
	Partial success	Drafted the essay. Needs editing and references.	Mostly done, but no cover. Diagrams missing and needs editing.
	Frustration	Printers not working. Forgot to spell check.	We can't find René who has it all on disk!
↓	**Success**	Final version handed in.	Report completed.

Figure 16.1 Natural reactions to group work.

16.1 Researching in groups

Groups can cover more material than an individual, but having decided to share research outcomes, recognize there will be difficulties and tensions at times. Group members are only human. Everyone has a different way of researching and note-making, so shared information will 'look' different on paper, BUT you can learn from the way other people note and present information. Figure 16.2 summarizes thoughts from three groups after a shared research task. They give some insights into what can happen.

One meeting or three? How often does a group need to meet? Generally:

Two or more meetings → more chat → greater exchange of views → more interactions → more learning. Have electronic meetings (see **Try This 16.1**) when time is tight.

16.2 Writing in teams

Team writing is a normal business activity. Typically it involves a group brainstorming an outline for the document, individuals researching and drafting sub-sections, circulation of drafts for comment, the incorporation of additional ideas and views, and someone editing a final version. The same approach can be adopted in university writing. Like ensemble recorder playing, writing as a team is difficult and discordant the first time you do it, but a very useful experience.

One valuable approach involves team members volunteering to research and draft specific sub-sections and volunteering for a 'writing role' (Figure 16.3). Discussions are more lively and focused when individuals can use their role to offer alternatives and new approaches. 'The Critic' has the licence to criticize, the linker can say 'yes but how does critiquing the paradigmatic exchanges amongst sailors relate to the Saussurian model of discourse?' Adopting writing roles can depersonalize criticism, which is especially important when working with friends. Be critical but stay friends.

Style and layout

Decide on the general layout at the start – the format, fonts and style of headings, and the format for references. Make decisions about word length, be firm – 'each subsection has a maximum of 200 words'. Early word length decisions limit waffle. Nevertheless, length needs looking at later in the project. Some parts of the argument will deserve expansion. Keep talking to each other about ideas and their relative importance and position in the narrative.

Finally, someone (or some two) has to take the whole document and edit it to give it a consistent voice and style, BUT everyone needs to provide graphs, diagrams and references in the agreed style.

Task	Reflection
Tutorial essay on Martial Themes in Spanish Novels. Individual Essays. Three-week deadline.	We had three weeks to do this but we were none too fast at getting started. No one wanted to jump in and lead. So we wasted the best part of ten days before really getting going. We didn't use e-mail and that might have helped. We did not really focus much at the first meeting. Everyone went off to do their own research. We could have done more to pool references. The two people who photocopied things for the whole group were really helpful. We did have a good discussion three days before it was due in, and we got to know each other which was great. Now it is over I can see how it could have worked well. We could have started sooner, shared more through two/three meetings, used e-mail to get organized. I found extra references and looked harder to find things to share, and got a couple of good points from the group that I wouldn't have mentioned but I could have got lots more from it.
Seminar preparation. Narrative strategies in French films of the '50s. Six people. 15 minute presentation followed by 10 minute discussion. Class of 40	We started with a meeting over beers in the Union and talked about what we could do. Everyone had lots of ideas and views and we talked a lot about films and plots we liked. Began to realize that we were going to need some more factual material and references. Peter decided to see if the Cinema literature had anything to say. Mike and Sue said they would do a www and newspaper search. Tim offered to do a Web of Science search. Agreed to meet to watch a couple of videos and organize the next stage. Downloaded video covers from www to make cool OHTs and got posters from the video shop for displays. As the seminar was at 3.00 we met in the morning to sort itout. Bad idea. Should have met the day before, had too many ideas, not enough structure and everyone wanted to get their piece in. We got a running order but no real introduction and we hadn't got a good OHT to finish. Questions went OK because everyone started offering their experience of cinema but it wasn't a very academic discussion so I don't think we will get that many marks. It was great getting to know the group and it was a really interesting subject but we were probably too general and not analytical enough.
Group research. Social engagement in Ibsen. Six people. Group report.	We got this started as a class exercise and had a good structure because we had just completed an Ibsen module. We had lots of IT traumas as we tried to send material to each other and discovered everyone had different ideas about structure. It became increasingly important that, for sub-sections to be compiled individually, everyone knew what they were supposed to cover, and had similar ideas about the arguments we wanted to make. Once we had a first draft other people added further information and someone else did the draft introduction and conclusion. We argued about individual sentences and words. I learned a lot about revising writing from this. Editing the final document meant five people sending me an assortment of materials and I felt that I was making a patchwork of a report – I learned a lot about the formatting features and generated the Table of Contents electronically. We had a big argument about whether the conclusion should be an optimistic paragraph on 'where do we go from here' or a summary of the content. Some members didn't like sentences starting with And or But. Eventually they 'let the editor make the final decision' but I think this was with some reluctance as they wondered if I would make the right decision. Too much material, we needed to plan earlier and make decisions sooner. Six people writing gave us too much text. Next time we need to set word limits for each section.

Figure 16.2 Experiences of group research.

Writing Role	Responsibilities
Summarizer	Introduction, Conclusions, Abstract
Visuals/Graphics	Smart indexes, contents page, pictures, drawings and figures
Critic	Faultfinder, plays devil's advocate
Academic content	Subject reporters
Linker	Checks connections between arguments, sections and the introduction and conclusion
Discussant	Evaluates and discusses

Figure 16.3 Roles in writing.

Duet writing

Two people sitting at a PC can be very effective in getting words on disk. The exchange of ideas is immediate. Two brains keep the enthusiasm levels high and you can plan further research activities as you go. It is also advantageous to have two people together doing the final edit, keeping track of formats, updates and being cheerful.

Timetabling issues

A team writing activity cannot be done like the traditional language essay, on the night before submission, after the pub. People get ill and things happen, so the timetable needs to be generous to allow for slippage AND team members have to agree to stick to it. It usually works. It is too embarrassing to be the only non-contributor. It may assist planning if you put some dates against the points in Figure 16.4.

1.	Brainstorm initial ideas, assign research tasks and data collection *(Day 1)*
2.	Research topics *(Day 2–5)*
3.	Draft subsections and circulate *(Day 6–9)*
4.	Meet to discuss progress, decide on areas that are complete, assess where additional research is needed, assign further research and writing roles and tasks *(Day 10)*
5.	Redraft sections and circulate *(Day 10–14)*
6.	Are we all happy with this? *(Day 15)*
7.	Editor's final revisions *(Day 16–18)*
8.	Finalization of cover, contents and abstract. Check and add page numbers. Check submission requirements are met *(Day 18)*
9.	Submit *(Day 18!)*

Figure 16.4 Timetabling team writing.

Keeping a team on track? Need a Chairperson?

One of the pitfalls of working with a group of friends is that more time is taken making sure everyone stays friends, than getting on with the task. One vital issue that emerges is the initial division of labour (see Figures 16.2 and 16.3). It is essential that everyone feels happy, involved and equally valued, so the chairman, or the person who emerges as the chairman, must endeavour to ensure there is fair play, that no-one hogs the action excluding others, and equally that no one is left out (even if that is what they want). The chairman is allowed to goad you into action – that's her/his job. It is unfair to dump the role of chairman on the same person each time, share it around. Chairing is a skill everyone should acquire.

If a group feels someone is a serious dosser they may want to invoke the 'football rules', or ask the module tutor to do so. The rules are one yellow card as a warning, 2 or 3 yellow cards equal a red card and exclusion from the group. The yellow–red card system might be used to reduce marks (p. 183). A red-carded person does not necessarily get a zero but in attempting to complete a group task alone, they are unlikely to do better than a bare pass. Remember:

- ✔ It saves hours of work if everyone agrees at the start on a common format for references, and everyone takes responsibility for citing the items they quote.
- ✔ The time required to tidy up, write an abstract, make a smart cover, do an index, acknowledgement page and cross check the references is 5 times longer than you think. Split the jobs between the team.

The key to team writing is getting the STYLE and TIMETABLE right, although CONTENT also matters.

Plagiarism

Where group work leads to a common report then collaborative writing is involved. BUT, if you are required to write independent reports from group research or group activities you must ensure your reports are independently written, not copies or cut and paste versions of each other's documents. In this situation share reading, float and discuss ideas, BUT write independently. This means planning to finish the research three days, or more, before the deadline so everyone has time to draft and correct their reports.

16.3 COMMUNICATION BY E-MAIL

'I think there is a world market for maybe five computers' –T. Watson, Chairman of IBM, 1943.

It is vital that everyone has access to a group report, therefore a method of circulating the most recent version of a document is needed. Using e-mail with attachments is ideal, and saves printing costs. You can share thoughts, drafts and updates, while working at the most convenient place and time for you. Have a go at **Try This 16.1**

TRY THIS 16.1 – E-mail in action

Research a tutorial essay or practical report, sharing resources and ideas, without physically meeting. HINT: the first time, it helps to have everyone in the same computer laboratory, you can resolve any problems quickly.

Open a new Word processing document and:

1. Type in the title, the keywords you would use in a library search and write very briefly about two or three issues, say 3 sentences for each.
2. Then save the document. Open e-mail, attach and mail the document to your mates.
3. With a bit of luck other people will be doing the same thing at the same time, so there should be e-mails arriving from them. Save your colleagues' files in your own workspace, but check whether they have used the same file name as you. If so, it will need changing to avoid over-writing.
4. Return to the word processing package, open your original document and the new ones. Copy the material into a single file and re-organize it to make a coherent set of comments. While collating, keep track of ideas, perhaps through

sub-headings. Reflect on your colleagues' comments. At the immediate supportive level there is the 'that's a new/good/middling idea'. More actively, think around variations on 'I was surprised by ... because ...' 'I disagree with ... because ... .' 'We all agreed that ... because ...'.

5. Now look at the *style* of the responses. What might you need to do as an editor to make these comments hang together?
6. Finally, get together and decide how you will organize your research and writing to maximize the opportunity to share resources and information.

Bigger documents

Imagine a report constructed by four people, being edited and updated daily. How do you keep track of what is going on? There needs to be an agreed system. Adapting elements of the following might be a useful template for action:

- The start of the document needs:
  - ✔ header page with title and the outline plan;
  - ✔ section which everyone updates when they change the document e.g. Rakesh modified section 2.6 and 3.2 on Wed 1 April at 10.00;
  - ✔ an agreed working order, e.g. Georgio drafts section 2, then Marie-Claire revises it. All revisions circulated by ... day.
- Decide that citations will be added to the reference list in the agreed format.
- Agree to check e-mail and respond every ... days.
- Use the 'Revision Editor' in your word processing package. The person responsible for section X will not necessarily welcome 5 independent redrafts. A 'Revision Editor' highlights revision suggestions for the subsection editor to accept or reject as desired. By opening multiple copies of the document you can cut and paste between drafts.
- DO NOT USE PAGE NUMBERS TO REFER TO OTHER VERSIONS. These change with almost every version. Use section numbers and date each version carefully.
- Ensure at least one or two people keep an archive of all drafts so that you can revive an earlier version if disaster strikes.

Use e-mail to brainstorm ideas among friends, tutorial and seminar groups and old school friends. People like getting messages and usually respond. E-mail is a quick and cheap way of discussing points. There are a great many people you could brainstorm with. Think more widely than just you and your lecturer.

16.4 Assessment of Team Work

Assessment tends to generate discussion about 'fairness'. There are dark hints about cheerful dossers getting good marks when their mates have done all the work. How is this handled? Most staff will offer some variation on the following approaches for assigning marks, some of which involve team input. If the 'football factor' is in play, there may be an agreed penalty, say –10% for a yellow card.

The simple approach

Each member of the team gets the same mark, so it is up to everyone to play fair.

The private bid

Each individual fills in a form privately, and the assessor tries to resolve discrepancies. This style:

Name ....

Names of other Team Members ....

I feel my contribution to this project is worth ....% of the team mark.

This is because ....

....

Signed ....

This approach may lead to discussion amongst your assessors, but it lets people with personal problems acquaint staff privately. It can require the 'Wisdom of Solomon' to resolve. Remember, a marker will take note of what you say, but not necessarily change the marks.

Team effort

A form in this style asks everyone to comment on the contribution of each team member. Summing the totals constructs an index of activity, which is used to apportion the marks.

Estimate the effort made by each team member, 0 = no effort, 2 = did a bit, 3 = average, 4 = really useful, 5 = outstanding contribution.	Paula	Max	Mika
Attended all meetings			
Contributed ideas			
Did a fair share of the writing			
Other – detail particular contributions:			
TOTAL			

16.5 Comments on team work

Staff comments: 'Initially students are very democratic and give equal marks. With experience, they choose to raise the marks of those who have done more of the task'. 'The amount of chat was enormous, and between them they could tackle a more difficult problem than as individuals'. 'The team writing exercise made everyone think about the order and quality of the material. The report was more thoughtful and detailed than one person could do in the time'. 'One team was happy to have this year's "mine's a third" candidate because s/he happily did the activities like taking books back to the library and making OHTs with Powerpoint, while cracking jokes and keeping the team cheerful'.

Figure 16.5 details reflections of second year language students following a group research and report writing session. Overall, they see the exercise as positive and the disadvantages as surmountable with experience. Their reflections may be worth considering as you start team activities.

Team research and writing at university usually produces better documents than individual responses. This is not because the academic content is necessarily substantially better, but because team activities generate a series of drafts and more thinking about the topic and audience, so that the final product is more polished. Make the most of group work activities on your CV. It isn't the academic content that matters. Highlight the skills you used in delivering a group product, like negotiation, meeting deadlines, allocating tasks, collaborative writing, editing and co-ordinating research.

What were the advantages of team work	What were the disadvantages of team work
We were well organized, we decided which texts to use and who was reading what. Between us we collected more critical texts than any of us could have managed on our own. Everyone got on, talked about the extracts and there was general agreement as to where the writing should be focused. Our group report had an odd diversity of style and opinions at first because there were so many ideas and approaches. We found more critical L2 material and struggled to understand it. On my own I would have ignored the L2 references. It was really good fun sharing ideas and suggesting different ways to organize the writing. I really hated the idea of group work in advance, but I found I had things to say and when the others took my suggestions seriously, I really got involved.	Timetabling times to meet – nightmare scenario. Having someone who only turned up half the time. Not being able to include everyone's ideas in the end. Choosing was really difficult. I like working in a certain way but other people don't do the same things as me. I felt I wasted my time while others were doing things in a slower way than I liked. Having to compromise on common topics and ideas. Not really knowing who was doing what all the way through. We needed to be more efficient at finishing off.

What will you do differently next time you work together?
Be more focused in meetings, and get a list of what people agree to do. Get the books and the secondary literature earlier. Set criteria and dates for reading, drafting, thinking about the draft and revising the final document! Use e-mail with attachments as well as the mobile phone to move documents about and chivvy the group. I discovered I have strong Plant and Company Worker strengths (Belbin 1996). Next time I will try to work on some of my less strong team player characteristics.

Figure 16.5 Students' opinions on team work, 2000.

16.6 References and Further Reading

Anon, (1995) How to Build Effective Teams. *People Management*, 23 February, 40–41.

Belbin, R.M. (1996) *Management Teams: Why they Succeed or Fail.* Oxford: Butterworth Heinemann.

Gibbs, G. (1994) *Learning in Teams: A Student Manual.* Oxford: Oxford Centre for Staff Development.

Analysing Language Wordsearch

Just 46 language related words to find, Answers p. 280.

A	N	O	S	R	E	P	I	L	O	G	U	E	S	A	C
D	A	E	S	S	H	U	M	O	U	R	I	B	A	R	S
V	E	R	B	O	A	S	E	F	N	E	V	I	T	C	A
E	A	F	N	F	I	C	T	I	O	N	O	B	A	H	L
R	P	E	I	M	K	L	R	T	C	N	N	L	Y	E	L
B	M	A	I	N	U	A	E	O	O	U	A	I	T	T	I
E	A	L	I	S	I	O	T	M	P	R	S	O	T	Y	T
R	E	L	A	C	I	T	A	M	M	A	R	G	I	P	E
U	U	M	L	A	U	T	E	R	O	H	T	R	D	E	R
T	O	N	E	A	O	E	Y	A	Y	S	T	A	N	Z	A
A	S	L	C	P	D	R	R	M	R	I	P	P	A	E	T
C	I	L	O	C	U	B	E	M	D	T	D	H	L	R	I
I	R	E	M	I	M	I	G	R	E	R	I	Y	E	D	O
R	I	T	E	S	Y	L	A	N	A	O	T	C	L	R	N
A	I	L	D	O	O	M	M	S	I	S	P	I	L	L	E
C	I	R	Y	L	A	C	I	R	O	H	P	A	T	E	M

17 ABSTRACTS AND EXECUTIVE SUMMARIES

I have told you billions of times to avoid hyperbole.

Abstracts and Executive Summaries (ES) inform readers about the contents of documents. While both approaches summarize longer documents, they have different formats and serve different purposes. Writing an abstract or an ES enhances your skills in reading, identifying key points and issues, structuring points in a logical sequence and writing concisely.

Some journal articles include an abstract that summarizes the contents; they are more likely to be found in linguistics journals than traditional literature journals. Abstracts also appear in bibliographic databases to notify researchers of an article's content. You may write an abstract as part of an extended project or dissertation report. The executive summary appears more often in business related courses and workplace activities. They are normally 1–2 page summaries placed at the start of reports and documents. Depending on the context, the style may be more dynamic and less formal than an abstract. You may be asked to do an ES exercise as part of a recruitment assessment to see how you handle and digest information. Writing an ES is a workplace skill – condensing and presenting key facts to a meeting or managers who do not have time to read lengthy documents.

While an organization may not translate whole reports they sometimes present executive summaries in more than one language as part of their marketing strategy (and if they don't you could suggest it).

17.1 Abstracts

Look at some well-written abstracts or résumés before writing one. *Applied Linguistics, Deutsche Vierteljahrsschrift für Literaturwissenschaft und Geistes-geschichte, La Linguistique, Modern and Contemporary France* and *Zeitschrift Für Deutsche Philologie* contain examples. For a splendid group of abstracts see *Nineteenth Century French Studies (1999–2000)* volume 28 (1 and 2) which contains the abstracts of all the articles in that journal 1972–99. Use **Try This 17.1** to look at the wider role of abstracts. An abstract should be a short, accurate, objective summary. It is not the place for interpretation and criticism. Abstracts should do the following:

☺ Enable the reader to select documents for a particular research topic.

☺ Substitute, in a limited way, for the original document when accessing the original is impossible.

☺ Access, in a limited way through translations, research papers in other languages.

Some departments expect abstracts with practical reports and dissertations, but not with every tutorial essay. When preparing an abstract of a paper or book, it might be useful to check off these points:

✔ Give the citation in full.

✔ Lay out the principal arguments following the order in the full text.

✔ Emphasize the important points; highlight new information, omit well-known material.

✔ Be as brief, but as complete, as possible.

✔ Avoid repetition and ambiguity. Use short sentences and appropriate technical terms.

✔ Include the author's principal interpretations and conclusions but do not add your own commentary. This is *not* a 'critical' essay.

Aim for about 120–250 words. The first draft will probably be too long, and need editing.

17.2 Executive summaries

An effective ES is a very much shortened version of a document and the style is generally less literary than an abstract. The format often involves bullet points or numbered sections. The general rule on length is 1–2 sides only, on the basis that really, really, really busy people will not read more. An ES can be part of an organization's promotional material, in which case an upbeat, clear style with lots of impact is advantageous. Longer ESs can be found on government web sites, summarizing longer documents. These may have a PR aim, for example to acquaint the reader with government policy in an accessible manner, rather than expecting a reader to tackle a draft Act of Parliament or Congress or EU legislation.

The essential element when writing an ES is to eliminate all extraneous material. Do not include examples, analogous material, witticisms, pictures, diagrams, figures, appendices, or be repetitious or repetitious or repetitious. An ES is:

- ✔ Brief;
- ✔ Direct;
- ✔ Indicates impacts, pros and cons;
- ✔ Includes all main issues;
- ✔ Places stress on results and conclusions;
- ✔ Includes recommendations with costs and timescales if relevant.

Chapter headings and subheadings may present a starting scheme for bullet points. Look at the discussion and conclusion sections for the main points the author is making. See also Asner (1999).

On p. 162 using abbreviations was suggested as a way to speed up writing, dealing with longer words or with phrases repeated regularly, and the L1/L2 convention is used throughout this book. Are you comfortable with this usage? Is it a style to adopt? Note that when the phrase first appears, (ES) is added afterwards to indicate that this abbreviation will be used thereafter.

TRY THIS 17.1 – Abstracts

Next time you read a journal article, read the paper first and make notes without looking at the abstract first. Then compare your notes with the abstract. Are there significant differences between them? Think about how you can use an abstract as a summary. (Remember, reading abstracts is not a substitute for reading the whole article.)

17.3 References

Asner, M. (1999). *A few pages may dictate your proposal's fate: Executive summary lays foundation for success* [on-line], http://www.gtreseller.com/publications/may99/winningproposals/winningproposals.shtm Accessed 30 July 2000.

Language Quick Crossword 2
Answers p. 280.

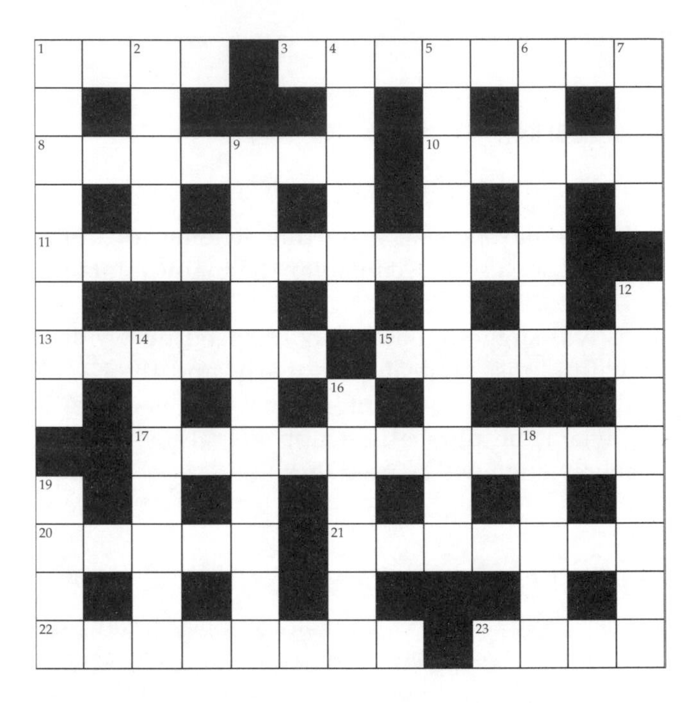

Across
1 Machine component (4)
3 Philosopher, arouse us (anag.) (8)
8 Scrap of cloth or news (7)
10 Standing above a plane (5)
11 Battle of opinions (11)
13 Modern Greek (6)
15 Upper section of windpipe (6)
17 One being questioned (11)
20 Native of Caribbean island (5)
21 Spanish or Portuguese (7)
22 Burlesque poetry (8)
23 Shout (4)

Down
1 A picture with a message (8)
2 Rule of a monarch (5)
4 Eight leaves to a sheet (6)
5 Raised above all others (11)
6 Giving name to a place or work, like Tristram Shandy (7)
7 Language of Pakistan (4)
9 Obstinate perseverance (11)
12 Lying outside (8)
14 Carrier for letters (7)
16 Highly commend (6)
18 Communicate by letter (5)
19 Sharp, sour (4)

18 REVIEWING A BOOK

Authors love criticism, just so long as it is unadulterated praise.

At some point in your student career, a tutor will explore your skill in summarizing and identifying the principal points in some aspect of your language studies by asking for a book review. With luck it will involve a text of only 5 zillion pages and a two-week deadline. This all adds to the fun (possibly), and admit it, given six weeks you would probably put off doing any preparation until two weeks in advance!

Before embarking on this exciting venture, read a couple of academic book reviews. The majority of literature and language journals publish book reviews in most issues. Look for ideas of style and content. If you can find a copy of the book being reviewed in order to compare it with the reviewers' comments, then so much the better. Have a look at **Try This 18.1**; it gives an insight into the types of comments made by reviewers.

There is no right way to write a book review but there are some general guidelines. Book reviews are highly personal, reflecting the opinions of the reviewer, but think about the audience first. It will help you decide where to place the emphasis of the review, and guide the formality and style of the writing.

There are two general types of review:

1. *Descriptive* – an objective summary of the contents, scope, treatment and importance of a text.

2. *Analytical or critical* – an objective appraisal of a text's contents, quality, limitations and applicability. It should discuss the text's relative merits and deficiencies and might compare it with alternative texts. This may require allocating time to browse through other material to place the book in context.

TRY THIS 18.1 – Book reviews

The following extracts are reproduced with permission from book reviews published in *The Russian Review*, 2000, 59, 2 (*RR*) and *Language Teaching Research*, 2000, 41,1 (*LTR*). The page numbers are indicated. To get a feel for the approach and style of review writing, make a brief comment on each of the quotations. It is hard to make objective judgements without reading the original text and the whole review; aim here to distinguish style and content points. Some potential responses are on pp. 280–81.

1. Struminski's impressively researched book is a set of two dozen essays grouped under six broad topics having to do with the linguistic systems of early East Slavic, Nordic and Finnic. They deal primarily with phonetics and lexicology. Although several of the essays will be of interest to historians ... the primary readers for this book will be linguists. Since relatively few will have the command of Old Nordic, Finnic (and, more broadly, Uralic), and East Slavic that Struminski seems to have, any given reader will probably find certain parts of the book more useful than others. The audience of linguists would certainly include Germanists and Uralists, not just Slavists. (*RR*, p. 285).
2. Some of Struminski's assertions contradict the consensus opinion without explaining why that opinion is rejected. For example he flatly assumes 'the fall of all the jers in Rus' by the early eleventh century' (p. 274). On page 78 he moves that date back still further 'After the jers had disappeared throughout Rus' by the end of the tenth century' (*RR*, p. 285).
3. Baudin's study is truly impressive in its scope and a great achievement in interdisciplinary research, covering the complex interplay of party politics and the arts as it can be seen in the role of Soviet artistic institutions and of art criticism, the training of artists and exhibition policy. Special attention is given to the specific relation of the fine arts to literature, both governed by the principles of Socialist realism that gave prominence to content, to the narrative. Focusing on the public distribution of fine art from 1947 to 1953, Baudin does not simply draw on a few exemplary paintings or sculptures but instead on all works of art presented in the yearly All-Union Art exhibits and on the vast amount of reproductions published ... (*RR*, p. 297).
4. Cohen provides valuable discussion of the topics that have already been extensively researched as well as many others about which little is known and further examination is needed, thereby creating a wide scope of investigation. The different themes researched in the book, ranging from multilingual thinking to testing, are organized into a general framework that helps readers to focus on second language use and strategies from a learner's perspective. Examples and practical explanations, often supported by research references and reviews of the literature, reinforce his arguments. (*LTR*, p. 87).
5. Arguably, Chapter 2, 'Construct definition and validity inquiry in SLA research', is one of the less penetrable articles in the book. Although fundamentally interesting and relevant to the general theme of the book, the degree of detail may well appeal to researchers, but is likely to deter the broader readership that this book is intended to attract. (*LTR*, p. 83).
6. As Donald Rayfield indicates in his introduction, this book is an updated version of his *Chekhov: The Evolution of his Art* (1975) ... Although *Understanding Chekhov* includes a useful select bibliography of recent work on Chekhov, relatively little of this work seems to have been drawn upon in updating the text. (*RR*, pp. 286–87).

7. The whole approach in which the author writes and presents his topics is carefully planned, clearly set out and rigorously presented. Each chapter has a similar structure and presentation style, and ends with discussion questions and activities. This structure allows readers to put into practice the ideas and the knowledge gained from the sections of the book dealing with research and theoretical explanations. It also highlights the author's choice to remain practical. (*LTR*, p. 88).
8. *Magic Mirror* is well-illustrated and provided a useful filmography. It is an important contribution to the emerging field of prerevolutionary film studies (*RR*, p. 294).
9. It would be condescending toward an important discipline to suggest that this farrago belongs on the African–American, not the Slavic, shelves of our libraries. The truth is that this carelessly edited volume, furnished with neither an index nor a bibliography, and padded with French translations which often have little to do with the subject, can make only very tenuous claims to scholarly worth. (*RR*, p. 286).

To get a good perspective on a text, set aside time for reading well in advance. Leave time for your brain to develop opinions. The SQ3R technique (p. 65) is certainly valuable here, especially if you have a short time limit.

A *descriptive review* might include a combination of some of the following elements:

- an outline of the contents of the book;
- a summary of the author's aims for the book and the intended audience;
- an evaluation of the material included and comments;
- quotations or references to new ideas to illustrate the review;
- a brief summary of the author's qualifications and reference to his/her other texts;
- citations of the linguistic, literary and other texts that this book will complement or replace, in order to place this text in its academic context;
- a summary of any significant areas omitted.

Including long quotations is not a good idea unless they really illustrate a point. A reference list is required if you refer to other texts in the review.

A *critical book review* gives information about the book and expresses an opinion on it. It should include a statement of what the author has tried to do, evaluate how well the author has succeeded, and present independent evidence to support the evaluation. This type of review is considerably more time-consuming than a descriptive review. While reading, note passages that illustrate the book's purpose and style. Remember to balance the strengths with the weaknesses of the book and also consider how the author's ideas, opinions and judgements fit with our present knowledge of the subject. Make sure that where you are critical this is fair comment given the author's stated aims for the text. Reading the preface and introduction should give you a clear idea of the author's objectives.

A critical review might include:

- a description of the author's purpose for writing, and qualifications;
- the historical background of the work;
- the main strengths and weaknesses of the book;
- a description of the genre to which the work belongs, its academic context;
- a commentary on the significance of the text for its intended audience.

- Read the book!
- Make notes on the principal themes and conclusions, then look at the book again.
- Think about the content and decide on a theme for the review – look at the book again.
- Draft the outline to support the theme of the review and check that nothing vital is missed – look at the book again.
- Draft the review – look at the book again.
- Edit and revise the final version.

You must include a full reference (see Chapter 15) so a reader can locate the original text. You may also include the price and perhaps compare prices of competitive texts. Hard and softback prices can be found through booksellers or the www.

You may want to comment on the style of the writing and the ease with which you think the intended audience will understand the contents. If it is well written then say so – 'this text is clearly written with examples illustrating key points' or '... although intended as an undergraduate text its style is turgid, the average undergraduate will find the detail difficult to absorb'. People read reviews to find out which books to read, and they like to know whether the material is written in an accessible manner. The real skill in reviewing involves giving yourself enough time to absorb the content of the text and then letting your brain make the connections to other pieces of reading so that you offer valid links, complements and criticisms.

A Book Review Cannot Be Completed In One Draft On The Night Before A Tutorial!

18.1 References and Further Reading

Forum for Modern Languages Studies, German Life and Letters, Eighteenth-Century Studies, Europe–Asia Studies, Harvard Journal of Asiatic Studies, MLN (Modern Language Notes), MLR (Modern Language Review), Textual Practice, The Australian Journal of Chinese Affairs, The Russian Review are a small selection of journals that have book reviews. Some may be available to you over the www.

The Times Literary Supplement always has well-written book reviews, and can be found electronically at http://www.the-tls.co.uk/ Accessed 30 July 2000.

The Book Review site at http://www.bath.ac.uk/~ma9map/index.htm will give you further insights. Accessed 30 July 2000.

19 POSTERS

I like snappy, but concise does have its virtues.

Posters are one of the ways researchers share results at seminars and conferences and advertise activities. You may be asked to prepare a poster to show the results of some research work, or as part of a display for new students. On school placements they are very useful for presenting ideas and displaying students' work. Posters may be part of a passive presentation, or more interactive when the authors are available to answer questions. The key skill is communication – getting a message across clearly and concisely.

Posters have limited space, so the presenter is forced to concentrate on the essential elements, and express them creatively through brief, concise statements and explanations. There is no room for flannel but plenty of room for creative visual elements. Most departments display the posters produced by staff and postgraduates for conference presentations; corridor, office and foyer walls are likely sites. Take a critical look at them. How effectively is the 'message' communicated? Can you read the main points at 1–2 m? Are you enticed into going closer and reading the detail? Do you like the colour combinations? Is there too much or too little material? Is there a good mix of pictures and text?

First check the presentation guidelines. There are often size limitations relating to the size of display boards and making sure everyone has a fair share of the space. Then find out about the audience. Whether it is children, fellow students or a presentation for a company, each would benefit from a tailored design and presentation, even though the basic information might be the same.

One of the fastest ways to lose marks is to overload with information. Printing an essay in 14pt type and sticking it on card will lead to instant failure, no matter how good the academic content. Sound-bite length messages are wanted. However, this is still an academic exercise, so a sound-bite alone will not do. The academic argument and evidence are required on a poster, as in an essay.

The main difference between posters and essays is that essays let you explore the highways and byways around ideas whereas in a poster you summarize to leave only the highlights. Be selective, you are trying to communicate your ideas simply and quickly enough so that a distracted reader understands your message, BUT please don't leave out essentials, it still has to be self-explanatory.

Table 19.1 describes some poster ideas to inspire you. Some attention should be paid to getting a 'grabbing' headline to encourage people to read further. Which of those in Table 19.1 do you find intriguing? The general advice is to go for simplicity and impact. Consider using a question and answer format to draw the reader into the topic.

The posters described in the table all contain visual elements, hand drawn,

Autobiographies Reveal Writing Styles: with pictures of the students in the background, mini autobiographies overlaid and a large summary statement that classified their writing development styles.

Promoting Learning Japanese: colourful display of curricular and extra curricular aspects and activities in promoting Japanese language.

Narrative Pictorial Map: A poster that showed through examples how narrative mapping can be used in literary character analysis and improving text comprehension.

The Ultimate Dessert: Rather fine foodie photos and graphics, linked to menus, used to highlight the excellence of gourmet cuisine of an area.

Joan of Arc: A Pictorial Figure: A time line, illustrated with copies of art works and literature extracts pick out elements of her life.

Libraries are Crossroads: Signpost and crossroads background highlighted text making points about libraries as multi-cultural, multi-lingual community, co-operative, information centres for all.

Environmental Politics in France: Set on a green map of France; pick out 4 examples from 1999, and use newspaper clippings to make points well.

Escaping Stereotypes: Used 5 stereotypical images from current print materials to explore ideas of xenophobia.

Poetic Structure in Chinese Literature: Great use of mixed calligraphy and prints to illustrate points made in 2 poems.

Youth Culture and Disillusionment: A Chinese student poster contrasting 1999 youth with traditional cultural values. Almost entirely pictorial – a montage of pictures.

Really Fundamental? – Jewish Studies poster contrasting 'Abrahamic' monotheistic religions and contemporary 'fundamentalist' re-assertions of those ideas resisting western cultural ideas. A flow chart approach with some very big ideas.

Post-Communism: Set against a picture of tumbling playing cards this 'list' style poster gave examples of some of the problems and some successes in Europe since the fall of the Berlin Wall.

Table 19.1 Some poster ideas.

montaged from newsprint, prints, photographs – any and every visual media. The academic argument or evidence needs to be added in text boxes to any poster but one test of the impact of a poster is that the message is almost carried by the visual items. Drafting a poster first without text can help you produce a creative image. Figure 19.1 is a starting point – a graph which carries the main message or

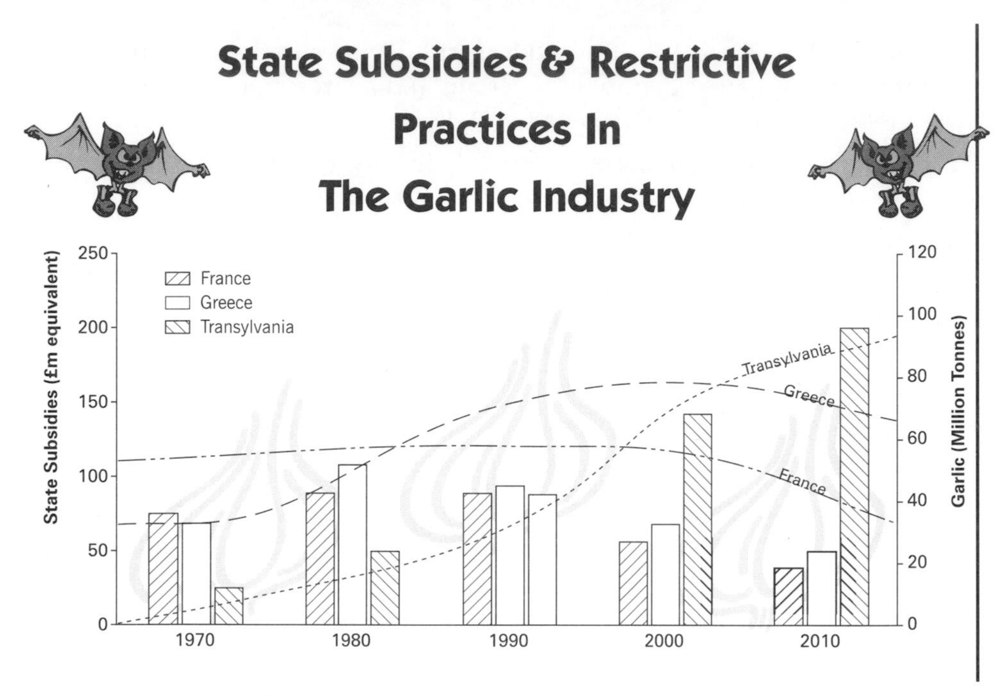

Figure 19.1 First draft ideas for a poster.

evidence. The vampire and garlic motifs are fun. Text can be placed around the images and the vampires may multiply or be enlarged in the final draft. Figure 11.1 (p. 123) could equally be a first draft poster, now add the text.

Imaginatively shaped posters – a medieval parchment roll for Early French, a stage for theatre-based posters, a hamburger for modern cultural impacts – will attract attention. Be careful not to let the background overwhelm the message – the background should complement and enhance, not dominate. It is also important when choosing a background, not to bias the message with an inappropriate, stereotypical image. Amongst a gathering of 50 posters on Flaubert or Hesse how many times do you want to see a portrait, and is a country's flag either in colour or in background always appropriate? There should be a limit to the number of bulls that are cut from brown card for Spanish cultural posters. Using a different background might make your poster stand out. Whatever the shape, ensure the width and height are within the maximum size guidelines.

Mount pictures and text on to contrasting coloured card or paper to highlight them. You could put primary information on one colour paper and supplementary information on another. Being consistent in design format assists the reader; for example, by placing argument or background information to the left of an image, graph or picture, and the interpretation, result or consequence to the right. Using two different paper colours or textures to distinguish argument

Syntax

Background Noise

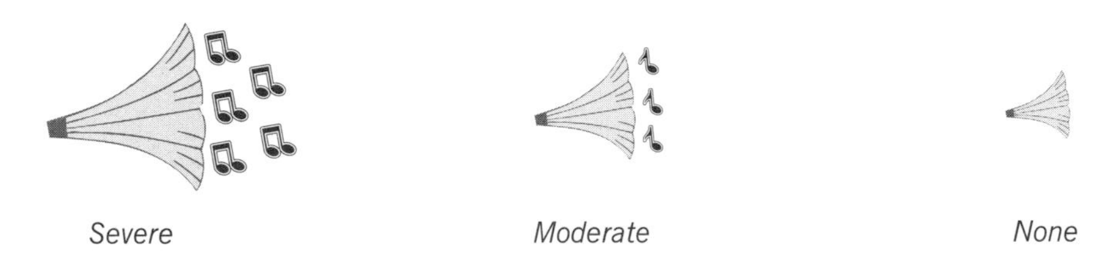

Figure 19.2 Examples of visual codes or classifications.

statements from consequence statements will reinforce the message. It may be effective to have a hierarchy of information with the main story in the largest type, and more detailed information in smaller type. By coding levels or hierarchies of information consistently, the reader can decide to read the main points for a general overview, or to study the whole in detail as desired.

Posters can do a 'compare and contrast' exercise. It may be advantageous to use creative visual coding to indicate examples of good and less good practice (Figure 19.2) but remember to include a key somewhere.

Remember to acknowledge sources and add keys and titles to diagrams, and you must put your name somewhere.

There are costs involved in poster production, including card, paper, photocopying, enlarging and printing photographic material. Colour printing is expensive so be certain everyone is happy with the size and shape of each diagram before printing. A rough draft or mock-up, in black-and-white, before a final colour print will save money. The first five to seven drafts are never right; font sizes that seem enormous on a computer screen look small on a poster board viewed from two metres away. Any poster produced by a group will be the subject of much discussion and change before everyone is happy! SPELL CHECK ALL COPY BEFORE PRINTING.

Interactive posters with pop-up book effects, wheels to spin, time lines to journey along or nests of overlays that slide away can be very effective. Take care that the structure is solid enough to cope with handling. Use a good glue, reinforce cut edges and ensure the poster is very safely attached to the wall or board. Multi-layered card is heavy and likely to fall off.

Show your mock-up, pilot poster to a few people. Ask them what message it conveys? Is it what you intended? Are they following through the material in the order you wish? Can they distinguish major points from support material? What do they feel about the colour scheme? Are the font sizes large enough? Does the overall effect encourage them to read further? Are the main arguments supported by clear evidence? Decide whether the design promotes the delivery of the message and then do the final version. If the poster is to be assessed, self-assess using your departmental assessment form or Figure 19.3. How are the marks assigned? If need be, change the design to meet the criteria for a higher grade.

Group Names ....
Poster Title ....

	1	2:1	2:2	3	Fail	
Poster Structure (20%)						
Well organized						Disorganized
Single topic focus						No clear focus
Research and Argument (60%)						
Main points included						No grasp of the main issues
Points supported by evidence						No corroborating evidence
Good use of relevant examples						Lack of examples
Ideas clearly expressed						Muddled presentation
Design and Presentation (20%)						
Creative layout and design						Poor design
Good graphics						No/poor graphics
Good word processing						No/poor word processing
Key points readable at 2m						Key points unreadable at 2 m
Comments						

Figure 19.3 Poster assessment criteria.

19.1 VIRTUAL POSTERS

Virtual posters are designed electronically in word processing or graphics packages. They have the advantages of being low cost, easy to store and can be viewed via the www projected in class.

A virtual poster may be an electronic version of a physical poster and the guidelines above apply in the same way. Think about size. The maximum size will probably be defined as part of the project, probably 1–3 screens. Use a typeface and font size that is attractive and clear. Think about whether you find CAPITALS EASIER TO READ or a Mixed Case style. Use different typefaces, colours and shading to highlight different types of information. Sans serif fonts, such as Arial, are generally more legible than serif fonts, like Times Roman, for poster work.

A virtual poster can be more fun IF it is possible to include electronic elements. Add HTML links to web sites elsewhere, video, photographs, animated cartoons, short interactive computer programmes to demonstrate a model in action, and so on. There are many possibilities. The facilities and the expense of scanning material into digital form will govern your creativeness. Beware of limits on file size, which may be set as part of the exercise, and check and recheck that links and animations work as you wish. Also recheck the final file size; anything that takes too long to load is unhelpful.

Author Word Ladder

Change one letter at a time to make a new word each time you move down the ladder. Answers on p. 281.

F	O	R	D		H	I	N	E		K	A	N	T		M	A	R	X		M	I	L	L
S	A	D	E		L	A	M	B		R	E	A	D		P	O	P	E		W	E	S	T

20 DISSERTATIONS

The First Law of Dissertations: anything that can go wrong, does.

Dissertations and final year research projects form a significant part of many language degrees. They are a personal opportunity to look at an aspect of a language-related literary, linguistic, historical, cultural, artistic, philosophical, religious, or business topic. Each department has its own timing, style, expectations of length, and monitoring procedures. Most departments run briefing sessions so everyone is aware of the rules. Missing such briefings is a BAD idea; one of your better ideas will be to re-read the briefing material every six weeks or so to remind yourself of milestones and guidelines.

This chapter does not in any way attempt to replace or pre-empt departmental guidelines and advice. It does aim to answer some of the questions asked by students in the first two years of a degree when a dissertation is sometimes viewed as a kind of academic Everest, to be assaulted without aid of crampons or oxygen, and to say something about timescales for effective planning. More detailed information will be found in Hampson (1994). Skills addressed during dissertation and project research include autonomous working, setting and meeting personal targets in research, problem solving and professional report production. Your dissertation may be written in your first language, or more probably in the foreign language, there is no hard and fast rule, so check it out.

20.1 Dissertations are not essays. What is the difference?

Getting a dissertation together is a very different activity, requiring different skills from those used in assembling essays. You look in **detail** at a particular topic, take stock of current knowledge of an issue, and offer some further, small, contribution to the academic discussion. The project is an opportunity, given a great deal of time, to explore material, develop your ideas, design and conduct studies, analyse information and draw mature conclusions from the results. The results need not be mind blowing – providing a whole new interpretation of Strindberg's dramaturgy is rare, and the world will not end if your research produces a completely unexpected answer.

Essentially these are opportunities to enquire systematically into a topic that interests you, and to report the findings for the benefit of the next person to explore that material. Dissertations are sometimes published. Aiming to produce a product that is worthy of publication is a wholly appropriate goal.

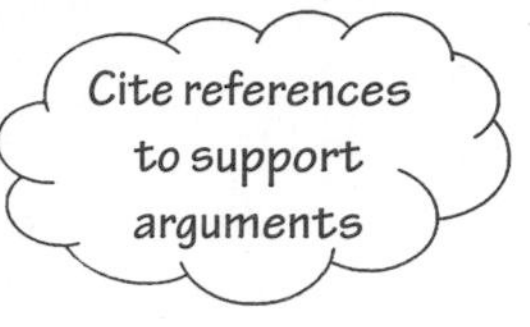

20.2 Time management

Typically you will explore a topic by yourself, making all the decisions about when, where, how, and in what detail to work. While supervisors will advise, give clues as to what the department expects, basically it is down to you to plan and organize. Dissertations are usually final year events, but what can you do in advance or while abroad to get started?

If you are leaving planning to the final year, look at the handing-in date, say May 1st; now work backwards:

1. Allow three weeks for 'slippage': 'flu, visitors, Easter, career interviews, despondency (April).
2. Writing up time – allow 3–4 weeks. OK, it should take 6–7 days but you have other things to do in March (March).
3. Analysing the information, devising new ideas, thinking of alternative interpretations (February).
4. Recovering from New Year, start of year exams, career interviews (January).
5. End of term parties, ModLangSoc Ball, preparing for Christmas, end-of-term exhaustion, Christmas (December).
6. Reading texts, chasing obscure texts, gathering evidence, rescheduling discussions when you get the 'flu, have visitors, etc. Allow 6–8 weeks (October and November)
7. Have an idea (no idea), check out the library, think about it, talk to supervisor, have more (too many) ideas, feel confused and worried, talk to supervisor, ... settle on a topic, allow 6–8 weeks.

A final year project or dissertation, designed to be done between September and May, will consume chunks of time throughout the period. With an early start date (meaning late October, because the first couple of weeks are needed for recovering from the vacation, starting new modules, catching up with friends and partying) a May 1st finish is very close. Is it worth planning ahead? Can texts be located in advance? Can you check out potential discussants while you are abroad? Try to get your research questions organized and a workable, planned timetable.

A dissertation should not be rushed if it is to get a high mark. Most low marks are won by those who start very late and those who leave the crucial thinking elements to the last week. You may have noticed useful thoughts occurring a couple of days after a discussion or meeting. You wake up thinking 'Why didn't I say … .' High marks become attached to dissertations in their third, rather than their first, draft. This means being organized so that there is ample thinking time, and keeping a small notebook near at hand to jot down ideas as they occur.

20.3 Choosing topics

It is your choice but there may be some house rules. Usually you cannot study texts that have featured heavily in your modules. So no matter how much you admire Umberto Eco's *Il Nome Della Rosa* you cannot base your dissertation on it if it is a key text in a module ('Toughioso' as we academics say). One novel or poem will probably be too slim, but equally taking on a discussion of the entire *Works of Tchaikovsky and their influence on European literature 1870–2000* is too large. Try to ensure you have a coherent study that can be completed in appropriate depth within the word limit.

If your degree combines the language you are studying with, say, management then you may be able to find a topic that combines subjects and gives you some bonus points when applying for gainful employment. There may be opportunities to use modern literature sources and newspapers or magazine articles to explore topics such as racism, political satire, terrorism, economic deprivation or migration.

Ideas might include:

☺ Analysing three or more (foreign language) novels or plays by an author or authors ignored in coursework.

☺ A critical study of a particular theme in the works of one or more poet, novelist or dramatist.

☺ Portrayal of the social, regional or historical setting in an author's work.

☺ The themes, settings or characterization in films made by a specific director in your foreign language.

☺ Discussion of an historical or contemporary figure (*Stalin's representation in 1950s and 1980s writing*).

Be careful to select a topic that falls within the expectations of a language degree. If you stray too far into pure historical, musical, sociological or art topics these may be viewed as inappropriate for your degree scheme and the marks may drop. Avoid this tank trap by talking to your supervisor and getting your topic and its scope approved.

Ideally your topic will capture your imagination. If you are not interested, you are unlikely to be motivated to give it time and thought. If you are stuck ask yourself:

What is my favourite genre? – poetry, novel, theatre, cinema …

What is my favourite period? – medieval, Renaissance, Romantic, modern, postmodern … . Then look at what is written for this combination of period and genre that was not a part of your modules – hint, try the library.

Any piece of research involves exploring a topic, examining it from a number of aspects and looking for solutions, interpretations or answers to issues or problems. The most awkward part of a dissertation is sorting out the questions to tackle. A good research topic will approach an interesting question in a way that can be addressed, to a reasonable extent, in the time and with the facilities available to you. Aim for a focused topic and avoid the 'Splodge' approach where too huge a topic is discussed too generally, like '*a study of theatre/postmodern French literature/Chinese poets*.

Questions that start 'How …?' 'To what extent …?' will help to focus thinking. Trying to come to judgements may be more difficult, as in 'Is a good memory more useful for language acquisition than a prolonged period of total immersion?' Topics that are both very big and largely unanswerable should be avoided, like 'Will Romanticism have relevance in the twenty-second century?' and avoid those where data are impossible to obtain, as in 'A quantitative evaluation of bilingualism and biliteracy in six-year-old Ewoks,' or 'Assessing language disorders among the Romulan, using personal interviews' or 'The role of Mexican didactic poets since the Aztecs …'.

- Think small at the start.
- Get a good balance between primary and secondary sources (original texts and critical materials).

Spotting gaps

Throughout the degree course make a note of thoughts like: 'Why is it like that?', 'Are these ideas also true for other people, groups, situations, adverts …?' 'Is that really right?' 'But Professor Reddit said …': also, when lecturers say 'but this area hasn't been explored yet', or '… was studied by Gone and Haddit (1936), but no developments since'. Another entry point is when an argument seems to have gone from alpha to gamma without benefit of beta. Now, it may be that the lecturer does not have time to explore beta on the way, there may be a great deal known. Alternatively, beta may be unexplored, a little black hole in search of a torch.

Having spotted an apparent 'hole' take a couple of hours in the library and on the www to see what is available. Many a tutor has sent a student to research a possible topic, to be greeted by the response 'the topic is not on because there are no references available'. SUCCESS IS FINDING LITTLE OR NOTHING. This is what you want – a topic that is relatively unexplored so that you can say something about it. When researching for an essay you want lots of definitive documentary evidence to support arguments, for a project or dissertation you want to find little or contradictory material to support your contention that this is a topic worth exploring. If there is lots of literature, that's OK too; use it as a framework, a point to leap off from, to explore and extend. Check out areas where the published literature goes out of date very quickly – can you cast 21st century ideas on an older topic?

Browsing

Browsing is a primary dissertation research technique. Try to immerse yourself in materials that are both directly related, and tangential to the topic. Wider reading adds to your perspectives, and should give insight into alternative approaches and techniques. You cannot use them all, but you can make the examiner aware that you know they exist.

There are still lots of questions to be answered; few of the lines of literature, linguistic and cultural enquiry have been definitively sorted out, though one or two are done to death. Topics go in cycles. There are fads that relate to whatever is taught in the two weeks before dissertation briefings, and standard chestnuts often expressed as 'I want to do something on – humour; asylum-seekers; cinema; the grotesque'. These are quite positive statements compared to the student who wants to do 'something social' or 'something to do with poems' or 'something while in France'. The choice of topic is ultimately your responsibility, but some projects are simply not feasible, and won't be approved by your tutor no matter how intriguing you may find them. 'The effects of BSE on aubergine sales in northern Portugal 1998–9', or 'The cost to British holidaymakers of cutbacks in road repairs in central Belgium in the summer months of 2000' will definitely not get your tutor's support. There may be a list of suggested areas or particular questions that tutors are happy to supervise, and some departments make past dissertations available to read and consult. It can feel hard and confusing but thinking around possible topics and deciding on a valid research question is part of the dissertation activity.

Take care if you choose to investigate a personal interest. You might do an extremely good dissertation on 'The 199 beers of Bavaria', 'Tapas bars in Toledo' or 'Dim Sum or Sushi: a report on a comparative blind tasting', but you will get into deep water, and probably lower marks, if you interpret all your data in the form of a graduated hangover index or a collection of restaurant bills. Writing from these perspectives would be fine in a newspaper article that seeks to put across a single viewpoint but researching is an objective academic exercise and requires objective reporting. If you feel extremely strongly about an issue you might write an excellent or a direly unbalanced report. Think about it.

20.4 Different Types of Project

Once you've decided on your topic it's time to think about the research strategy that best fits your needs and interests. The methodology or standpoint you use is as critical as your choice of evidence. If you are doing experimental studies with a linguistic edge you will need to use standard methodologies or devise your own approach such that anyone else could repeat your work and get similar results. If your topic is more discursive, literary or historical analysis for instance, you need to ensure that your findings are supported by evidence from primary and secondary sources. Look carefully at the research methods used by academics working on similar studies, read a few articles. Whatever your approach and topic you must be able to show that your findings are the result of mature thinking and evaluation, not a collection of ideas based entirely on your personal tastes, opinions and emotional responses.

Beware

There is a temptation to feel you should show one thing or another, that there is a definitive answer. Often in language studies it is a matter of balancing subjective and objective opinions. Aim to have the best information available at the time. Interview-based information is subjective, relying on people's openness, there being time to collect enough material, and one's own subjectivity. Authors of criticisms or historical studies are also people – they have opinions that reflect their background and beliefs, their place in time and space, but ideas evolve. Knowledge is partial, go for your best interpretation on what you know now, but keep looking, and recognize the areas of doubt in your arguments.

A tutor is important, especially in warning against falling for trite arguments that can appear beguiling. Watch for moral arguments that are acceptable in one culture or time, but inappropriate in another. Evaluating gender roles among the Azande using the standards and attitudes of a twenty-first century northern European will not work. Arguing that something 'is the best' is also fraught with danger. There is a good case to argue that Proust is the greatest novelist, but that accolade, we could argue, goes to either Dostoyevsky or Kafka. Some less well-read person might want to give this credit to Musil or Dickens. (These two sentences could keep a tutorial group going for some time.) These last two sentences are extreme, unbalanced and unsupported as they stand. (The answer, of course, is Sir Walter Scott.) Avoid unsupported arguments and strong language unless there is overwhelming evidence.

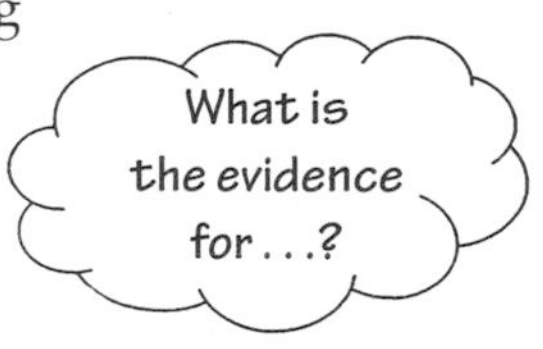

20.5 Preliminary thinking

Resources

How accessible, and in what form, are the texts or data you need? In linguistic studies, what are the implications of choosing the right number of texts to examine, or the way in which you construct your interview questions for a survey? How long will it take to get your materials together? How will you organize the printing and copying of your questionnaire? Do you need to book the tape recorder, interview space ... ? Finding out about the availability of resources is something you need to get done early on. Pilot work helps here.

20.6 Pilot work

Just about every lecturer nags every student to do a rough draft or pilot; about 99 per cent of students do not bother and about 99 per cent regret it. PILOT WORK IS A GOOD IDEA. It allows you to have a first run at the texts or, in linguistic studies, to try out a questionnaire or run a mini discussion group. Life is too complicated and too complex for anyone to get everything right first time. A pilot study shows there are other angles, other people to consult, suggests other critics to consider and indicates other things you could do to enhance the research. More than one student has discovered that texts are out of print and unobtainable, e.g. collections of ephemera or anthologies of underground poetry from the German Democratic Republic.

At the end of the pilot ask yourself:

- Is this the best approach?
- Can I get all the information I need to address the hypothesis in enough depth?
- Can the project be done in the time allowed?

If not, revise your methodology or the whole topic.

20.7 The real thing!

OK, you have found the books, photocopied various papers, posed your research questions – what next? Well reading is a good idea (essential), but you need to keep track of ideas and evidence. A (big) piece of paper may help you keep track – put down those research questions, link them to your first ideas for the argument, then keep adding and revising this sketch/plan/lists. Add new ideas, draw in links in the argument, note the reasons for and against. Track those odd ideas that seem off-the-wall or beyond the initial scope of your study – they may be valuable and link in later, or they may find a home in your recycling bin. Re-read the key texts; you will find new ideas.

Your examiner will be impressed by the logical progression of your arguments and high quality critical perceptions. You have had plenty of research time so you should have found a range of critical sources, comparable published materials and been able to synthesize these with your own ideas and results. Judicious use of quotations should provide evidence that you can link ideas together and support them.

Keep track of everything you read – can you put all your sources in an electronic bibliography such as EndNote or Idealist? Your references must be complete so you do need all the boring bits – author, title, source, publisher, place, date, page numbers (see Chapter 15). Note your quotations very carefully. Cutting and pasting from electronic documents may help but you still need to check the copy is accurate, especially if a web browser does not support umlauts, accents, pictograms and so on.

- Read carefully and deeply (Chapter 6).
- Re-read key material.

20.8 The Format and Assessment

A dissertation or thesis is a formal piece of writing. The reader expects the author to adhere to the 'rules', make the presentation consistent and tidy and observe the word limits. If possible ensure the same typeface is used throughout, that there are page numbers on ALL pages, and that you double check the university guidelines and follow them, especially the WORD LENGTH. The general format is roughly along the lines given in Figure 20.1. Treat the page lengths as suggestions. There are plenty of high quality dissertations submitted in different page combinations.

Find the marking guidelines your department adopts or see Figure 20.2. There are many variations. Some departments ask for an initial plan that counts, others do not. Some departments mark your first draft. Remember these percentage distributions are only a guide, mark distributions vary considerably depending on the nature of the dissertation.

Chapter	Contents		Page Length
0	Title page, Acknowledgements, Abstract, Table of contents, Table of figures.		
1	Introduction: brief background, research aims, signpost thesis layout.		2–3
2	Literature review, summary of material relevant to this research. General links to the topic		4–8
3	**Qualitative Thesis**	**Quantative Thesis** (comparatively rare in languages)	2 – piece of string
	Methodology, a description of your research approach *or* Discussion and evaluation of first theme/idea/concept.	Methodology – your research process, techniques used, criticism of techniques and evaluation of their accuracy and representativeness.	
4	Discussion and evaluation of second theme/idea/concept.	Results, with tabulations, graphs as required.	Piece of string
5	Discussion and evaluation of third theme/idea/concept. Synthesis of themes and alternatives.	Interpretation of results. Evaluation of accuracy and representativeness, sensitivity analysis if relevant.	Another piece of string
6	Findings, implications for future research. 'What I would have done if I had known at the start what I know now.' Conclusions.		1–2 1 1
Bibliography	Full references to material referred to in thesis.		As required
Appendix	Data sets if required. Example copy of Questionnaire(s). Sample of interview transcripts.		Minimize

Figure 20.1 Typical dissertation formats.

Dissertation Assessment	Please comment using following headings as appropriate
Planning phase *Clarity in formulation of project? Originality in formulation of project? Independent development of project?*	5%
Abstract	5%
Literature review/bibliography/use of sources *Relevance of literature selected? Comprehensive? Critical comments on literature?*	10%
Methodology *Appropriate to topic? Successful in execution? Followed plan and adapted it appropriately?*	5%
Analysis and interpretation *Planned? Appropriate? Extent to which aims were met? Consciousness of limitations?*	20%
Discussion/quality of argument *Logical and thought through?*	20%
Conclusions *Sustainability of conclusions? Suggestions for future research?*	15%
Quality of language *Grammatical accuracy? Appropriate register, vocabulary, syntax?*	15%
Presentation *Quality of figures, tables and photographs? References? Appendices? Page numbers? Appropriate length?*	5%
Degree of supervision required *Did the student take the initiative? Any illness or personal problems?*	
Further comments	

Figure 20.2 Dissertation assessment criteria.

20.9 Writing and writing up

'Writing up' rather implies that it can be done in one go, and as a one off. Developing ideas and seeing the implications of results takes time. Remember to write as you go. GET SOMETHING ON PAPER EVERY WEEK. Read a couple of things and then draft some paragraphs. Add to it when you read the next book or paper. Writing is part of the research activity, you read a bit, write a bit, think a bit; and the combination of these three activities tells you what you might do next. The project can also exemplify your time management skills. Typical research patterns are mapped in Figure 20.3; the optimist's pattern is sadly misleading.

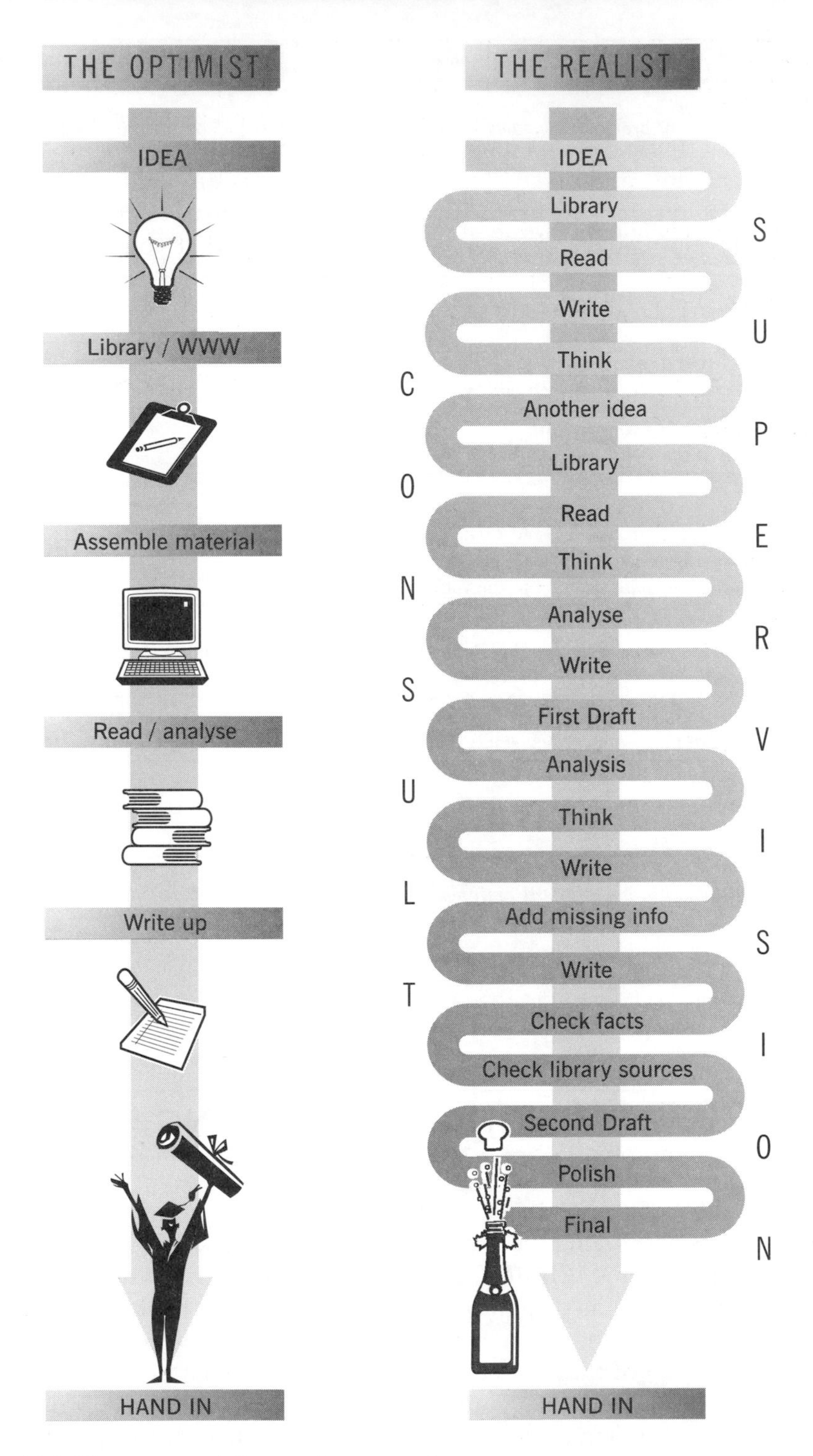

Figure 20.3 The process of dissertation research.

You cannot hope to have read all the critical and comparative literature and to research all aspects of a topic. Much of dissertation management is about drawing a line, stopping reading, starting thinking and starting writing. You are aiming to synthesize what you have read and discovered. You base your opinions on your personal judgements and on cited material. If you took another year over your project, you would still be reporting on partial information and your ideas would continue to develop. Your examiners are looking to see that you have tackled a reasonable topic in a relevant manner and drawn sensible inferences and conclusions from the findings. They do not expect you to explain why anti-Semitism exists, account for all the different attitudes and beliefs about Molière or explain why sonnets rhyme. Don't get overwhelmed by reading, keep it in balance. Remember to balance 30 minutes of www, or on-line bibliographic searching, with lots of hours of reading.

Top Tips

- **Start writing**, the draft will not be right the first or second time. Ask tutors how often they rewrite before sending a piece to a publisher. 'Lots' is the only answer worth believing.
- **Spell check everything**, whatever the language.
- **References matter**; check that your references are properly cited. Put them at the end of the document from day one. Realising in the last week you have kept no record of references is like getting to within 6 inches of the summit of Everest and having to go back to base camp for flag and camera.
- **Proof read** what you have written, not what you think you wrote. Check quotations especially carefully, and that the title page, abstract, acknowledgements and contents page are in the right format for your department.
- **Proof reading is not easy**; get a flat mate to read through for grammar, spelling, bias and general understanding. If your friend understands your 'Linguistic norms in Ibiza nightclubs' then so, probably, will your tutor. You can repay the favour by checking out your mate's dissertation on the 'The reading habits of Pokemon'. If you can leave a little time between writing and proofing, you spot more errors.
- **Abstract.** Write this last.

20.10 References and Further Reading

Hampson L. (1994) *How's Your Dissertation Going? Students Share the Rough Reality of Dissertation and Project Work.* Lancaster: Unit for Innovation in Higher Education.

Hennessy B. (1994) *How to Write an Essay: Winning Techniques and Skills for Students.* Plymouth: How to Books.

Suffering from stress? Take our advice:

Make up your own language, then go and use it –
to ask people in the street for directions.

21 REVISION SKILLS

Assessment does not have to be the ultimate journey into an uncharted wilderness.

'I finish five modules this week, have three essay papers and a translation to hand in on Friday, and the first exam is on Monday – so when do I revise?' Well the answer is that you don't revise in this style. Revision at the last minute – 'cramming' style – is really a school concept. It is part of a 'Get the facts → Learn them → Regurgitate in examination' process. It is characteristic of surface learning. In 'real life', you don't revise, you have an accumulating body of knowledge and apply it continuously. University is a transition phase, but all your deep reading and learning activities should mean that revision as cramming becomes a small proportion of your activities. (However, mugging up more vocabulary at the last minute may calm nerves!)

Re-reading and reviewing material needs to be an on-going process built into your weekly timetable, because it improves the amount of detail that you recall. So normal learning activities should reap rewards at exam time because they are also 'revision' activities that reinforce your learning, and you have been doing them all term. Keep a balance between content revision and language modules revision – going over 'content' material often seems more attractive than doing language drills. The following ideas may help:

- ✔ Make notes in your foreign language.
- ✔ Get your brain in gear before a lecture by reading last week's notes.
- ✔ Re-read notes from discussions.
- ✔ Use SQ3R (p. 65) in reading and making connections to other modules.
- ✔ Think actively around issues (see Chapter 7).
- ✔ Check that you have good arguments (see Chapter 8). Look for gaps in the evidence and use that information to determine what you read, don't just take the next item on the reading list.
- ✔ Actively ask questions as you research (see Chapter 7).

Timetable 'revision slots' to continue these learning processes.

Tight deadlines are a feature of university life. Most tutors will be blissfully unaware, and emphatically unsympathetic, when you have five essays due on the last day of term or semester and examinations two days later. Sorting out schedules is your problem not theirs, an opportunity to exercise your time management skills.

21.1 Revision aims

Exams test your understanding of interrelated language and content materials from coursework, personal research and reading. You will need to have overview information on a large number of topics and detailed knowledge, examples and evidence to back it up.

We could put this next section in the exams chapter but by then it might be too late! Understanding, relevance, analytical ability and expression are listed by Meredeen (1988) as the Holy Grail of examiners, keen to donate marks. What do you need to do while revising to demonstrate these attributes to your nice, kind examiner?

Acquire new words

1. UNDERSTANDING. Have you shown you understood the question? Keep answers focused.
2. RELEVANCE. There are no marks for irrelevant inclusion of material no matter how interesting. Stick to the issues and points the question raises. Don't let yourself be side-tracked. In exams, or when writing essays, keep re-reading the question to ensure that your answer is still relevant.
3. ANALYTICAL ABILITY. Aim for a well reasoned, organized answer. Show that you understand the meaning of the question and can argue your way through points in a logical manner.
4. EXPRESSION. Clear and concise writing that makes your ideas and arguments transparent to the examiner helps enormously. The length of an answer is no guide to its effectiveness or relevance. A well-structured short answer will get better marks than a long answer padded out with irrelevant details.

Plan revision to match these goals.

21.2 Get organized – time management again

If from the start, you take 30 minutes each week for each module, to review and reflect, to think around issues, and decide what to read next, you will also be revising. It is an on-going process, and you will be well ahead of the majority! As exams get closer, sort out a work and learning timetable – say for the five weeks before exams. Put every essay, oral and presentation deadline on it, add the exam times, lectures, tutorials and all your other commitments, and have a little panic. Then decide that panicking wastes time and sort out a plan to do six essays and revise twelve topics and include social and sporting activities to relax, and block the time in two hour slots, with breaks to cook and eat. Then organize group revision, discussion and sharing opportunities.

- Start earlier than you think you need to!
- Put revision time into your weekly plan, use it to think.
- Keep a revision record and attempt to allocate equal time to each paper or module.
- Speaking an idea aloud, or writing it down, lodges information in the brain more securely than reading.
- Attend revision classes, they almost always go over new ground and the people running the class know what will be the most helpful for you.

Revising is not something you have to do alone. Think with friends and colleagues. Group revision assists:

☺ By giving you language practice – is there a native speaker to practise with?

☺ By generating comments on your ideas, adding the perceptions of others to your brain bank.

☺ Because it is easier for two or three brains to disentangle ideas about existentialism, Keynes or Zen Buddhism.

☺ Because it's more fun (less depressing?).

☺ By making you feel less anxious about the exam, more self-confident.

☺ Because the challenge of explaining something to a group will help you understand the points and remember details more clearly.

☺ By showing where you need to do extra study and where you are already confidently fluent with the material.

Don't be put off by someone claiming to know all because they have read something you have not. No one reads everything. If it is so good, ask for an explanation.

21.3 What do you do now?

What were your thoughts as you left your most recent exams? Ignoring the obvious 'Where's the nearest bar?' jot down a few thoughts and look at **Try This 21.1**.

TRY THIS 21.1 – Post-examination reflections

Write down your thoughts about your last examinations, and then look at the list below. These are random, post-examination thoughts of rather jaundiced first years. Tick any points you empathize with. Make a plan.

- ☹ No practice at timed essays since A-level. I'd forgotten how after eighteen months.
- ☹ Not enough time to write a full answer.
- ☹ My mind went blank, couldn't remember a thing.
- ☹ I knew what I wanted to say in my first language but couldn't think of the words in the foreign language.
- ☹ Hadn't revised things that came up.
- ☹ Missed the point of the last essay.
- ☹ Put in a load of things that were not relevant, because I could remember them.
- ☹ Was thinking about going to the bar after, most of the time.
- ☹ Needed more direction towards the questions.
- ☹ Had loads of facts in the lectures, but nothing to apply them to.
- ☹ Mostly relied on common sense and made something up.
- ☹ I had all this stuff about tragic theory and mimesis and he asks about humanist values.
- ☹ I spent so long on the first six lines of the translation that I couldn't finish it all. (A BAD idea, always finish translations, the examiner can't give you marks if you haven't written anything, and you might just get it right!)
- ☹ None of the quotes I mugged up were relevant, but I put a few in anyway (another daft thing to do, it just irritates the examiner!).

21.4 Good revision practice

The rubrics (headings and special instructions) for papers are usually displayed somewhere in a department, possibly in the course outline or on the examination noticeboard. Find out about the different styles of questions, how many questions you have to answer and what each question is worth. Plan your revision activities to match the pattern of the paper.

Revise actively

Sitting in a big armchair in a warm room reading old notes or a book is almost guaranteed to send you to sleep! Try some of these ideas:

- ✔ Make summary notes in your foreign language, ideas maps, lists of main points and summaries of cases or examples.
- ✔ Sort out the general principles and learn them.
- ✔ Look for links, ask questions like:
  - 'Where does this fit into this course? – essay? – other modules?'
  - 'How important is it? – a critical idea? – detailed example? – extra evidence to support the case?'
  - 'Is this the main idea? – an irrelevance?'
- ✔ Write outline answers to essays, then apply the criteria of Understanding, Relevance, Analysis and Expression. Ask yourself: 'Does this essay work?' 'Where can it be improved?'
- ✔ Practise writing a full exam paper in the right time. Sunday morning is a good time! Put all the books away, set the alarm clock and do a past paper against the clock. DON'T PANIC, the next time will be better. Examination writing skills seize up, they need greasing before the first exam.
- ✔ Remember you need a break of 5 minutes every hour or so. Plan exercise into your revision time, swimming, walking or going to the gym; the oxygen revitalizes the brain cells (allegedly).
- ✔ Apply the ideas in the Active Reading SQ3R technique (p. 65) to your revision. Use it to condense notes to important points.
- ✔ Aim to review all your course notes a week before the exams! Then you will panic less, have time to be ill without getting behind, and feel more relaxed for having had time to look again at odd points and practise a couple of timed essays. (OK, OK, we said AIM!)
- ✔ Staying up all night to study at the last minute is not one of the best ideas in life.

Reviewing the first four weeks of a module should, ideally, be completed by weeks 6–8, so that the ideas accumulate in your mind. The rest of the module will progress better because you understand the background and there is time to give attention to topics in the last sessions of the module. But then, who is ideal?

Outline essays

Outline answers are an efficient revision alternative to writing a full essay. Write the Introduction and Conclusion paragraphs in full, NO CHEATING. For the central section, do one-sentence summaries for each paragraph, with references. Then look carefully at the structure and balance of the essay; consider where more examples are needed and whether the argument is in the most logical order.

Keywords

Examiners tend to use a number of keywords to start or finish questions. Words like discuss, evaluate, assess, compare and illustrate. They all require slightly different approaches in the answer. Use the **Try This 21.2** game to replace keywords and revise essay plans.

TRY THIS 21.2 – Replacing keywords in examination questions

Take a question, any question that has been set in an examination or tutorial in your department. Do an outline structure for your answer. Then replace the keyword with one or more of: assess, compare, criticize, explore, illustrate, justify, list, outline, trace, verify. Each word changes the emphasis of the answer, and the style and presentation of evidence, think how to slant your answer to reflect this.

Here is a list of keywords used in essay questions and 'possible' meanings, (adapted from Rowntree 1988, Lillis 1997).

Analyse	Describe, examine and criticize all aspects of the question, and do it in detail.
Argue	Make the case using evidence, for and against a point of view.
Assess	Weigh up and make a judgement about the extent to which the conditions in the statement are fulfilled.
Comment	Express an opinion on, not necessarily a long one, BUT often used by examiners when they mean describe, analyse or assess – (cover your back).
Compare	Examine the similarities and differences between two or more ideas, theories, objects, processes etc.
Contrast	Point out the differences between ... could add some similarities.
Criticize	Discuss the supporting and opposing arguments for, make a judgements about ...; show where errors arise in ... use examples.
Define	Give the precise meaning of ... or show clearly the outlines of ...
Describe	Give a detailed account of ...
Discuss	Argue the case for and against the proposition, a detailed answer. Try to develop a definite conclusion or point of view. See Comment.
Evaluate	Appraise, again with supporting and opposing arguments, to give a balanced view of ... Look to find the value of ...
Explain	Give a clear, intelligible explanation of ... Needs a detailed but precise answer.
Identify	Pick out the important features of ... and explain why you picked this selection.
Illustrate	Make your points with examples, or expand on an idea with examples. Generally one detailed example and a number of briefly described, relevant supporting examples make the better argument.
Interpret	Using you own experience, explain what is meant by ...

Justify	Give reasons why ... Show why this is the case ... Need to argue the case. See Argue.
List	Make a list of ... (usually means a short/ brief response). Notes or bullets may be OK.
Outline	Give a general summary or description showing how elements interrelate.
Prove	Present the evidence that clearly makes an unarguable case.
Relate	Describe or tell a story. See Explain, Compare and Contrast.
Show	Reveal in a logical sequence why .... See Explain.
State	Explain in plain language and in detail the main points.
Summarize	Make a brief statement of the main points. Ignore excess detail.
Trace	Explain stage by stage .... A logical sequence answer.
Verify	Show the statement to be true. The expectation is that you will provide the justification to confirm the statement.

The quiz approach

Devising revision quizzes can be effective. You do not need to dream up multiple answers, but could play around with a format as in Figures 21.1. and 21.2. These are two short factual quizzes based on journal articles, but tragically the answers in the second column are out of order. Can you sort them out?

1. What is Koineization?	*a. About 16 years (Gass and Selinker 1994).*
2. At what age does language-learning aptitude level off?	*b. No.*
3. What is the timescale for koineization as suggested by the Milton Keynes results?	*c. The development of a new mixed language variety following contact between people with different dialects.*
4. Is the London cockney influence a significant element in the Milton Keynes study?	*d. Britain (1997).*
5. Which group shows the clearest features of the new dialect?	*e. Focusing, as yet incomplete, is taking place amongst the second generation.*
6. Who studied dialect contact in the English fens?	*f. The older children and the youngest mothers.*

Figure 21.1. Quiz questions for an article by Kerswill and Williams (2000) [Answers at the end of the chapter].

Note the inclusion of references in the answers, they provide the evidence that increases your marks. The questions in Figure 21.1 cover facts, and are good for MCQ (multiple choice question) revision. Now consider the style of these questions:

- What are the theories that are considered in this article?
- Why was this research approach adopted?
- Why was Milton Keynes a suitable site for this study?
- What are the factors which influence the outcome of dialect contact?
- Outline the research process adopted by Kerswill and Williams (2000).

These questions demand similar factual knowledge as those in Figure 21.1, but a more reasoned and extended response. They are useful for revising short answer questions and essay paragraphs. Helpfully, the first two questions apply to every article. You may feel this approach works best for more technical papers but can be applied to literature studies, it may be less easy to find factual questions but searching for them gets your brain in action and memorizing points and evidence. See for example Figure 21.2, based on an article from *German Life and Letters.*

1. What was the 'Kulturbund zur demokratisschen Erneuerung Deutschlands'?	*a. In this autobiographical novel, which concerns a young man's break with his bourgeois family and involvement with radical politics, Becher promotes the idea that his psychological problems and difficulties in being a good Party man can be explained by conflicting social categories.*
2. What is meant by the 'kulturelles Erbe'?	*b. He was too open to bourgeois writers and politicians.*
3. Who appealed for 'Goethe-Gesellschaften' to be set up throughout Germany?	*c. A self-inflicted act of violence.*
4. What evidence does Davies draw on from Becher's novel *Abschied?*	*d. The theory that the great literary works of the German humanist tradition form an opposition to nationalism and irrationalism.*
5. How does Becher characterize the German invasion of the Soviet Union in *Erziehung zur Freiheit?*	*e. One aspect of Becher's programme for German renewal, the moral education of the masses and a promoter of high culture.*
6. Why did the Soviets consider replacing Becher as 'Kulturbund' President in 1946?	*f. Friedrich Meinecke (1946).*

Figure 21.2 Quiz questions for an article by Davies (2000)). [Answers at the end of the chapter].

Or more generally:

- What is the evidence that Becher saw himself as the embodiment of an aspiration to unite 'Geist' and 'Macht' in Germany?
- What was the relationship between the Kulturbund and Becher's programme for German renewal?
- How is the role of 'purity' evidenced in Becher's work?
- How did Becher's work influence GDR literary life?

Questions do not have to be profound to help your revision, you are trying to cast the information in a new and memorable light. To get into the swing have a go at **Try This 21.3** and **Try This 21.4.** The first asks for quiz questions based on your notes from lectures and additional reading, and the second uses the same technique with a journal article.

Revision is an opportunity to think about and continue to look for explanations and insights. Revision is therefore a creative process, with ideas gelling and developing as you re-read and reconsider. Note-making is therefore an integral part of revision. Some general questions running in your head will encourage a questioning, active approach to revision. Have a go at **Try This 21.5** to explore this approach further.

TRY THIS 21.3 – Quiz questions from notes

Pick a set of notes and create a short quiz, 10 questions, in each of the two styles. First short factual questions then some more extended questions. Write the questions on one side of the page and answers on the reverse, so you can use them (without cheating too much) for revision.

TRY THIS 21.4 – Quiz questions from a journal article.

Read an article from any reading list and, rather than making notes, devise a set of 5 short and 5 extended questions that explore the topic. Again, write the questions on one side of the page and answers on the reverse, for revision purposes.

TRY THIS 21.5 – Generic questions for revising your language exams

Compile a list of questions that could be used in revision. Some suggestions are on pp. 281–2, but have a go at your own list in L1 and L2 before looking.

21.5 Grabbing New (Forgotten) Words

This has to be an ongoing activity (see Chapter 2) but keep your word lists, paragraphs with gaps and pictures and look at them again. Pictures are good – can you name all the items and a few verbs to describe the actions. Play word association games, alone or with friends, to pick up vocab. Go for the fun elements. Can you translate those chart topping lyrics into your foreign language (though why you should want to …)? Get the headphones, tapes, radio … in action.

What works for you? Find it and use it.

21.6 References and Further Reading

Davies, P. (2000) Johannes R. Becher and the Agony of Responsibility 1945–1949, *German Life and Letters*, 53, 2, 243–260.

Kerswill, P. and Williams, A. (2000) Creating a New Town koine: children and language change in Milton Keynes, *Language in Society*, 29, 65–115.

Rowntree, D. (1988) *Learn How To Study: A Guide for Students of All Ages* (3rd edn.) London: Warner Books.

Answers to Quiz, Figure 21.1: Kerswill and Williams (2000) 1c, 2a, 3e, 4b, 5f, 6d; and Figure 21.2: Davies (2000) 1e, 2d, 3f, 4a, 5c, 6b.

Anagrams 4

Try These Language anagrams, answers p. 282.

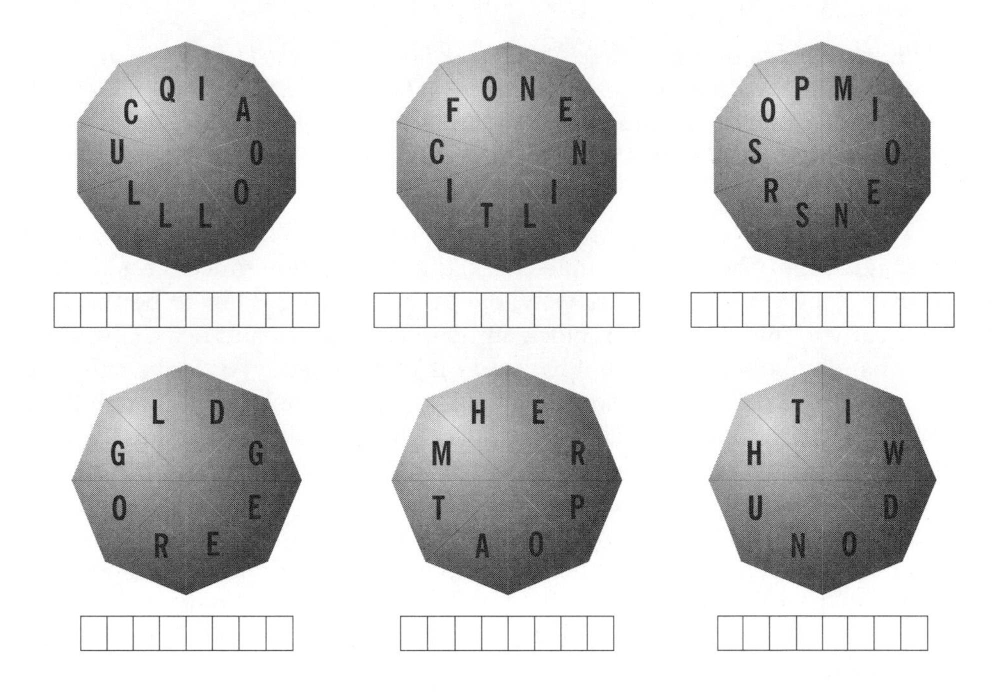

22 EXAMINATIONS

Explore and illustrate all aspects of Chinese literature in the last 5000 years in relation to ogham and cuneiform writings, European and Japanese literature from the medieval to postmodern, and second millennium Arabic literature. Time allowed: 45 minutes.

Relax, you did all that reflection, reviewing and revision, so the examinations will be most agreeable. Check, and double-check, the examination timetable and room locations – they can change. Know where you are going. Plan to be there 20 minutes early to find your seat or block number, visit the loo and relax. Check the student handbook so you know what to do if you are delayed. Make sure you have a pen, spare pens, pencils and highlighters and a watch (even though there ought to be a clock in the room). Take heed of anything the invigilator has to say. If you think there is a problem with the paper tell an invigilator at once, so the Languages staff can be consulted.

Find out well in advance how the paper is structured and use the time in proportion. The usual convention is that if the marks for individual questions are not stipulated, the questions will all be worth equal marks. So, if you have to answer four questions in a two-hour paper, allow equal time for all four, i.e. 25 minutes per question + 10 minutes to read the paper and plan your answers + 10 minutes to check through your answers. Be strict with yourself about running over time, and if you can shave a couple of minutes off one or two of the questions, you gain another 5 minutes for extra checking or emergencies. In a three-hour paper with five short questions worth 10 per cent each and two essays worth 25 per cent each, allow 16 minutes for each of the short questions, 40 for each of the essays, and 10 + 10 minutes for reading, planning and checking, as before. Do all this arithmetic in advance, and try writing some timed answers to an old exam paper to get yourself tuned in. For language exams, where it is the quality of the language that determines your mark, you will need to adjust the time allocation so as to allow sufficient time for checking what you have written for spelling and grammatical accuracy.

Make sure you read the instructions at the top of the exam paper (the 'rubric') very carefully. Don't rush to answer the first question on the page. Read through all the questions before you put pen to paper, and make a rough plan of every answer (including any quotations or references you intend to use) before you start. Answer the number of questions required, no more and preferably no less. Leave time to do justice to each question, and don't leave your potentially best answer until the end. Equally, don't spend so much time on it that you have to skimp on the remaining essays.

Should you be seized with anxiety and your brain freezes over, use the 'free association', brainstorming approach. Write out the question and then look at each word in turn scribbling down the first words that occur to you, anything ... authors' names, examples, and related words. This should generate calm and facts, and you can plan from the spider diagram you have generated.

Double check exam locations and times

22.1 EXAMINATION ESSAYS

In languages, as in most arts and humanities areas, discursive essays will feature prominently in your exams. The minimalist advice here is: re-read the advice on argument (Chapter 10), revision (Chapter 21), and writing essays (Chapter 14), and write fast. Essays allow you to develop lines of thought, draw in diverse ideas and demonstrate your skills in argument, analysis, synthesis, evaluation and written communication. Remember to keep the linguistic/cultural/historical/literary content high, use evidence to support your arguments wherever you can and cite supporting references.

Top Tips

- If all questions look impossible, choose the one where you have the most examples to quote, or the longest question. Long questions usually give more clues to plan the answer. '"What was assuredly the main attraction of '*Werther*' for the discerning eighteenth-century reader turns out to be the very factor which alienates the modern student of this work: the hero's extreme 'sensibility'." Comment on this statement,' is a question with loads of clues and parts to answer, whereas 'Discuss why Werther is a difficult character to empathize with?' is essentially the same question, and could be answered with the same information, but will be a minefield if you do not impose structure and facts.

- Plan your answer even if short of time. Underline or highlight keywords in the question, like <u>Discuss</u>, or <u>Compare and contrast</u>, note the period, areas and issues the answer should cover, and don't stray into irrelevancy. Don't make generalizations if the question asks about specific authors or texts or historical events, but if the answer calls for a wider-ranging treatment, make sure you supply it, along with relevant examples. Do a quick list or spider diagram of the main points, and note ideas for the introduction and conclusion. Then rank the points to get a batting order for the sections.

- On a three question paper, plan all three questions before writing the answer to Question 1. Your brain can run in background mode on ideas for Questions 2 and 3 as you write the first answer.

- Watch the time. Leave a couple of minutes at the end of each answer to check through, amend grammar, spelling, add extra points, references and tidy up diagrams.

Does not address the question. 25%
Swarming with factual errors. 35%
Fine answer to a question about David Hume; pity the question was about European Enlightenment. 38%
Very weak effort – no attempt to explain examples or definitions. 42%
Somewhat confused but some relevant points. 42%
Good background but little analysis on the question set. 44%
A scrappy answer with some good points. 45%
Started fine then got repetitive. 49%
Decent attempt, some examples but not focused on the question. 50%
Not sufficient explanation/evaluation; you list some ideas at the end but these needed developing to raise the mark. 52% (2 sides only)
Reasonable answer but misses out the crucial element of … 54%
Has clearly done some reading but fails to write down the basics. 54%
Reasonable effort as far as it goes, but does not define/explain technical terms – no examples. 55%
Accurate but generally descriptive, never really got to the 'evaluate' section. 55%
Needs to learn about paragraphs, then fill them with organized content. 55%
Reasonable effort – covers many relevant points, structure adequate but you need to organize points in shorter paragraphs. 57%
Too much description – not enough argument. 58%
Good – but needs to be more focused on key points. 58%
Good discussion but needs to emphasize international aspects more. 60%
Good introduction and well argued throughout, although with no evidence of reading. Good use of examples but unfortunately only from class material. 62%
Has done some reading and thinking. 65%
Quite good – a general answer, omits existentialism but lots of non-lecture examples. 64%
Excellent; clearly structured, to the point. 70%
Outstanding. Persuasive argument and a comprehensive answer to a complex question. 85%

Figure 22.1 Comments on examination essays.

Some of the points examiners search for may be deduced from Figure 22.1, which lists comments from a random selection of examiners. They concentrate on the lower end of the marking scale and from it you may gather that examiners cannot give marks unless you tell them what you know: explain terms, answer all parts of the question, use lots of examples – remember you're a ~~Womble~~ language student. Everything needs setting in a language context. If you do not demonstrate your powers of argument and include language-related material and examples, connecting what the examiners are asking with what you know, you are not going to hit the high marks. Organize your points, one per paragraph, in a structure that flows logically. Set the scene in your first paragraph and signpost the layout of the answer. Be precise rather than woolly, for example rather than saying 'Early on ...' give the date; or for the general 'In many parts of Europe we see ...' use examples like 'In Aachen, Amsterdam, Liège and Strassburg we can see ...'. Try to keep an exciting, interesting point for the final paragraph. If you are going to cross things out, do it tidily.

Take-away or take home examinations

Essays written without the stress of the examination room can seem a doddle, but still need revision and preparation. Get the notes together in advance, make sure you have found the library resources you require before the exam paper is published; at that point people are trampled underfoot in the race to the library. Think around possible essay topics to get your brain in gear. Do not leave it all to the last minute.

22.2 Short answer questions

Short answer questions search for evidence of understanding through factual, knowledge-based answers and the ability to reason and draw inferences. For short answers a reasoned, paragraph answer is required to questions like 'Briefly describe humanism', 'Explain the difference between a diphthong and a ligature' or 'What was Helene Lange's main contribution to the German women's movement?' Questions like 'Outline four characteristics of the courtly epic' or 'Suggest four reasons for the increased popularity enjoyed by right-wing politicians in central Europe in the early years of the 21st century' require four, fact-rich answers, and can be answered as a set of points. Take care to answer the question that is set – 'Define and demonstrate the importance of the following four aspects of Dadaism: its mocking of traditional European institutions and art forms; its emphasis on odd conjunctions of everyday objects; its left-wing, anti-war thrust; its international dimensions'. This is a really helpful question, provided you answer all eight parts, (define and demonstrate * 2!).

22.3 MCQs

MCQs (multiple choice questions) test a wide range of topics in a short time. They may be used for revision, in a module test where the marks do not count, or as a part of module assessment where the marks matter. A class test checks what you have understood, and should indicate where more research and revision is required. In a final assessment watch the rules. With on-line assessment, once the answer is typed in and sent, it cannot be changed.

Look carefully at the instructions on MCQ papers. The instructions will remind you of the rules, such as:

There is/is not negative marking. (With negative marking you lose marks for getting it wrong).
One or more answers may be correct, select all the correct answers. (This is how you can get 100 marks on a paper with 60 questions.)

General advice says to shoot through the paper answering all the questions you can do easily, and then go back to tackle the rest (but general advice does not suit everyone). Questions come in a range of types:

The 'Trivial Pursuit' factual style

These questions aim to test your recall of facts and understanding of theories. They usually represent only a small proportion of the total number of questions. Answers on p. 282.

The term *Gesamtkunstwerk* was coined by:
- a. Johann Nestroy
- b. Bertolt Brecht
- c. Richard Wagner
- d. Richard Strauss

Antoine de St Exupéry's *Vol de Nuit* is about:
- a. Wildlife
- b. Aeroplanes
- c. A burglary

RAF stands for:
- a. Royal Air Force
- b. Rapid Artillery Fire
- c. Rote Armee Fraktion

In this last example there are two correct answers, (a) and (c), and both should be indicated for full marks.

Reasoning and previous knowledge style

Reasoning from previous knowledge gives rise to questions like:

In each of the following lists of language families, which is the 'odd-one-out'? (Answers p. 282)

a. Gaelic, Armenian, Manx , Breton.
b. Faroese, Norwegian, Latvian, Icelandic.
c. Bengali, Gujarati, Kurdish, Urdu.
d. Catalan, Romansch, Romany, Romanian.

Some questions give a paragraph of information and possible responses. You apply theories or knowledge to choose the right response or combination of responses. Some tests combine information from more than one course, as here where a second year European art history paper requires information from a first year society and culture module:

> 'In the strictest sense, the term "classical" is used to describe the art and literature of ancient Greece and Rome. More broadly speaking, the term "classical" refers to any style or period exhibiting characteristics derived from classical Greek or Roman art or literature. Which of the following countries embraced neo-classicism in the early 18th century (tick all that apply)?
>
> a. Mexico
> b. Italy
> c. Poland
> d. England
> e. Denmark
> f. America
> g. Scotland
> h. Portugal

22.4 Gap-filling or cloze test

These are peculiar to language learning, especially interactive CALL (Computer-Assisted Language Learning) drills, and used wisely they have a powerful re-inforcing effect (because you can learn by your mistakes, go back and try them again). But there is also a sudden-death paper-based form much-beloved of language teachers out to probe (as in 'dentists' instruments') students' knowledge of grammar, where they can be profoundly demoralizing! You are given sentences or a passage containing a series of gaps which represent missing adjectival endings, articles or verbs, and you are required to fill the gaps by adding the correct form. With these tests there is no grey area, only black and white, right and wrong, and the only sensible way to approach them is in the sure and certain knowledge that comes from learning the rules off by heart ... (see also Chapter 3, grammar ...) and get some past exam papers to practise on.

22.5 Types of written examination

The traditional tests of a language student's ability, still widely used, are a series of three-hour exams involving translation in and out of your L2 ('prose

Read and re-read the question

composition' and 'unseen translation' respectively), an essay in the L2 ('free composition') on some inspiring topic like 'The prospects for Europe', 'The humour of Cervantes', 'Patriotism', or 'The legacy of Calvinism', and a short oral examination. The common factor in all of these is the element of surprise. Essay titles and chunks of prose are laid before the candidate, and the trick in responding is to display a sophisticated command of language and high-level powers of analysis, synthesis and rhetoric under acute pressure of time. Nice work if you can get it! The 'prose' and essay are tests of grammar in action, but with the translation passages and essay questions all drawn from a virtually boundless pool, it may seem like a bit of a lottery, but luckily you have loads of experience to call on.

There are numerous variations on these traditional tasks, along with alternative forms of assessment. *Translation* still figures prominently in testing language acquisition (as in re-inforcing the language-learning process), and presumably always will. But there is a shift of emphasis away from the unexpected towards the expected, from rewarding a combination of reading at large and luck, to rewarding careful attention to detail and reading around the material covered in the course. This in turn reflects a general trend towards clearly defining aims and objectives, syllabuses and outcomes of courses in advance. Typically, candidates have to translate a passage or sentences, or write an essay, on a topic that relates more or less closely in subject-matter, style and lexis to work done during the year. Preparation for this type of exam pays off, and there are three main ways:

- Go over the course material again and again, learn all the vocabulary in the texts. Look up associated terms and phrases and memorize them. Study the grammar and syntax of the texts and try to imitate them.
- Get hold of non-syllabus material related to the texts and study them in the same way. Many tutors make dossiers of newspaper clippings and articles available, or use the www.
- Do practice runs with material linked to the topics, e.g. if the course topic is the euro, search the web for news items in both your L2 and L1 and use these to practise translating both ways and essay writing.

For essays, here is another important tip:

- Study the 'functional terms and phrases' section of your dictionary or grammar book, particularly the L2 expressions for introducing, developing and concluding an argument, expressing opinions and doubts, making concessions, emphasizing points, making transitions from one part of an argument to the next. Most of these are set, ritualized words and phrases, and without them you will be unable to construct a convincing-sounding argument in L2, no matter how persuasive your actual argument is.

In line with this growing tendency to construct language exams around known bodies of material, there are numerous other exercises where a passage or passages are used as a springboard for tests other than translation. These include:

- *The guided essay.* You are provided with an essay title along with a short passage on the topic in question, or some bullet-point notes and vocabulary to help you write the essay.
- *Reconstruction.* You are given a series of headings (e.g. the outline of a short story or description of a scene or situation) and asked to expand these into a longer account.
- *Summary or précis.* You are given a long passage (in L1 or L2) or several, and the task is to write a condensed version of the main arguments or points in L2. Variants permit or forbid the use of vocabulary found in the original.
- *Commentary or interpretation.* Here you have to answer questions on a passage, in either L1 or L2, or write a critique of the text.

22.6 Oral examinations

Oral examinations in L2 are an integral part of all language degrees. **Vivas in English** exist as part of some modules in some degree schemes, and there is also the hybrid form, the **viva in L2**.

In the *Oral exam* (anything from 10 to 40 minutes) you have a conversation with one or sometimes two examiners (perhaps one of the native-speaker language assistants plus a lecturer or external examiner), either on a topic you have chosen and prepared in advance, or on a subject determined there and then by the examiner(s). Either way, it is a test of your conversational skills, aural and oral. You may also be asked to read a passage out loud, to test your pronunciation. With a topic chosen beforehand, it is up to you to research it and practise the vocabulary connected with it, but many people think that if you don't know the subject until you enter the room, there is nothing you can do to prepare for the exam. Not so. As with writing an essay (see above), there is a lot you can do to help yourself.

Top Tips

- Track down useful conversational gambits and responses and learn them.
- Drill yourself until your grammar (especially endings, which always go first under strain) is as rock-solid as possible. If you make a grammatical error and correct it, you will rewarded for spotting the mistake, too many candidates aren't even aware they have made a mistake.

- Second-guess which topics will come up, and rehearse conversations around them with your friends or kindly language assistants. Even if you guess wrong, all practice is good practice, but realistically, the examiners are quite likely to ask you something vaguely related to your course, your residence abroad, the country itself, your plans for the future, or ...?
- Practise reading aloud (a variety of material, anything will do) to a friend or a tape-recorder until you are satisfied with your accent and intonation and confident about reading a new passage at short notice.

In some universities, *vivas* are part of the final examination process. The thought of a viva has been known to spook candidates. Don't panic! Vivas are an opportunity to talk about a topic or subject in detail, and are a skill that should be more widely practised, since in the workplace, you are much more likely to 'explain an idea or project' than to write about it.

At Ph.D. level, the ***Viva Voce*** examination is the occasion when the candidate 'defends his thesis', that is, answers questions and engages in debate on aspects of his written dissertation. For finalists the viva is generally part of the degree classification process. When all the assessments and examinations are over and the marks are sorted out, some people are 'borderline specialists' – people so close to the boundary that another chance is given to cross a threshold. A viva may also be given to candidates who have had 'special circumstances', such as severe illness, during their studies. The viva will be conducted in L1 and is usually run by the external examiner – a delightful professor or senior lecturer from another university. DO NOT PANIC. In all the departments we know vivas are used to *raise* candidates. You have what you have on paper, things can only GET BETTER. So if your name is on a viva list that is good news, sigh with relief, remember all that revision you did before and check out some answers to the questions below. Get a good night's sleep and avoid unusual stimulants (always sound advice). Examiners tend to appear in suits but are interested in your brain not your wardrobe; but wear something tidy just the same. Celebrate later.

Typical viva topics

Dissertations are a frequent opening topic. You are the expert, did all the research and wrote it up. So the **Top Tip** is to glance through your dissertation – you will have kept a printout or it is on a disk somewhere.

Rehearse answers to questions like:

- What were the main language/literary/historical/cultural issues you addressed?
- What do you feel are the two main strengths of your dissertation research?
- Please will you outline any weaknesses you feel the research has?
- Can you explain why you adopted your research strategy?

- Since you started on this topic I see you did a module on ... How might you have adapted your research having done this module?
- Can you talk a bit about how your results relate to language studies generally?
- Obviously in a student dissertation there is limited scope for assembling and analysing information, how might you have speeded up and extended the process of gathering and evaluating your information?
- Which items of secondary literature did you find most helpful, and why?

Try to keep answers to the point and keep up the factual content. Any examiner recognizes flannel. Waffle cannot reduce a mark, but you are trying to raise it. External examiners have supervised, marked and moderated thousands of dissertations during their career. They know every dissertation has strengths and weaknesses, they are impressed by people who have done the research and realize there were other things to do, other ways to tackle the issue, other techniques, more data to collect ... so show them that you know too.

Use your 'languages speak' skills. Asked about the Pacific Rim, you could say: 'Strictly this means the islands situated in the Pacific Ocean, plus the countries which border on it, but the term is most frequently used in an economic context to refer to commercial links forged since the late 1980s between the nations of South East Asia, Australasia and the west coast of the American continent.'

It is a general answer, but in the 2.2 class. You could say, 'Some 21 countries, including the USA, Canada, Japan, China, Russia, Australia, New Zealand and Brunei belong to APEC (Asia-Pacific Economic Co-operation), founded in 1989 to promote trade. The success of the initiative may be judged by the fact that within seven years of its initiation the aggregate GDP of its members totalled over $16 trillion per annum, and that it accounted for over 40 per cent of global trade. In 1994 APEC agreed to establish a common market – akin to the EU, with which it has developing links – free from all trade and investment barriers among its member states, by 2020, starting with its industrialized states by 2010 and incorporating the developing economies by 2020. Given the economic, social, ethnic, political, religious and – last but not least – linguistic complexities of this vast region, the Pacific Rim initiatives are a remarkable demonstration of the potential for co-operation that exists between the nations of the world.' A longer and more balanced answer, the detail is there, the policies, the internal and external links, a more considered opinion. This answer has the evidence and should merit a good 2:1 or First. If you can work some references into the answer so much the better. So think a bit and support your answer with sound facts and balanced views, just as in an essay.

You cannot do much more preparation. The examiner can ask about any paper and question, about the degree as a whole and language studies in general. If you missed a paper or question, or had a nightmare with a particular paper, and if you are still awake, think around some answers to the questions BUT the odds are they will not be mentioned.

After every exam, aim to review your answers as soon as you can. What did you learn from the exam process? University exams are a little different from school ones; a spot of reflection on your revision and exam technique might be useful before next time, but don't dwell on your mistakes, everybody makes them. Questions that might occur to you include:

- Had I done enough revision? The answer is almost always no, so ask 'Where could I have squeezed in a little more revision?'
- Was there enough detail and evidence to support my answers?
- Would different revision activities or emphases be useful next time?

Writers Wordsearch

Forty to find. Answers p. 282.

C	O	N	G	R	E	V	E	I	Z	N	E	K	C	A	M
H	E	V	O	L	T	A	I	R	E	E	R	A	L	C	A
E	T	S	E	Y	H	T	R	O	W	S	L	A	G	Y	U
K	O	I	T	L	A	H	D	N	E	T	S	O	T	E	P
H	I	A	H	A	P	A	S	T	E	R	N	A	K	C	A
O	L	L	E	D	N	A	R	I	P	A	D	A	D	N	S
V	E	E	S	T	M	M	I	R	G	Y	E	T	N	I	S
O	E	B	E	E	R	W	E	A	R	K	S	O	U	U	A
M	O	A	N	T	H	I	L	S	E	S	C	H	O	Q	N
I	S	R	N	U	E	L	A	D	E	V	A	P	P	E	T
S	B	S	I	H	I	D	D	U	N	E	R	P	U	D	U
A	O	R	E	S	N	E	I	M	E	O	T	A	S	I	T
K	R	E	T	C	E	R	V	A	N	T	E	S	H	R	U
F	N	A	S	N	O	O	S	S	A	S	S	L	K	G	O
A	E	S	O	P	O	G	U	H	R	O	T	C	I	V	L
K	I	E	R	K	E	G	A	A	R	D	L	O	N	R	A

23 LEARNING A LANGUAGE FROM SCRATCH – *AB INITIO*

In the beginning there was ab initio.

Top Secret – This chapter is ONLY for first-time language learners

'I didn't do this language at A' level'. OK, so you are starting from scratch in a new language, which is admittedly a bit scary. BUT you have made a conscious decision to acquire a new foreign language. WHY? (... you want enough Yiddish to get by on vacation in Tel Aviv, or as an automotive engineer you need to read Fiat technical manuals in Italian?)

Before reading further, complete the following sentence: 'I am learning .... because I ....'.

Having a good reason for starting is the best motivation for giving it a real go. Remind yourself WHY regularly. This chapter is about attitudes, strategies and tips to help you cope with what at times may seem a long and daunting task. No two people are alike, we all work in our own ways. Mastering a new language requires not just practice but passion. Starting a new language is like getting fit – it is easier to slump with a smoothie. Language learning is a lot of work. If your heart is really not in it, do something else.

All language students have skills to exploit. If you are starting Russian but have already learned a little Spanish or French you have language skills, you know about vocab and grammar. So you are an engineer with no language background – but you do have study skills, a logical brain and a memory that you have been accessing since birth. That is how you got to university.

How will you be taught?

FIND OUT NOW. The spectrum for *ab initio* language acquisition stretches all the way from intensive class teaching in large groups, to working alone at home or in college with tapes and textbooks – how you are tutored should influence your study plans.

? If your new language is a named part of your degree, you will have 15 to 20 timetabled hours per week, with a mix of learning activities including language-centre sessions as well as tuition. Normally the aim is to get you to A-level standard in a year, so that in your second year you can join the next set of students with A-level qualifications. This is quite a tall order when you think that these students have up to seven years of learning the language behind them. They may not be that far ahead in grammar but will have soaked up a considerable amount of vocabulary in that time. So you get lots of tuition, but it needs building on.

? If your language is an extra or elective subject, teaching will be less intensive. You may not need to delve into so much detail but your language learning will have to play second-fiddle to your main subject. You need to organize to give yourself time to get good.

What is the fundamental problem?

We think it revolves around vocabulary. A tourist can get by on a hundred words or less (some manage holidays for two in France by asking for 'Deux comme ça' everywhere from boulangerie to bistro). A child of six has a vocabulary of around 2000 words (Lewis, 1999). How far would the vocabulary of a six-year old take you? Well you can probably ignore all dinosaur, Pokemon and junior monster terminology every street-wise six-year-old has, but you need the basics. Fantastically usefully, in most languages the 2000 most frequently used words make up 80 per cent of most texts, and 3000 words cover 95 per cent of most texts. Many words and phrases are repeated – they, or members of their family, keep turning up and become familiar. Then add the specialist vocabulary in areas that interest you – politics, sculpture, tai chi and bierkellerei.

There's no easy answer to all this. It is tough and you just have to enjoy yourself to working at it! Extra hours beyond the timetable are needed on a regular basis. Languages are best learned by the drip-feed method into long-term memory, not by cramming in the night before the class test. You pass the test with your short-term memory skills and then forget 98 per cent. Try to focus on vocabulary that matches your learning aims – get lists of gearbox parts, gastronomic menus ...; find some books on these topics in your new language and keep your interest up by focusing on your long term goals.

But first, a thought; having got your reasons for starting another language clear, what will constrain or hamper you? Add your own thoughts below:

- Language learning is not my main subject
- I ....
- I ....
- I ....
- I ....
- I find learning vocabulary difficult
- I ....
- I ....
- I ....
- I ....
- I don't like talking to others too much

DON'T let this list put you off – you have good reasons for starting your language studies. Keep them in mind, recognize that it will not be easy, and get planning. The key to language learning is:

⊶ Establishing a routine is vital for those moments when your resolution wavers under the conflicting pressures of reams of vocab that won't stick in your head, and a beckoning hostelry ... Do different things each time to keep boredom and choredom at bay.

... and it also helps if:

- you are well organized and have a clear set of goals.
- you have a set of strategies for memorizing and collating information.
- you practise being less shy. Building up confidence is especially important if you're shy, and the best way to do this is to stay ahead of the game and know that little bit more than those who are fearless.
- you are self-motivated, resilient and have a will to succeed.

Well some of these, some of the time.

Learning a language is a marathon rather than a sprint. You need signposts and refreshments along the way, and you need to break your race up into stages. So set yourself two kinds of quite specific goals,

Long-term:
'By the end of this year, I want to be able to ... Read the business opportunities pages in *Izvestia*/Attend lectures on "Design considerations for tall structures" at the University of Pisa/Write simple but accurate reports in L2 on sharp practices by the Spanish Inquisition'. And,
Short-term:
'Every week I aim to ... learn a minimum of x new words and y new grammatical constructions', (20 may be more realistic than 50?) or 'Next week I intend to ... revise the forms of the subjunctive in French.' You might also want to set yourself some **intermediate targets**, things you want to achieve by particular stages in the year, '... get my larynx round the glottal stop by Week 7/master the twelve non-verbal modes of affirmation and negation in Mezzo-Kabardian (without the use of mirrors) by Week 18.' Use **Try This 23.1** to set your own agenda.

TRY THIS 23.1 – Language targets

Make a list of your long-term and short-term goals. Three of each. Look at your time management planner and plan ways to achieve them (See **Try This 3.1** and **Try This 3.3**).

Pin your list of aims on your notice-board or underneath a fridge magnet, and review them regularly, that is, check whether they are realistic and still relevant, and whether you are achieving the tasks you set yourself. Revise/update them weekly. Give yourself treats or rewards when you think you have earned them. Above all, stay motivated!

23.1 MUTUAL SELF-HELP – CHATTY STUDY BUDDIES – LANGUAGE EXCHANGE PARTNERS

Alone you can memorize and revise new words and grammar points in whichever way suits you best (repeating lists out loud, drawing mind-maps, in time to the beat on your early-morning jog, etc.), BUT a study-pair/buddy/exchange partner/group will reinforce your learning. Arrange to meet and chat. You will improve faster by reciting and checking each other's work, exchanging new phrases, practising transactions (buying a ski pass, arranging an overdraft), making up role-plays and conversations, ... Take care of your group – it needs to be fun and useful but not overwhelming if it is to work. Some ideas to help meetings continue include:

- ✔ Find an exchange partner, a real Italian or Finn, . . . because this is what it's all about.
- ✔ Sort out a rough *plan*, e.g. meet for an hour every Tuesday at . . . to discuss *a*, practise *b* or revise *c*. Check next week is available each time and if not try to find another time that week – it is all too easy to skip one. (Tea-time, after class and before evening socializing is good.)
- ✔ Vary your activities. Don't try to plan the semester in too much detail. You won't know the priorities yet so just block the time in your diaries and decide what to do from week to week at the end of each session. (Take it in turns to lead or organize the activity?).
- ✔ Ring the changes. Meet in different places (the pub or local curry-house are prime candidates, but use them sparingly, it's hard to do serious work against a lot of background noise, or with a chappati in one hand and a lassi in the other). Share a take-away pizza in one person's flat (*cook Italian, speak Italian*); have a meal in someone else's; arrange to watch a foreign-language film in the language centre and discuss it afterwards over a few beers . . . (Make it fun).
- ✔ (N.B. a student's suggestion –) '. . . this may sound swotty, mad even, but suggest that there be a 5 minute vocab test at the start of each lesson. Take the initiative and get keen! It's easier than testing yourself at home which you just (probably) won't do on a regular basis.'
- ✔ Make it fun – TV, radio, games (Taboo, Scrabble). Try to get hold of target language CDs, if only to gain an insight into that culture (get to know what your Russian or Danish peers are doing!). You will build up a little resource centre full of interesting films/tapes/music.

It may be harder, but it is more vital to set up this sort of arrangement if your language-learning doesn't involve regular class contact. Support and discussion with ~~fellow sufferers,~~ sorry, fellow-learners, makes the pain vaguely bearable. Try putting a notice up in the language centre, or ask the staff there if they can put you in touch with other people in your situation; they may know a native speaker who will spend time speaking their language in exchange for some English conversation.

If your main (or only) objective is to acquire a *reading* knowledge of the foreign language, you will be spared the many hours of tape and video drill, but in their place you will have many hours of grammar, syntax and vocabulary exercises. Take your pick! Virtually every university and college now has some sort of 'Languages for All' programme, a language centre and CALL (Computer-Assisted Language Learning) facilities. Don't be afraid to ask your tutor and the language centre staff for advice on the best materials for your purposes – they are there to help. In the best cases, if you are learning without tutor support, they will give you specialist guidance in constructing a sensible learning programme.

- Don't panic.
- Get yourself sorted! Devise a workable timetable (see Chapter 6 and **Try This 23.1**) and stick to it.
- Record new vocabulary systematically on index cards or on computer, noting essential grammatical information (e.g. gender and plural of nouns, principal parts of verbs) at the same time. Remember, writing things down is also a form of reinforcement.
- Persevere, practise, repeat, rehearse, share – repetition is the most powerful method of learning the sort of information that language-learners need to learn and you can't have too much of it.
- Find a balance between autonomous and group learning that suits you.
- If faced with modules like Pacific Rim Politics or Spanish history since 1580 for the first time, go to the lectures and get the general idea of the topic and material. Sort out the focus of the module.
- Doing background reading in advance can confuse, but it may be worth looking in local libraries for 'A' level texts, to pick out the background either before a course starts or during the first couple of weeks. An 'A' level text is likely to have the essentials, with less detail than a university text, BUT you must move on to university level texts. School texts are starting, not end points.
- Take your 'A' level notes to university – your Spanish Golden Age notes may help someone who can help you via their Contemporary French History notes.
- If you are having difficulty with essay writing now is the time to get a grip.

Find someone who did English for 'A' level and pick their brains about writing. There are plenty of people with excellent English language skills who will be happy to explain how to use semi-colons.

- Ask people which reading they find accessible and comprehensible.

And in no time at all you'll be able to write a classy CV in Italian, negotiate yourself a cushy *au pair*'s job in Tuscany, order *vitello alla marsala con fettucini* as you sit sipping a glass of crisp Pinot Grigio, or settle down with a *caffe latte* or an *espresso lungo* to read Dante in the original . . . .

23.2 References and Further Reading

Chambers,E. and Northedge, A. (1997) *The Arts Good Study Guide,* Milton Keynes: Open University.

Gass, S. and Selinker, L. (1994) *Second Language Acquisition. An Introductory Course.* Hillsdale, NJ: Erlbaum.

Lewis, M. (1999) *How to Study Foreign Languages.* Basingstoke and London: Macmillan.

The Nuffield Language Inquiry (2000) The Nuffield Foundation, London [online] http://www.nuffield.org/language/index.html (Accessed 30 November 2000)

Alcoholic Texts

The Advocaat by John Grisham
The Old Curaçao Shop by Charles Dickens
Dai Quiri by Joanna Trollope
Tequila Mocking Bird by Harper Lee
Vodka Godunov by Alexander Pushkin
War and Pissed by Leo Tolstoy
Lucky Gin by Kingsley Amis

24 THE YEAR (OR TERM) ABROAD

Language is the means by which mistakes are propagated. Get propagating.

Many new students and some older ones wonder/panic/fantasize about their year ~~off~~ abroad. This chapter is less about study skills when you get there and more about pre-departure action. Get organized.

On most modern language degrees you don't just read great (but ancient) works of literature, translate stylishly in and out of the foreign language and gen up on key cultural achievements – you also get to spend time at another university or on work placement, getting to the nitty gritty of local language and culture. You may fix it up yourself or through university links. The experience may be good, bad or life-enriching (wildly awkward). That's life. What you make of your year out mostly depends on you. You can look forward to a life experience combined with linguistic gains. Expect (unless you organize otherwise) to be far from home, friends and significant others; expect to have nowhere to stay on arrival, have difficulty being understood, get lost when others are talking, be short of money, and … to have the best year of your life so far.

Get the facts: can you choose what you do? Studying at a university or college (p. 255); working for a commercial organization (p. 255)? or working as an English-language Assistant (p. 247)? Will you stay in the same country for the whole year, or divide your time between two countries? Some students on two-language degrees spend six months in each place, which (irritatingly) makes them ineligible for school Assistantships, which run for a complete academic year. Where you go depends on:

- Your own university's regulations. Some departments stipulate study at another university or a particular placement, whilst others allow their students a great deal of choice.
- The range of options you find, based on your department's contacts and your own enquiries.
- And, lastly (firstly?) – your personal preferences, who else is going where.

24.1 Briefing and Preparation

Your time abroad is a mega adventure (possibly *the* adventure of your life), but needs a military planning operation. All departments have year abroad tutors (YAT) and most produce detailed guidance notes and organize briefing sessions where you also meet students who were abroad last year. Returning students are always keen to pass on tips and relate anecdotes, so this meeting is A MUST!

But beware! Students who have just returned from a summer in some sun-drenched foreign clime are not necessarily reliable witnesses. They usually end the year abroad on a high, having made scores of friends, savoured the good life, and had to tear themselves away from what is now their second (and often, preferred) home. Happily most forget about their first weeks, with no proper place to stay, dodgy cashflow, aching homesickness and all the rest. You may have a tough start but 99.99 per cent have a great finish.

What else can you do in advance?

- ✔ Find out as much as you can about where you are going (library, bookshop or websites).
- ✔ Make sure all your paper work is in order – passport, birth certificate (yes, your date of birth is on your passport, but some officious bureaucrat will insist on seeing your *actual* birth certificate), driving licence, International Students' Union card, health documents, home university registration documents . . . .
- ✔ Put your affairs in order at home! This may or may not include tearful farewells (think of it as character-building), but MUST include a session with your bank manager. Sort out what you need by way of cards, loans, overdraft facilities, etc.
- ✔ Check out alternative (cheaper) travel arrangements, including group travel and web sites.
- ✔ Glean tips on accommodation and dealing with red tape from returning students.
- ✔ What clothes?
- ✔ Learn as much as you can about etiquette and cultural do's and don'ts (ask the language assistants and exchange students in your department).
- ✔ **Lists** – you need a few: Essential Things to Do, and Essential Things to Take. Assess your personal needs and preferences: list what you think are your strengths and weaknesses; what you're good or not so good at; things you'd like to accomplish or get better at while away. Include personal achievements to aim at (e.g. learning to cope with starting work at 6 a.m. in temperatures of –20°C), AND places you want to visit AND activities you want to carry out. Revisit these lists during the year, assess what you have accomplished, plan to achieve the goals you have forgotten about and revise these challenges for your stay. (See **Try This 24.2** and **Try This 24.3**).

24.2 University

Numerically, this is probably the most popular option for the year abroad. You live amongst people of your own age, learn the language (including the latest slang) and study worthwhile subjects at the same time. In some countries, such as China and Egypt, for diplomatic, political or cultural reasons there is no realistic alternative to going on a university course arranged by your department. In such cases, the department will be pro-active about organizing your stay, possibly including group travel, accommodation and specially laid-on courses.

There are snags about studying at a foreign university. The first of these is financial. Departments sending students abroad normally pay the fees (if any) for you – so these aren't usually an issue. But the cost of living may be high and you won't be earning a wage. The university may be very large and socially less cohesive because students often live at home. You may have to try harder to meet local students than you expect. It is not good to spend all year socializing with ex-pat students.

- Take, or make, opportunities to strike up conversations, in lecture-theatres (difficult), seminar-rooms (a bit easier), cafés, bars and refectories (should be a cinch). Most people want to learn or improve their English and appreciate genuine efforts to learn their language. Dangle the chance of speaking English, but balance this with an equal dose of L2 speak.
- Speak the language to your landlady, in shops and restaurants, on public transport and ...
- Consider joining university sports or other clubs or societies (though these are generally scarcer than in Britain).

Ask returning students what they would add to this list.

24.3 Business based

Your department may have links with businesses, and the YAT will brief you on what to expect from the job. Really lucky students are paid the same as local new graduates, with access to sports and social facilities, and subsidized travel and accommodation. Others have to find their own job and accommodation, establish their own social circles, etc., using the tactics described above.

Applying for a post is a marvellous demonstration of initiative. There are three keys to finding a work-placement:

- Start early – launch your campaign about a year before you need the placement.
- Create a hit-list of potential employers, long enough to allow for rejections, and realistic as regards your skills and abilities.

- Prepare your application meticulously – a CV and a letter of application.
- Persevere.
- Use you Careers Centre. They have country and company directories and they will help with CV preparation.

Here is one Leeds University student's account of how she got a year's placement with a prestigious German motor manufacturer:

Anne Macdonald 12 Month Internship , BMW AG

I first made a list of all the German companies or international companies with large bases in Germany, which were known to me.

My sole mode of research was the World Wide Web. I used various search engines, both German and international, to find the web sites of these companies. The majority of home pages had the address of the Personnel department, many had specific contact names. A number of web sites offered information on specific internships available. However my applications were all blind.

My next step was to formulate my application.

I created my CV in the German language and German CV format.*

I composed a covering letter in German.* This was short and concise:

Who – student of German, who has to spend minimum 10 months in Germany as part of the BA Honours degree.

My interest – marketing/sales department or the contract/legal department.

When and how long – 10–12 months , available from September 1998.

Interview availability – available for telephone or personal interview at their convenience.

I then had my CV and covering letter proof read by a native speaker, with knowledge in the business field.

I included two references, proof of education awards, and proof of being a student. My application had a cover page.

I sent off 20 applications during November, 10 months prior to my possible internship.
I had a lot of negative replies, but finally the positive reply from BMW AG came at the end of January.

* Information on the differing CV formats and covering letters are available at the Careers Service.

A business placement abroad is a unique opportunity to enhance your CV. As well as learning the specifics of the business, you hone your personal and interpersonal skills day in, day out. Working a 12-hour day starting at 7 a.m. and coping with a stressed, ill-tempered boss is a traumatic but effective apprenticeship for a later career. We hope your boss is calm, considerate and enlightened! Have realistic expectations. At first you will know little or nothing about the company – be prepared to be bewildered as you learn the ropes and don't expect to be entrusted with sensitive or specialized work straight away. Also remember that most companies see you as an asset. Unless you are pretty unlucky you will be given a mentor to show you what to do and to look after your needs in general. Just remember s/he is also a Very Busy Person. S/he will value a rookey colleague who makes a real effort to learn and work independently most of the time, which should get you a good reference.

24.4 Language assistant

If you studied a modern language at school, you already have a pretty good idea about this job because most schools and sixth-form colleges have foreign language assistants on one-year placements. Your job is to provide native-speaker, authentic backup to the English teachers: take conversation classes, do role-plays (maybe put on a real play), help with lessons, correct exercises, and be a walking dictionary and world expert on all things L1. Usually, you are a valued player in the school community, acquire an instant social circle, and have opportunities to gain a close-up view of local life. You develop your personal and interpersonal skills – organizing your timetable, planning lessons, sampling teaching as a career and testing yourself in a leadership position. And all this with relatively good pay, not too arduous hours and plenty of time to travel and enjoy your financial independence.

24.5 Hidden gains

Once you have recovered from the initial excitement and trauma of leaving home and setting up on a distant shore – it's just like being a fresher all over again – the Year Abroad is the icing on the university cake .... It involves self-reliance writ large. You develop life skills you never even realised you had, great for your CV, and should be valuable for years to come. Life skills include 'survival' skills – independence and coping alone in an alien environment – a host of personal and interpersonal skills – managing your time (possibly too much of it) and your finances (almost certainly too little); planning a sensible work and leisure routine; working alone; working with others; negotiating, and ....

24.6 Medical matters

Have a thorough medical check-up. Many placement schemes require a medical certificate in advance confirming your fitness for the job or course. If you suffer from a chronic ailment, such as diabetes or asthma, your doctor is required to mention this on the certificate, but this will not (usually) disbar you from going. Ask your doctor what to do about medication and routine treatment. Carry a written note at all times stating any existing medical conditions, together with a list of any medication (the proper names, not just the proprietary names) and doses you take.

The YAT arranging your placement will tell you about medical cover. It may be arranged by your employer and paid for by the firm or by monthly deduction from your salary, or you may have to pay for it before you leave home or when you arrive, and it doubtless involves some serious trekking around to sort out. (Check your Students' Union for study and work abroad, and insurance information.)

24.7 Health insurance

YOU MUST HAVE IT. Arrangements vary between countries. From the UK there are different arrangements depending on whether you are going to an EU country or a non-EU country. Get *Health Advice for Travellers* (1999), free from Post Offices, which contains an E111 application form. Your YAT knows the answers! If you plan to be an English-language Assistant in a school placement organized by the CBEVE (Central Bureau for Educational and Vocational Exchanges), they organize and explain insurance cover details when your appointment is confirmed.

Whatever the type of placement, get forms E111 and E128.

- Form E111 provides emergency medical and hospital cover for travellers in other EU countries, but it is not, repeat NOT, a substitute for proper cover for routine or ongoing medical matters,
- Form E128 provides health cover for students: those studying abroad and those on work placements.

It is your responsibility to make sure you are equipped with the necessary forms. You are also strongly advised to register with a doctor as soon as possible after you arrive at your destination. This entails bureaucracy, and bureaucracy is best coped with when you are fighting fit. PLEASE DON'T WAIT UNTIL YOU ARE AT DEATH'S DOOR!!

For Non-EU countries get country-specific advice. Your YAT will advise you. The basic rule of thumb is, the more exotic the placement, the more you can reasonably expect the sending department to take charge of insurance (and other) arrangements connected with your stay.

TRY THIS 24.1 – Which of these are not members of the EU? **Answers p. 282**

France	Sweden	Israel	Belgium	Portugal
Hungary	Italy	Netherlands	Germany	Luxembourg
Spain	Romania	Norway	Poland	United Kingdom

24.8 Advice to women students (but men might find bits useful too!)

OK, you are over 18, are careful and know all about the dangers of going out alone after dark, walking in lonely places and wearing 'provocative' clothing. You strike a balance between sensible precautions and living your life as a free agent. BUT if you are unlucky, living abroad may expose you to potentially threatening situations. Compared to home:

- ☹ you are more likely to be on your own, especially at first.
- ☹ initial language difficulties coupled with a lack of experience of cultural differences may make it hard to recognize a potentially threatening situation.
- ☹ the kind of situations you find yourself in – looking for accommodation or a job, meeting new people and trying to establish a social life, using unfamiliar public transport systems – are precisely the ones that require caution.

So, while no one can advise you on how to cope with every possible situation, you are more likely to be able to deal with – or better still, avoid – unpleasant or dangerous situations if you have cast a wary and critical eye over your new circumstances and thought about strategies beforehand. Before you go, talk to fellow students or other women who have spent time abroad who can give you a realistic picture of what to expect. Look out for yourself and have a great, safe, enjoyable stay abroad.

Top Tips

- **Attracting attention** If you have no desire to be immediately noticeable as a foreigner:
  - ✔ take your cue from the local women as regards dress and behaviour.
  - ✔ try to use the local language as much as possible.
- **Travelling**
  - ✔ Plan your travel carefully. If possible, find out about bus and tram fares and timetables in advance.
  - ✔ If travelling alone, especially at night, look for a compartment with at least one other woman in it, and be prepared to move if she gets off before you do.
  - ✔ DON'T HITCH – it's not worth the risk.
  - ✔ Don't travel on public transport without a valid ticket unless you fancy being forced off the bus by an inspector in the middle of nowhere – not much fun late at night!

- **Finding somewhere to live**
  - ✔ The best (safest) way is through personal contacts, school, business or university links.
  - ✔ The worst (dodgy) is following up a newspaper ad on your own. Take someone with you. Don't be bashful about asking – most people are pleased to help.

- **Making friends:** It's hard to make friends if you feel obliged to view each new male as a potential rapist or murderer, but equally dangerous if you are too trusting. To avoid offence whilst minimizing the risks:
  - ✔ keep meetings to neutral territory such as cafés, concerts, pizzerias etc.
  - ✔ let someone know where you have gone, with whom, and when you expect to get back.
  - ✔ only go back to private accommodation as part of a group until you feel happy about the person.
  - ✔ don't be too liberal at first about private information, such as where you live.

- **Night life:** Of course nobody wants a self-imposed curfew, but the sad fact remains that the streets might not be safe for you on your own after dark.
  - ✔ Try to arrange to be picked up/dropped off by friends or stay overnight with someone you can trust(!) after a party or concert.
  - ✔ If you must go out alone, always carry enough money for a taxi (expensive but safer).

- **Making money:** Offering English lessons is a very tempting way of supplementing your income, and provided you go about it the right way, it should be unproblematic.

- ✔ The safest way to find clients is by personal recommendation. Your landlord/landlady, fellow workers or students may know friends who want to brush up their English.
- ✔ Many English-language School Assistants find pupils willing to pay for pre-exam tuition. Approach local schools and language schools if you are not teaching.
- ✔ Advertising your services or answering an advert in the paper – Bad Idea. At best you are embarking on a trip into the unknown, at worst your innocent quest for work will be misconstrued. In many countries, the phrase 'English lessons' is the equivalent of 'Swedish massage'.
- ✔ Even if you are satisfied with the credentials of your clients, take common-sense precautions – don't give out your address and hold the lessons somewhere neutral, like a café.

And talking of cafés: working in a café, bar or restaurant is a popular and generally safe way to make extra money. Your knowledge of English can be a big plus for the proprietor. This type of work has opportunities galore to improve your spoken language, and your listening comprehension, especially if the bar is noisy!

24.9 Money matters

Indeed it does! Brace yourself, your year abroad will probably be the most costly in your university career. Travel costs, incidental expenditure such as getting/renewing your passport, student Railcard and International Student ID Card, registering with the authorities when you arrive, and so on. Even if you are going somewhere in Europe rather than to a high-cost country like Japan, the mere fact of being abroad will mean that you do more phoning, more travelling around and probably more eating for pleasure and hanging out in pavement cafés than you would do at home. You may also find that accommodation is scarce and expensive, and there isn't a European tradition of student halls of residence, though many universities have a limited number of self-catering rooms in residential blocks. It is worth considering these, as flats are especially scarce and rents correspondingly high in university towns. But if L2 is Chinese, your money will stretch farther than back home.

Phone bills will be higher when you are abroad as you find yourself ringing parents and friends to remind them that you exist, to stave off boredom and/or homesickness. Your fellow-students are scattered around the globe, so you will almost certainly spend time talking to them too, arranging your next reunion and trips to Prague or Florence.

Which is another thing. What's the point of being in a foreign country if you don't make the most of the opportunities to see the sights? So you'll want to travel, every vacation, every month, every weekend, according to your resources. Fun it is, cheap it ain't!

✔ **Make the most of e-mail.** Note all your friends' email addresses and find out (a) where you can send and receive e-mail (preferably free of charge) and (b) the e-mail addresses of all the people you want to stay in touch with whilst you are abroad.

✔ **Take advantage of all the freebies and discounts available ...**

23.11 Mature, part-time, disabled or with special needs?

Section 26.2 discusses some of the problems and special considerations affecting mature students. The compulsory year abroad opens up an additional set of impossible-looking challenges for students with family commitments, a different set again for students with disabilities, and yet another set for part-time students. We cannot generalize solutions, everyone and each situation is unique, but we *can* suggest how to *tackle* them. Every department has someone designated to handle special needs. There is a University Special Needs and Disabled Students office with specialist advisers who are experienced in assessing potential difficulties and suggesting solutions. Discuss your needs with your tutors from the start. Finding a way around the foreign residence requirement that is acceptable to you, the department and the university calls for discussion and negotiation skills. Make sure an agreement is reached very early, ideally before embarking on the course. Alternatives to a full academic year abroad include short courses abroad, immersion courses in the home university, short residential courses at UK-based foreign institutes, language buddy schemes and self-study packages for use at home (*LARA Report on Special Needs, 2000*). Whatever arrangements are made, make sure they are written down and fully understood by all parties.

23.12 Logs or portfolios

Many students are required to maintain a diary, learning log, portfolio ... (the terms vary, we shall stick to 'log') whilst abroad. It may be assessed, or remain private to the student but form the basis for an end-of-year report, or be read by a tutor and discussed in a debriefing session. Some departments require regular reports throughout the year, written in English, or in L2. Just about the only common factor is that, generally, completing the log is a condition for gaining the course credits attached to the year abroad.

Some language departments also encourage students to enter portfolios, based on their logs, for external qualifications such as the LCGI (Licentiateship of the City & Guilds Institute, London) (Donald, 1996).

But why should I bother? Credits apart, ex-users agree that logs are a 'Good Thing'.

- They provide you with a permanent record of your year, not just where you went and what you did, but – easily forgotten – how you felt at the time.
- They can help you set objectives and review and reflect on the 'year abroad experience.'
- They can prompt you to identify and reflect on your skills and capabilities (see Chapter 4).
- They provide you with material for your CV and your tutor with material for references.

Not bad for a simple diary, and there is lots more ... Students' comments on keeping a log include:

'I thought it was a rubbish idea, but when I started listing all the things I had to do before I went, I realised it had a point. But I was a bit sporadic about writing it up.' 'It really came into its own in the first 3 or 4 weeks. I was so homesick and lonely, I used it as a sort of confessional. But after Easter I was so busy I hardly wrote a thing.' 'I keep a diary anyway, so it was no hassle, but the really private bits went into my diary, not the log.' 'Once I got into the way of it I kept it fairly religiously. The best aspect was setting targets and being able to tick them off when I'd done them.'

Logs range from totally free-form to tightly structured. Typically, they break the year up into stages:

- pre-departure;
- the year, again divided up;
- end-of-year review (and report?);
- debriefing.

Use **Try This 24.2** as a starting point, and follow up with **Try This 24.3** especially if a log is not part of your scheme.

TRY THIS 24.2 – Reflect and go

Before setting off for abroad, complete this table and plan.

Preparations	List up to 10 things you must get sorted before you go.
Expectations	List 5 things you expect to encounter or hope to see and do.
Worries	List 0–5 things you are concerned about in connection with the year (ideas for overcoming them?)
Strengths and weaknesses	List your three greatest strengths or assets, and your 3 greatest weaknesses (and areas and ideas for improvement).
Goal-setting	Things you hope to achieve in the year, with time-scale.

TRY THIS 24.3 – Reflect and go again

Revisit your **Try This 24.2** list after 3 months, again after 6 months, and finally at the end of the year. Update it and add new aims.

24.10 MAKE THE MOST OF YOUR YEAR ABROAD

Primarily for UK students. You will have a great time in your year abroad and may want to go back after you graduate. If that is your aim then you need to use your year abroad to get contacts, research opportunities, and find and impress the people who can help you return. BUT you will also discover that this is very difficult. A French company will not employ you for your French language skills, after all, they have plenty of French speakers already – you would usually need additional business qualifications. UK graduates are usually aged 21–22, which is a lot younger that European graduates, so you may appear to be very inexperienced. BUT don't despair – with planning and forethought you can achieve what you want (see Chapter 25). Some planning ideas for your term/year abroad:

- Visit companies/organizations, talk to human resources staff, stress your interests and qualifications. Can you work with them part-time or voluntarily?
- Participate in local societies, get to know local people.
- Get involved in the social activities at your placement organization.
- Find out how the country's employment system works.
- Review your progress after the first two months and make a plan to get further involved.

- Are there specific skills you would need in your future employment? Can you find some part-time or voluntary work that would help you get experience and look good on your CV?

It is about networking, developing contacts and then using them when you graduate. You may not get exactly what you want, but your year abroad could be a big help towards your next activity.

If you are a non-UK student the paragraphs above may or may not be helpful. Investigate the different opportunities that will let you build on your year abroad. See your careers service staff before you go and make a check-list of their suggestions for maximizing your networking skills and researching further opportunities.

Finally (seriously). Remember that during your stay you are also an ambassador, and possibly the only person your hosts have ever met/worked with from your university or your country. This matters anyway, but it *really* matters if you are on a placement that your department has used in the past and hopes to use again.

24.11 References and Further Reading

Donald, S.G. (1996) *From Logs to Licentiateships: a case-study in natural progression* [on-line]. http://www.lle.mdx.ac.uk/hec/journal/ccss/sdonald.htm Accessed 30 July 2000.

DISinHE (2000) *Disability and Information Systems in Higher Education.* [online] http://www.disinhe.ac.uk/ Accessed 31 July 2000.

DSS (Department of Social Security) (1999) *Health Advice for Travellers.* London: HMSO. [For information concerning Form E111, and to obtain Form E128, contact: Contributions Agency International Services (EU), DSS, Longbenton, Newcastle upon Tyne NE98 1YX]

LARA (2000) *Learning and Residence Abroad Project.* [online] http://lara.fdtl.ac.uk/lara/index.htm

LARA (2000) *LARA Report on Special Needs.* [online] http://lara.fdtl.ac.uk/lara/spclneeds.html Accessed 30 July 2000.

Rapport (2000) Residence Abroad @Portsmouth [online] http://www.hum.port.ac.uk/slas/fdtl/traffic-light.html

Study Abroad (2000) [online] http://www.studyabroad.com/

The University of Sheffield Interculture Project (1999) *Report on the Sub-Project: Diaries as Learning Support for the Year Abroad.* Sheffield: University of Sheffield.

What is the greeting you use in Siberia when meeting a Russian soldier wearing 6 balaclavas? – Anything you like – he won't hear a thing!

Language Cryptic Crossword 2

Answers p. 282

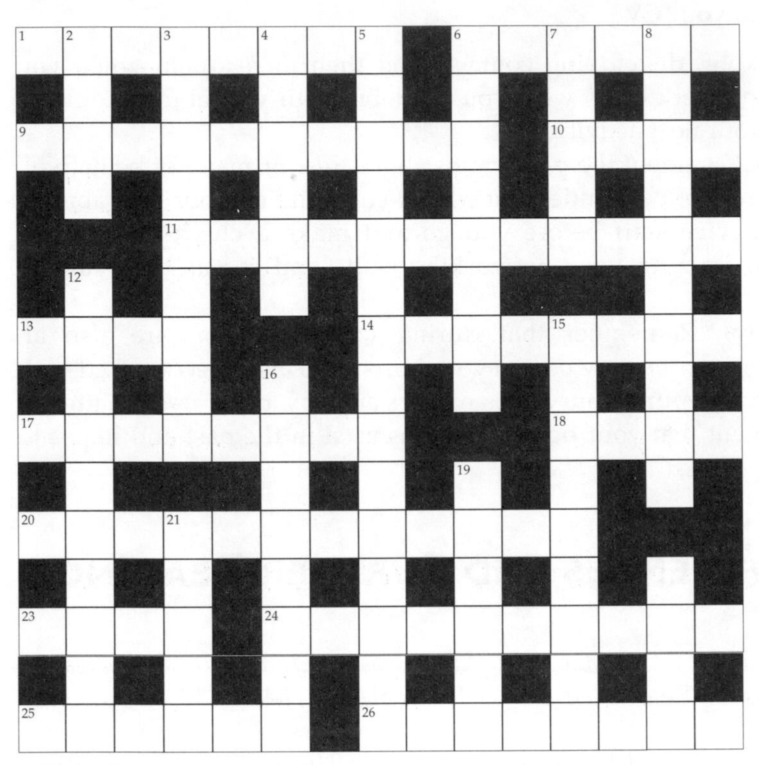

Across

1 Gets information together, but loses halter end on Devon hill (8)
6 Fourfold, more origami than clover (6)
9 Writing at the edge (10)
10 Questionable meat for group (4)
11 Racist banter is out of place at dizzy party (12)
13 Positioned between Buffalo circuits (4)
14 Sound chest to check larynx (5-3)
17 Leave standing in away football kit (8)
18 Grave bloom without Rose (4)
20 Pedlar of traditional songs (12)
23 Totally tropical swing to the song (4)
24 Indifferent to Capital Oil take-over (10)
25 Round table spiritual encounter (6)
26 One's days were itemized (8)

Down

2 Testimony without a moral lead (4)
3 Ways to work out? (9)
4 Metal fellow, kept Dorothy company (6)
5 Who or whom to renovate, purloin which or whose?(8-7)
6 Latin who might start rolling stock on four-liner (8)
7 Player in multi-factorial number(5)
8 Laugh and cry? the theme of the piece? (5-5)
12 Advertise the air upslope to the people (10)
15 When pére exits we find what we really need (9)
16 Qualified to be argued at (8)
19 No shortage of self-interest (6)
21 Los Angeles metal is considered, to be dead (5)
22 Often blank attendant (4)

25 CAREERS FOR LINGUISTS

Veni, vidi, veal parmagian: I came, I saw, I ate Italian.

'You have a degree in Chinese – to get that you must have the skills we want in car sales management' said an employer who knows language graduates have loads of skills. If you really want to waste your degree (narrow your options) think 'the only skill I got at Uni was to speak in . . .'. OK, there are some specifically language-related jobs, like translating, but you miss the whole point of a degree if when your aunty asks what you learned at Uni you don't reply 'I learned to work in teams, got confident about presenting to groups from 5–60, improved my logical reasoning ability, discovered I was really good at organizing when I took the French Soc. to Lausanne for the weekend, enjoyed . . .' And if you can explain that to your aunt you can express it more fluently for an employer. Applying for a job with a degree in Russian or Chinese has given even the dimmest employer the idea that you have your language skills, so make the most of the rest. Look back at Chapters 1 and 4, and list the skills your degree is giving you (**Try This 4.6**). Are they highlighted on your CV? Higher education changes people. Attitudes and values develop and perspectives evolve. It is worth reflecting on how you are altering as a person during your degree course, and thinking about how that might influence your choice of career. Ask yourself 'How does what I now know about myself, and my personal skills and attitudes, influence what I want to do after I graduate?'

The real problem for language students is that almost anyone wants to employ you. Your degree shows you have cultural and historical awareness and the self-confidence to communicate with all sorts of people. You survived your year abroad – which proves you have resilience and organizational skills – and, as a graduate, you are critical, logical and a creative thinker. Tourism, translating and interpreting may seem obvious routes – but check out the need for Master's qualifications in the last two before rushing in. Companies like language graduates, so take a good look at accountancy, international banking, retailing, human resources, advertising, marketing, the media . . . . You have all the skills that other graduates have AND you can speak a foreign language.

Knowing what you want to do when you graduate is difficult and there is an enormous choice of careers available to you where your language degree is helpful but not essential. Your first advice point is your Careers Centre. In the absence of a Careers Centre do a www search for your local region using careers+centre/service+university. or careers+languages, UK students *may* be able to access http://www.prospects.csu.man.ac.uk/STUDENT/CIDD/startpts/casinfo.htm Accessed 30 July 2000. Use **Try This 25.1** as a way of focusing some thoughts as you search through careers information.

TRY THIS 25.1 – What shall I do?

In your Careers Centre office, or while surfing the electronic careers nets, use the following questions to focus your thoughts.

1. Pick a career/occupation you think you might like.
2. Make a quick list of the things you think this job will involve.
3. Find literature/web site for 3 potential companies – what skills do they say the job will need?
4. Make quick list of the skills and the evidence you can quote to show you have these skills?
5. How did your original ideas about this occupation match your first ideas?
6. Is this the right type of company for you?
7. Now research another career.

Why wait until you graduate? Get involved with your Careers Centre from year 1. They have lots of information about summer placements and internships. Why not be paid to work in accountancy, sales or banking and find out if it is really for you?

Possible Careers (just a few, there are thousands out there)

Translator: An MA/Diploma in Interpreting and Translation may be essential. Most translators' work tends to be freelance, which can be useful if you want to work independently from home.

Interpreting: Needs Master's qualifications to ensure you have a clear future. Check up on current details. There are not too many jobs available so be prepared for competition.

See http://www.wmin.ac.uk/courses/languages/pgdipconfinterptech.htm for one example.

Accounting and Finance: As international banking, insurance, and company management increases there are plenty of graduate opportunities. You will be employed because you have flair and potential as a financier or auditor but if you remind your managers that you have language skills that could get you the overseas postings as well.

Civil Service: Look at the information for the Main Stream and the Fast Stream. A few people are needed each year for EU jobs and for the diplomatic service. You may find your niche in customs or immigration. Start at http://www.cabinet-office.gov.uk/index/civilservice.htm

Catering: Enjoyed all that great Chinese/French/Italian cuisine while abroad and fancy hotel and restaurant management? Again you don't need languages but they can help – go for your graduate skills.

Sales, Marketing, Purchasing: Commercial areas of business provide hundreds of opportunities.

Tourism: Just about every student fancies working as a courier so stress your experience overseas, your ability to organize, to sort out papers, to get people through customs ... Don't forget to explain that you are happy to add up figures and work out timetables. Fun and stressful!

Voluntary Organizations: will recruit graduates with any degree so your langage may give you an edge if it is an international organization.

Teaching: UK students looking to teach in the UK need a PGCE (Postgraduate Certificate in Education). To teach overseas look at the requirements for that country. You won't be let loose on a class without some preparation. Needs bags of energy, enthusiasm and patience. You don't necessarily get to use your advanced language skills much, but if you like small people . . . .

TEFL: (Teaching English as a Foreign Language): short term fun, can get you abroad, meet interesting people, but not necessarily a long-term career. Needs energy and flexibility in travel. See AGCAS (Careers) booklets that compare different training courses and describe the job. Amongst the most exciting is JET (teaching English in Japan), although the competition is fierce because it is open to graduates from every discipline.

For Graduates with *Linguistics* degrees see all the above and check out Useful Bookmarks for Linguists at http://ling.ed.ac.uk/~night/bookmarks.html Accessed 30 July 2000.

25.1 Applications

Make the most of your skills, the personal, transferable and academic. Look back at Figure 1.1, p. 2 and check off your skills. Be upfront about them. Tell employers that you have given 20 presentations to groups of 5–50. You have used OHTs, slides and electronic display material. Practical skills are easy to list on a CV, but often seem so obvious that they are left out. Familiarity with different databases, word processing packages, spreadsheets and CALL skills are all bonuses of language degrees. Tell employers you have these skills.

Building and updating a CV throughout your degree course will save time in the last year. There are plenty of texts on CV design. Do a key word library search, or check out the Careers Centre. There may be an on-line CV designer.

Top Tips

- Always write job applications in formal English or appropriate L2 style, not a casual style. As more applications are written and sent electronically via www site connections, it is easy to drop into a casual, e-mail writing style; it does not impress human resources managers.
- It may help you to focus your CV if you think about some of the questions employers ask. Try answering a few posed in **Try This 25.2**.

TRY THIS 25.2 – Questions from Employers

Before filling in your applications and before an interview think through (with a pen) some answers to these questions which are often asked at interview.

1. Why are you choosing to be a *solicitor, accountant, personnel manager, marketing manager ...?*
2. What prompted you to apply to this company?
3. What do you know about the company?
4. What interests you most about the job you have applied for?
5. Why does working in this area/organization/country attract you?
6. Why do you want to work in a large/middling/small organization?
7. Why should we offer you a job with us?
8. What were the three most significant/tough/traumatic things that happened in your year abroad?
9. Variations on: What are your strengths and weaknesses? What can you offer the company?

Check out Careers Centre sites that can help with interviews too. See for example http://www.topgrads.co.uk/ (Accessed 30 July 2000) which has some example answers to those difficult questions people ask at interview.

Think of yourself as a marketable product. You possess many skills that employers are seeking, it is a matter of articulating them clearly to maximize your assets. Get yourself well prepared and enjoy the job seeking process.

25.2 References and Further Reading

AGCAS (2000) *Using Languages*. Manchester: AGCAS Graduate Careers Information.

Ostarhild, E. (1997) *Careers Using Languages*. (8th edn). Richmond: Trotman.

Whetter, L. and Pybus, V. (2000) *International Voluntary Work* (7th edn). Oxford: Vacation Work Publishers.

There are three series to chase up in libraries and Careers Centres which include many useful texts:

How to ... *get into travel and tourism*. Plymbridge: How To Books.

Live and Work in ... *different countries*. Oxford: Vacation Work Publishers.

Careers using ... Richmond: Trotman.

Carpe Diem

Language Links 2

Add 2 letters in the middle squares to complete the 5-letter words to left and right. When complete, an 8 letter word can be read. Answer p. 282.

T	R	U			E	M	E
M	O	R			S	A	Y
T	E	M			T	C	H
S	E	D			G	S	T

26 'OF SHOES, AND SHIPS, AND SEALING WAX …' a few answers to things modern language students ask

Last but not least take the bull by the tail to eliminate clichés and mixed metaphors.

Here is a potpourri of topics and lists addressing queries raised by students. Some items may seem bizarre and irrelevant, but check out the headings so that, should something become relevant during your degree, you know where to look.

26.1 STRESS

Weight 11st 6lb, calories 7500, alcohol units 35, cigarettes 45 (v.b.), library hrs 0 (v.b.), essays by Fri. 4 (aargh).

All students suffer from stress, it is normal, but needs management. Stress is a bodily reaction to the demands of daily life, and arises when you feel that life's physical, emotional or psychological demands are getting too much. Some people view stress as a challenge and it is vital to them for getting jobs done. Stressful events are seen as healthy challenges. Where events are seen as threatening then distress and unhappiness may follow. If you are feeling upset, or find yourself buttering the kettle and boiling the toast, try to analyse why. Watch out for circumstances where you are stressed because of:

☹ Expectations you have for yourself. (Are they reasonable, at this time, in these circumstances?)

☹ Expectations of others, especially parents and tutors. (They have the best motives, but are these reasonable expectations at this time?)

☹ Physical environment – noisy flat mates, people who don't wash up, wet weather, hot weather, dark evenings. (What can be done to relieve these stresses?)

☹ Academic pressures – too many deadlines, not enough time to read. (Can you use friends to share study problems? Would it help to talk to someone about time management?)

☹ Social pressures, partying all night. (Are friends making unreasonable demands?)

Serious stress needs proper professional attention, no text will substitute, but how do you recognize stress in yourself or friends? Watch out for signs like feeling tense, irritable, fatigued, depressed, lacking interest in your studies, having a reduced ability to concentrate, apathy and a tendency to get too stuck into stimulants like drink, drugs and nicotine. So that covers most of us! DO NOT GET PARANOID. A few individuals do seem to have leapt into the gene pool while the lifeguard was having tea; their problems do not necessarily have to be yours. PLEASE do not wander into the Health Centre waving this page, and demand attention for what is really a hangover following a work-free term. Thank you.

Managing stress effectively is mostly about balancing demands and desires, getting the right mixture of academic and fun activities and taking time off if you tend to the 'workaholic' approach (the workaholic student spends nine hours a day in the library outside lectures, has read more papers than the lecturer and is still panicking). Get some exercise – aerobics, salsa, jogging, swimming, any sport, walk somewhere each day, practise relaxation skills – Tai Chi classes are great fun. Study regularly and for sensible time periods. Break down big tasks into little chunks and tick them off as you do them. If you are stressed,

✔ TALK TO SOMEONE.

26.2 Mature students (not to be read by anyone under 21, thank you)

'They are all so young and so bright and I don't think I can do this'. Oh yes you can. You have had the bottle to get your act together and make massive arrangements for family and work, so handling a class of bright-faced nineteen-year-olds is easy. Just keep remembering that all those smart teenagers have developed loads of bad study habits at school, are out partying most nights, are fantasizing about the bloke or girl they met last night/want to meet, and haven't got as many incentives for success as you. This degree is taking time from other activities, reducing the family income and pension contributions, which is a great motivation for success. Most mature students work harder than students straight from school and do very well in finals.

'I really didn't want to say anything in tutorial, I thought they would laugh when I got it wrong.' I'm nervous, you are nervous, he ...(conjugate in L2 to gain confidence or get to sleep). At the start of a course, everyone in the group is nervous. Your experience of talking with people at work, home, office, family, scout group, ... means YOU CAN DO THIS. It is likely that your age gets you unexpected kudos – younger students equate age with experience and are likely to listen to and value your input.

'I hated the first week – all those 18 year olds partying and I was trying to register and collect the kids'. The first term is stressful, but having made lots of compromises to get to university give it a go, at least until the first set of examinations. If life is really dire you could switch to part-time for the first year, gaining time to get used to study and the complexities of coping with home and friends.

Mature students end up leading group work more often than the average. Your fellow students will be very, very, very, very happy to let you lead each time – it means they can work less hard. But make sure they support you too!

'It takes me ages to learn things, my brain is really slow'. OK, recognize that it does take longer for older brains to absorb new ideas and concepts. The trick is to be organized and be ACTIVE in studying. This whole book should prompt useful ideas. The following suggestions are gleaned from a variety of texts and talking to mature students in Leeds. It is a case of finding the tips and routines that work for you, get used to practising oral skills at the bus stop, and the cat will like the attention if you talk Russian to it all week. Like learning to play the accordion, keep practising.

Top Tips

- Review notes the day after a lecture, and at the weekend.
- Check out your notes against the texts or papers; ask 'Do I understand this point?'
- Practise writing regularly, anything from a summary paragraph to an essay. Write short paragraphs, which summarize the main points from a lecture or reading, for use in revision. Devising quizzes is also fun (p. 221).
- Talk to people about your studies, your friends, partner, children, people you meet at bus stops, the dog or hamster. It gives great practice in summarizing material, and in trying to explain in an interesting manner, you will raise your own interest levels. Non-experts often ask useful questions.
- Try to visit the library on a regular basis. Timetable part of a day or evening each week, and stick to the plan.
- Meet a fellow mature student once a week or fortnight to chat about experiences and coursework over lunch, coffee or a drink.
- Have a study timetable, and a regular place to study – the shed, attic, bedroom or a corner of the hall.
- Stick a notice on the door that says something like:

Eintritt verboten!

or

I'm Studying
Keep Out,
unless you are really, really ill!

Be assured that, once the family knows you are out of sight for a couple of hours, they will find a series of devious things to do unsupervised. Remind yourself why you decided to do this degree, then ask is this essay on Sardinian devolution or your language lab practical really worse than anything else you have ever had to do? OK, so it is worse, but it will be over in x weeks.

Some time-management and a bit of organization will get you through and by the second year you will have so many more language skills, be giving the family fluent guided tours of Moscow, and know how to manage. When you have finished and got your degree your family will be amazed, stunned and you will have the qualifications you want.

Make specific family fun time and stick to it: 'As a family we really tried to go out once a week for an hour, an evening, or all day. This made a real difference. We did walks, swimming, supper at the pub, visits to friends and family and loads of odd things. We took turns to choose where we went, which the kids thought was great'.

Don't feel guilty, life-long learning is the way the world is going, and there is increasing provision and awareness of mature students' needs.

Problems?

Check out the Students' Union. Most Union Welfare Offices have advice sheets for mature students, advisers for mature students and a Mature Students' Society. If there is no Mature Students' Society then start one. Generally the staff are very experienced in student problems and in solving them. Most departments have a staff tutor or contact for mature students. Go and bother this nice person sooner rather than later. If you feel really guilty, buy him or her a drink sometime!

Family management

Even the most helpful family members have other things in their heads besides remembering that they promised to clean out the gerbils, vacuum the bathroom or pick up a ciabatta on the way home. On balance a list of chores that everyone agrees to and adheres to on 40 per cent of occasions, is good going. Thank the kids regularly for getting jobs done, and remember, this degree should not take over all their lives too. YOU NEED to take time away from study too – plan some trips to the cinema, games of badminton, yoga, visit the sports centre and get away from academic activities.

Short courses

If things get really rough it is possible to suspend studying for a semester or year, or stop after one or two years. Most universities offer certification for completion of each whole or part year. Find out about your options.

Useful sources are Rickards (1992) and Wade (1996) or do a library search using study, degree, mature as keywords and check your University Union website.

26.3 Equal opportunities, harassment, gender and racial issues

All universities have equal opportunities policies, they aim to treat students and staff fairly and justly. Happily most of the time there are few problems. This section cannot discuss these issues in detail, but if you feel you have a problem then here are some sources of advice.

Talk to someone sooner rather than later. There will be a departmental tutor who oversees these issues. Your problem is unlikely to be a new one, and there is normally a great deal of advice and experience available. It really is a matter of tapping into it. Check out your Student Union and your university or college handbook. There should be a contact name, someone who has a title like University Equal Opportunities Officer, or Adviser on Equal Opportunities.

Check out your own university web sites, or visit these:

Loughborough University (1997) *Equal Opportunities.* University Handbook Online, [on-line] http://www.lut.ac.uk/admin/central_admin/policy/student_handbook/section13.html Accessed 30 July 2000.

Liverpool John Moores University (1997) *Equal Opportunities in LJMU.* University Policy, [on-line] http://www.livjm.ac.uk/equal_op/opportun.htm Accessed 30 July 2000.

Useful texts to consult are: Adams (1994), Banton (1994), Carter and Jeffs (1995), Clarke (1994) and Davidson and Cooper (1992).

26.4 Dropping out

'I've been here for a month, no one has spoken to me and I hate it, I'm off'. Happily this is a rare experience for language students, but every year there will be a few people amongst the thousands taking language degrees who are not happy. The main reasons seem to be 'wrong subject choice. I should have done Philosophy, Quantum Physics, Mining ...', 'Everyone else is cleverer than me, I cannot manage ...', ' the course was not what I expected', 'I was so shattered after A-level and school I needed a break and a rest' and 'I really felt I didn't fit in and it wasn't right'. There are big differences between school and university, homesickness is not unusual. All university departments lose students for these kinds of reasons – you will not be the first or last language student feeling unsettled. There are tutors to give advice and people in the Union. Talk to someone as soon as you start to feel unhappy – waiting will probably make you feel worse.

The good news is that most people stick out the first few weeks, get involved with work, social and sporting activities, and really enjoy themselves. Remember, there are 6000–22,000+ other people on your campus; 99.9 per cent are very nice and at least 99.7 per cent feel as shy as you do. If you are really at odds with university life explore the options of suspending your studies, taking a year out in mid-degree or transferring to another university. Take the time to make this a real choice, not a rushed decision.

Question all unsupported statistics!

26.5 Latin words and phrases

amo, amas, where is that lass?

Few people do Latin in school but there are many Latin phrases in normal, everyday, usage. Understanding some of them will get you through university and assist in solving crosswords for life.

a priori	reasoning deductively, from cause to effect.
ad hoc	for this unusual or exceptional case.
ad hominem	to the man, used to describe the case where an argument is directed against the character of the author, rather than addressing the case itself.
ad infinitum	to infinity.
ad interim	meanwhile.
ad lib.	ad libitum, to any extent, at pleasure; (speak) off the cuff.
C.V.	curriculum vitae, a short description of your life, suitable for employers.
carpe diem	seize the day, make the most of your time.
cf.	confer, compare (*cp.* is sometimes used with the same meaning).
de facto	in fact, or actual.
e.g.	exempli gratia, for example.
et al.	et alia, and other persons, appears in references to multiple authors.
et seq.	et sequentia, that which follows, the following page(s).
et passim	(found) all over the place (in a text).
etc.	et cetera, and the rest, and never used in a good essay. It implies lazy thinking.
ex cathedra	authoritative.
ex officio	by virtue of office.
honoris causa	as an honour.
ibid.	ibidem, the same, used when a reference is the same as the previous one.
i.e.	id est, that is.
inter alia	amongst other things.
ipso facto	thereby or by the fact.
loc. cit.	loco citato, in the place cited.
mea culpa	it was my fault.
n.b.	nota bene, note carefully, or take note.
op. cit.	opere citato, in the work cited.
post hoc	used to describe the type of argument where because y follows x, it is assumed x causes y.
reductio ad absurdum	reduced to absurdity.
(sic)	sic, which means 'thus', is often printed in brackets to indicate that the preceding word or phrase has been reproduced *verbatim*, often to point up incorrect spelling or inaccurate quotation in the source text.

sic transit gloria mundi	Nothing to do with Gloria being ill on Monday's bus, it means 'thus passes earthly glory' (cf. *carpe diem* and *tempus fugit*!).
tempus fugit	time flies (cf. *carpe diem*).
verbatim	word for word.
vi et armis	by force of arms.
viva voce	by oral testimony, usually shortened to *viva*, meaning an oral examination.

And finally the motto for the end of many a good seminar:

ergo bibamus therefore let us drink

and for the end of a good university career:

grandeamus igitus therefore let us rejoice!

26.6 An acronym starter list

Most language students compile a personal acronym list depending on their interests. You need two lists, this one and one in your L2. Add acronyms to make a growing reference resource.

AP	Adjectival phrase
AI	Artificial Intelligence
ASL	American Sign Language
BAAL	British Association of Applied Linguistics
BEV	Black English Vernacular
BSL	British Sign Language
CALL	Computer-assisted language learning
CFG	Context-free grammar
CSG	Context-sensitive grammar
DO	Direct object
EEA	European Economic Area, the 15 member states of the EU, plus Iceland, Liechtenstein and Norway.
EFL	English as a foreign language
EU	European Union: Austria, Belgium, Denmark, Finland, France, Germany, Greece, Republic of Ireland, Italy, Luxembourg, the Netherlands, Portugal, Spain, Sweden, United Kingdom
IO	Indirect object
IPA	International Phonetic Alphabet
ITA	Initial Teaching Alphabet
L1	Your first language c.f. L2
L2	Language you are learning, c.f. L1
LARSP	Language, assessment, remediation and screening procedure
LF	Logical form

LSP	Language for special purposes
MLU	Mean length of utterance
NORM	Non-mobile, older, rural male
NP	Noun phrase
OSV language	Object-subject-verb
OVS language	Object-verb-subject
OED	Oxford English Dictionary
PC	Political correctness
RP	Received pronunciation
RRG	Role and reference grammar
S	Sentence
SLA	Second language acquisition
TESL	Teaching English as a Second Language
TEFL	Teaching English as a Foreign Language
TESOL	Teaching English to Speakers of Other Languages
T pronoun	Informal second person pronoun: du (Ger), tu (Fr), tú (Sp)
V pronoun	Formal pronoun: Sie (Ger), vous (Fr), usted (Sp)

26.7 Radio stations

Listening to radio broadcasts in the language you are studying gives you an insight into accents, culture and politics. Tune in your ears. Search the MIT List of Radio Stations on the Internet at http://wmbr.mit.edu/stations/list.html to find stations for the countries you are interested in. This is a very comprehensive listing. Find other web sites which list radio stations by searching using Radio+stations!

26.8 References and Further Reading

Adams, A. (1994) *Bullying at Work: How to Confront and Overcome It*. London: Virago Press.

Banton, M. (1994) *Discrimination*. Milton Keynes: Open University Press.

Carter, P. and Jeffs, A. (1995) *A Very Private Affair: Sexual Exploitation in Higher Education*. Ticknall, Derbyshire: Education Now Books.

Clarke, L. (1994) *Discrimination*. London: Institute of Personnel Management.

Davidson, M.J. and Cooper, C.L. (1992) *Shattering the Glass Ceiling: The Woman Manager*. London: Paul Chapman.

Rickards, T. (1992) *How to Win as a Mature Student*. London: Kogan Page.

Wade, S. (1996) *Studying for a Degree: How to Succeed as a Mature Student in Higher Education*. Plymouth: How To Books.

27 ANSWERS

Proof read everything to check if you any words out.

Anagrams I p. 13

P	O	R	T	U	G	U	E	S	E		A	N	G	L	O	S	A	X	O	N		V	I	E	T	N	A	M	E	S	E

G	U	J	A	R	A	T	I		S	A	N	S	K	R	I	T		E	S	T	O	N	I	A	N

Works and Author's Wordsearch p. 27

Alfred, Lord Tennyson, In Memoriam; Charles Baudelaire, L'Albatros; F. von Schiller, Don Carlos; Henrik Ibsen, A Doll's House; Jane Austin, Emma; Karl Marx, Communist Manifesto; Leo Tolstoy, Anna Karenina; Oscar Wilde, Lady Windemere's Fan; P.B. Shelley, Ozymandias; P.G. Wodehouse, Jeeves Takes Charge; T. Hardy, Jude The Obscure; William Wycherley, The Country Wife.

Language Quick Crossword I p. 36

Across 1 Tongue, 7 Truant, 8 Paradise, 10 Twister, 11 Friseur, 12 Meant, 14 Motto, 15 Print, 19 Glottal, 20 Passive, 22 Emergent, 23 Memoir, 24 Immesh.
Down 1 Typify, 2 Narcissi, 3 Undreamt, 4 Stew, 5 Pursue, 6 Intern, 9 Stratagem, 12 Monogram, 13 Aesthete, 16 Reader, 17 Nestor, 18 Blotch, 21 Verb.

Try This 4.3 – Reflecting on a class or module, p. 42

A selection of answers from level 2 students

- What I want to get out of attending this module is: 'This subject is new to me and I would like to find out about it', 'I did this at 'A' level, and I'd like to put it in a wider context', 'I need to learn something about the mechanics of language learning before I go abroad as an English language Assistant'.
- In what ways has this module/session helped you to develop a clearer idea of yourself, your strengths and weaknesses? 'Nothing: we were spoon-fed by the lecturer and never encouraged to ask questions or voice opinions', 'Before I took this module, I had no idea how to search for information in the library or on the internet, and now I can', 'This module has been great for career planning because it has helped me to find out what I am good at'.
- Record your current thinking about the skills you *can* acquire from this module. Tick those you want to develop, and make a plan. 'Improve my close reading technique', 'Learn more about the meta-language of literary criticism', 'Learn to work faster and assimilate more', 'Cope with very long reading lists', 'Get acquainted with 18th century women's writing'.

- I have discovered the following about myself with respect to decision making: 'I tend to avoid making decisions like the plague', 'I never realized how many decisions I take in a day', 'I have always loathed taking decisions, but I know I will have to face up to this when I get a job, so I might as well work on it from now on'.

Wordplay Word Ladder p. 47

BARD	CASE	COPY	MIME	PLAY
BARE	CAST	COPT	MIRE	SLAY
BORE	COST	COOT	WIRE	SLAP
BODE	POST	CLOT	WORE	SLOP
NODE	POET	PLOT	WORD	STOP

Try This 5.2 – WWW addresses p. 55

All Accessed 30 July 2000
Arnold http://www.arnoldpublishers.com
Chicano Database http://www.library.yale.edu/pubstation/databases/chicano.html
Consortium of University Research Libraries (CURL) Union Catalogue
http://www.curl.ac.uk/database/
Deutsche Bibliothek Database
http://portico.bl.uk/gabriel/en/countries/germany.html
Linguistics Abstracts Online http://labs.blackwellpublishers.co.uk/
Periodicals Content Index (PCI)
http://www.hull.ac.uk/Hull/Library_Web/helpsheet/edina.htm
Russian Academy of Sciences Bibliography
http://www.gla.ac.uk/Library/Resources/Databases/ras.html
ITAR/TASS. http://www.cs.toronto.edu/~mes/russia.html
Reuters Worldwide newswire. http://www.reuters.com/onlinemedia/

Try This 6.3 – Where do you read p. 66

'I can skim through an article on the bus and on the train home at weekends, which is good. For real reading I like to have some music on, so I use my room in the flat'. 'We try to have a couple of "quiet flat" hours each evening so that something gets done, and it mostly works'. 'I like using the library computer rooms where I can read and type in notes. It can be a bit noisy, but you don't notice most of the time, and friends don't interrupt, so I get quite a bit done'.

Try This 6.4 – Spotting Reading clues p. 67

I will start with a description of what might be considered the basic requirements ...; There will then follow a discussion of ...; Recent publications highlight ...; From these examples, it is clear that ...; The present study comprised ...; Consequently ...; In all of the above, the focus was ...; However...; Our study has revealed that ...; A key feature of the model is ...; Clearly there are some basic features of ...; One such feature is ...; One way to account for this is ...; Immediately apparent from the figure is ...; While the debate continues, I would argue ...; Finally ...

Book Link p. 70

Jane Eyre by Charlotte Brontë.

Authors, Poets and Philosophers Wordsearch p. 86

Atwood, Baroness Orczy, Beaumarchais, Coetzee, Flaubert, Frost, Garcia Lorca, Gogol, Hans Andersen, Houseman, Leacock, Macciavelli, Mann, Molière, Nietzsche, Omar Khayyam, Pope, Proust, Sade, Salinger, Sartre, Schiller, Solzhenitsyn, Spinoza, Tocqueville, Twain, Washington Irving, Wilkie Collins, Wittgenstein, Zola.

Author Anagrams 2 p. 96

ROSSETTI BETJEMAN DELAMARE

DEBEAUVOIR MAUPASSANT BAUDELAIRE

FLAUBERT VOLTAIRE SCHILLER

Try This 10.1 – Logical arguments? p. 113

Example comments:

1. 'It is evident from ...' They might be, or again the Italian system might be less efficient, less supportive of students than the British one. And how do we define 'educated'? Does it mean, for instance, that Italian students have read more books and written longer dissertations than their British counterparts? – Quite possibly. Or does it mean that they are more self-reliant, better equipped for the world of work? – Possibly not?
2. 'Although his father ...' Strindberg's ambivalence towards women is well documented, as is his sense of shame at his background. But a vital factor in his make-up, necessary to provide the link, has been omitted: his violent love–hate relationship with his mother, in which rebellion and intense attachment constantly vied with one another.
3. 'The outbreak of ...' A non sequitur. Certainly women at home in Britain and Germany had to take on jobs formerly done by men, to keep the economy going, but frequently they were forced to work for lower wages or simply to avoid eviction from a tied house; they still had to run a household as well; and they gained little politically from their new roles.

Try This 10.2 – Logical linking phrases p. 114

And; however; several attempts have been made; not infrequently, conversely; do not agree; if; subsequently; consequently, despite the fact; in addition;

notwithstanding, this is broadly similar to; such factors also; these conclusions differ from; in other words; coupled with; making a causal connection; given the pressures to; for instance; one additional mechanism; none the less; such as; how can this; there is evidence; see, for example.

Try This 10.3 – Fact or opinion p. 114–115

1. "It seems to me that Chomsky's MPLT ...' (p. 224) Pérez-Leroux and Glass cite Ellis's interpretation of Chomsky's MPLT theory and its implications, then proceed to challenge Ellis head-on by means of a number of categorical statements supported (a powerful weapon, this) by reference to Chomsky himself.
2. 'Given Grinstead's (1994; 1998) claim ...' (p. 174) Here the authors attack Grinstead on his home ground, by pointing to empirical data which cast doubt on Grinstead's claim.
3. 'It has sometimes ...' (p. 133) In this somewhat convoluted but no less forceful statement the authors challenge a whole series of assertions as being 'misconceptions', a polite way of saying 'misunderstandings' of the basic data. Apparently Carroll/Meisel, Ellis and Birdsong have all made false assumptions about the premises under which researchers in this field operate, which is a very basic error and one that, assuming Duffield and White's claim is correct, would seriously weaken the arguments of Carroll & Co. Duffield and White anticipate their 'misconception' statement by their use of 'in fact', which suggests to the reader that what is claimed by Carroll and the others is not in fact the case.

Language Cryptic Crossword 1 p. 119

Across 1 Customs, 5 Cyclops, 9 Melodrama, 10 Totem, 11 Conversazioni, 13 Optional, 15 Indent, 17 Crabby, 19 Encyclic, 22 Prelinguistic, 25 Uniat, 26 Eye-opener, 27 Largess, 28 Odyssey.

Down 1 Camp, 2 Solicit, 3 Olden, 4 Space-bar, 5 Clause, 6 Citizenry, 7 Outcome, 8 Semeiotics, 12 Conceptual, 14 Oubliette, 16 Anti-hero, 18 Atelier, 20 Lacunas, 21 Egress, 23 Tipsy, 24 Troy.

Play Link p. 127

Coriolanus by William Shakespeare.

Try This 12.1 – Working with a Brainstormed List pp. 129–30

CDU in crisis: A sorted version

Corruption in the CDU, why now? CDU in crisis. CDU too long in power. 'All power corrupts, absolute power corrupts absolutely': Kohl was near-absolute ruler; Kohl a virtual dictator; Leaders once in power are prone to arrogance vis-à-vis the electorate; Kohl's motive was retention of power at any price; Kohl had Germany's long-term interests at heart; Kohl did everything for the best;

Kohl's split loyalties: to party, to 'benefactors', to nation. Kohl also a great achiever – re-united East and West Germany BUT Re-unification an albatross around CDU's neck.

Politics and morality: Secret donations to political parties are illegal in Germany; All political parties are corrupt in one way or another; Sleaze endemic in government, all succumb in the end; Politics is about votes, not morals; General need to redefine values in German politics; Sleaze is a particular problem for a party that espouses 'traditional values'; The SPD is cashing in on CDU's discomfort with a holier-than-thou stance; Sleaze more than a German problem (Tories, Mitterand).

Politics and economics: Kohl would never have had a problem if German economy hadn't slowed down; CDU brought down by unemployment, not sleaze; Kohl's fall linked to Euro, demise of DM, loss of national pride.

Regeneration of CDU? CDU needs to atone for past mistakes; CDU needs new initiatives/programme; CDU needs new image; Schröder charismatic, Kohl dull and unappealing; Kohl: age problem – perceived as past it; New CDU leader, new hope: Angela Merkel female, young and squeaky-clean; SPD unpopular over its ecologically-driven policies – chance for CDU.

Tutorial Conundrum p. 138

Megan and Jack discussed the role of the narrator and got 78%, Natasha and Tim researched Tolstoy and got 72%, Sam and Georgia researched the epistolary novel and scored 63%, while Ann and Jordan looked at Flaubert and got 58%.

Word Ladder p. 144

C	E	L	T		C	O	P	T		M	A	N	X		P	I	C	T
C	E	N	T		C	O	A	T		M	A	N	E		P	I	C	K
C	A	N	T		C	H	A	T		M	A	L	E		T	I	C	K
C	A	N	E		T	H	A	T		M	O	L	E		T	U	C	K
D	A	N	E		T	H	A	I		P	O	L	E		T	U	R	K

Try This 14.1 – Keywords in essay questions p. 148

1. 'Political fragmentation, ...' Asks for 'weaknesses' and 'two' sectors only. Don't attempt to impress by covering all four factors and strengths and weaknesses. The question asks about the eighteenth century, so no brownie points for a potted history of the HRE either. And if you choose either of the first two factors, make sure that you concentrate on how they could have affected economic development and don't get side-tracked into theology or politics or social history.
2. 'To what extent ...' Keywords here are 'growth', 'change' and 'lingua franca'. Explore the connections between tradition and global communication and consider the 'against' factors as well as the 'fors' ('to what extent'). Take examples from across Latin America.

3. 'Critically explain how ...' Wants a statement of their theory and a technical account of the premises on which it is based. Call on pre-1994 work by both these and other authors, and evaluate the evidence used by Schwartz and Eubank and their contribution to the ongoing debate at that stage. In your closing paragraph you may refer briefly to subsequent developments, but any detailed discussion of post-1994 developments is beyond the scope of this essay.
4. 'Account for the ...' A two-part question with equal marks for 'account for' and 'assess'. Evidence and examples are required for both parts. The problem here is that there is no indication of whether this is a UK, Europe or world-wide question, nor are you given much help by the phrase 'graduates in languages other than English'. At first glance it could be a question about the prospects for either UK language graduates (at home or abroad), or graduates who have studied a language (including their own) abroad. Apply common sense. What topics were covered in the module? What would be the point of the second interpretation? Given the global nature of e-commerce and the dominance of English on the WWW, the question must be about the prospects for non-English language graduates in a predominantly English-speaking environment. Write about that, but complain about the sloppy question.
5. 'Evaluate the role of ...' In 'evaluating' be complimentary as well as critical – remember the pros in raising awareness as well as the disadvantages. Consider all types of mass media, different types of newspaper reportage – the news bulletin versus the considered documentary, and the print media, papers and magazines. The answer requires lots of diverse examples. Is this a UK question or should you comment on media activities in other countries? Incidentally, just because all the lecture examples came from France that is no reason to ignore examples from other countries, unless the module was called something like 'The French Media'.

Try This 14.2 – Evaluate an introduction p. 150

Discuss the validity of the concept 'Standard German' in the description of the language.

Version 1. This gets off to a promising start, apart from confusing 'media' (pl.) with 'medium' (sing.). However, problems of terminology and definition quickly arise (a serious matter in a technical essay of this type) when 'standard forms' are compared to 'other dialects', implying wrongly that the standard form is a dialect. The final sentence seems to advance the first argument, that it is difficult to identify a standard form, but raises other issues of accuracy: there may well be **norms** for different areas, but not standards, and there is certainly nothing as definite as Austrian or Swiss Standard German.

Version 2. The approach here is lively and engaging, if rather colloquial for a technical topic. More seriously, although the various forms of the language mentioned here do play a part in any discussion of linguistic norms and standards, what the author refers to as 'stylistic variation' is what is customarily called **register**, and to concentrate on this aspect alone, as is proposed, is to leave out some very important considerations, such as the regional dimension in the question of standard language.

Version 3. This version has a lot going for it: it appeals to common experience, it introduces the important concept of a linguistic continuum and notes that the 'Grammar Standard' is only one point on that continuum. On the down side, the implication that a speaker 'chooses' and 'switches' between different points on the scale conflicts with the statement that a person's speech is 'located' at some point on the continuum. Nor, having mentioned some of the factors that influence a speaker's language, does the writer mention one of the most important factors of all, that our language alters depending on the situation and the type of person(s) we are talking to. And – major flaws, these – in what is supposed to be an introduction, there is no indication of how the question is to be tackled, yet the discussion has already begun.

Version 4. This is very succinct and to-the-point and the thrust of the essay is clearly indicated. Somewhat naughtily, the writer doesn't plan to cover all three aspects of variation directly, but hints that the two aspects not specifically addressed may also be touched on in discussion.

Try This 14.3 – Good concluding paragraphs p. 154

Version 1

This 'conclusion' isn't really a conclusion at all. It comes from an essay which described and analysed the main issues very clearly, with good supporting evidence, but this lets the side down by the narrative approach and lack of any strategy for summing up.

Version 2

This is more of an attempt at a conclusion than Version 1. But it is marred by poor English (sentence 2 isn't a sentence at all; to whom does 'they' in sentence 4 refer?). There is very little sense of direction, and unhelpful statements: gaining the vote was an achievement for all German women, not just the working-class movement. The *Vereinsgesetz* (a repressive anti-association law) was very important and should have been part of the main text. It was added here as an afterthought, which is totally inappropriate. It makes a very weak unsupported ending.

Version 3

A tidy, competent conclusion, making it clear that the arguments have already been presented and this is intended as a closing summary and nothing else. Could still be improved, but the best of the bunch.

Try This 14.6 – Shorten/tighten up these sentences pp. 158–9

Wordy	Better
In a great many instances, the authorities were powerless to act.	Many authorities were powerless to act.
The use of case *is an important factor* in many inflected languages.	Case is important in many inflected languages.
In *much of* eighteenth-century Europe, the law of primogeniture applied and daughters and younger sons had no inheritance to look forward to.	In eighteenth-century Europe, primogeniture meant that daughters and younger sons could not inherit.
Moving to *another phase* of the project ...	The next phase ... or Part x
Dialect variations were studied in Provence and the Dordogne regions *respectively*.	Dialect variations were studied in Provence and the Dordogne.
Iambic pentameter *is a kind of* metre. (should read 'Iambic pentameter is a type of metre.')	Iambic pentameter is a poetic metre.
One of the best ways of investigating the women's movement in its early phases is ...	To investigate the early stages of the women's movement ...
The process of integrating genuine asylum-seekers into mainstream society continues *along the line outlined.*	Integrating genuine asylum-seekers into mainstream society continues
The nature of the problem ...	The problem ...
Child's speech is an *increasingly important, perhaps the most important* factor in their social interactions	Children's speech is the most important factor in their social interactions ...
One prominent *feature* of blank verse is the absence of rhymes.	Blank verse does not rhyme
It *is sort of* understood that ...	It is understood that ...
It is difficult *enough to* explore gender issues in the media without time restraints adding to the pressure.	Exploring gender issues in the media is time-consuming.
The *body of* evidence is in favour of ...	The evidence supports ...

Try This 14.8 – Synonyms, homonyms and look-alikes pp. 160–61

1 persistent; 2 (a)improve; (b)better; 3 (a)disinterested; (b)uninterested; 4 affected; 5 complementary; 6 unwonted; 7 practising; 8 tentatively.

Language Anagrams 3 p. 164

A L L U S I O N C R I T I Q U E L I M E R I C K

I M P E R S O N A L P A R A P H R A S E N O M I N A T I V E

F O O T N O T E O X Y M O R O N V I G N E T T E

Try This 15.1 – The nightmare reference list pp. 172–3

This is the list correctly organized. Errors included misplacement of stops and commas, authors' names with full given names, names without initials, italics in the wrong places, missing details about publishers, or details in the wrong order, missing volume and page numbers and the list was not in alphabetical order. Throwing marks away because of incomplete and inaccurate referencing is a real waste.

Air Pollution. 23 October 1999 Air pollution index of major Chinese cities. *China Daily*, 19, 6047, 2.

Bourges, É. (1987) *Le crépuscule des dieux*. Saint-Cyr-sur Loire: C. Pirot.

Ince, K. (1996) L'Amour la Mort: the eroticism of Marguerite Duras. In Hughes, A. and Ince, K. (eds.) *French erotic fiction: women's desiring writing, 1880–1990*. Oxford: Berg 147–181.

Kelly, K.E. (ed.) (1996) *Modern Drama by Women 1880s–1930s: An international anthology*. London: Routledge.

King, C. (1999) Michael Davitt and Lev Nikolaevich Tolstoy: Meetings 1904, 1905. *Irish Slavonic Studies*, 20, 71–87.

Kubicek, P. (2000) Regional Polarisation in Ukraine: Public Opinion, Voting and Legislative Behaviour. *Europe-Asia Studies*, 52, 2, 273–294.

Muñoz Molina, A. (1997) *Escrito en un instante*. Palma Mallorca: Calima.

Neilan, E. 3 June 2000. The siren song of 'the China market'. *The Japan Times*. [online] http://www.japantimes.co.jp/ Accessed 3 June 2000.

Polizzotto, L. (1998) Patronage and Charity in Savonarola's Reform. *Patronage, Piety, Prophecy: Savonarola and After, The Savonarola Quincentenary Conference*, Trinity College Dublin, November 1998.

Roskies, G., (ed.) (1989) *The Literature of Destruction: Jewish responses to catastrophe*. Philadelphia: Jewish Publication Society.

Walter, B.K. (1997) Web of Shudders: Sublimity in Kierkegaard's Fear and Trembling, *MLN*, 112, 753–785.

Xiguang, Y. and McFadden, S. (1997) *Captive spirits: prisoners of the Cultural Revolution*. Hong Kong and New York: Oxford University Press.

Language Link p. 174

Asterisk.

Analysing Language Wordsearch p. 186

Active, Adverb, Alliteration, Analyse, Archetype, Atmosphere, Ballad, Bibliography, Bucolic, Caricature, Case, Comedy, Definite article, Ditty, Drama, Ellipsis, Epigrammatical, Epilogue, Fiction, Haiku, Humour, Idyll, Imagery, Libretto, Link, Lyric, Metaphorical, Metre, Mime, Mood, Motif, Ode, Onomatopoeia, Paean, Persona, Phoneme, Poem, Pun, Rhyme, Scalar, Simile, Stanza, Style, Tone, Umlaut, Verb.

Language Quick Crossword 2 p. 190

Across 1 Part, 3 Rousseau, 8 Snippet, 10 Proud, 11 Controversy, 13 Romaic, 15 Larynx, 17 Interviewee, 20 Cuban, 21 Iberian, 22 Doggerel, 23 Yell.
Down 1 Postcard, 2 Reign, 4 Octavo, 5 Superlative, 6 Eponymy, 7 Urdu, 9 Persistence, 12 External, 14 Mailbag, 16 Praise, 18 Write, 19 Acid.

Try This 18.1 – Book reviews p. 191

Comments on the extracts:

1. 'Strumiński's impressively researched book . . .' (RR p. 285). This is a clear opening statement from a review that gives you essential information about the content and audience. The first sentence is both complementary and outlines scope. The paragraph concludes by identifying the linguistic skill areas that it addresses.
2. 'Some of Strumiński's assertions . . .' (RR p. 285). It may be difficult for you as a young researcher to spot gaps but it is worth looking for unsupported statements at all times. A lack of evidence is a real problem. The reviewer here has given the evidence for his argument with the page numbers – which is good practice.
3. 'Baudin's study is truly impressive . . .' (RR p. 297). This style of paragraph which describes content is essential in most reviews. What is nice here is that he points out that Baudin has done a better job than he might have by reviewing all the works, so it is description of content and praise for a job well done.
4. 'Cohen provides valuable discussion . . .' (LTR p. 87). Positive review that pulls out some reasons for reading this text rather than another.
5. 'Arguably, Chapter 2 . . .' (LTR p. 83). OK, so maybe the undergraduates will fall asleep part way through but you might still want to read the start and end of this chapter, you have been warned about the style but the content is still valuable.
6. 'As Donald Rayfield indicates . . .' (RR pp. 286–870). In reviews of second editions you might expect substantial change and updating – which seems to be missing in this case.

7. 'The whole approach ...' (LTR p. 88). A positive recommendation that encourages reading because the author is providing you with additional help in transferring ideas from the page to your practice through practical activities.
8. 'Magic Mirror is well-illustrated ...' (RR p. 294). Great, one to buy perhaps?
9. 'It would be condescending ...' (RR p. 286). Hmm, probably not one to buy – however you may disagree with the reviewer. If this is by an author you have trusted previously then maybe you should at least look at the book.

Author Word Ladder p. 201

FORD	HINE	KANT	MARX	MILL
FORE	LINE	KENT	MARE	WILL
FARE	LIME	RENT	MORE	WELL
FADE	LIMB	REND	PORE	WELT
SADE	LAMB	READ	POPE	WEST

Try This 21.5 – Generic questions for revising p. 224

Can you translate each of these into your L2?

What is the purpose of ...?
Why is ... an inadequate explanation of ...?
Who are the three main authorities to quote for topic ...?
Name two examples not in the course text or lectures for ...?
Explain the findings of ...?
What are the main characteristics of ... *Fodorion notions of informational encapsulation* ...?
Outline the evidence from ... *Le Roman de la Rose* which supports/confutes ideas of ... *courtly love.*
What are the chief merits and limitations of ... *Epic Theatre*?
Define ... ?
What does ... mean?
What methodology can be employed to research *the workings of the economy in post-1989 Russia*?
What is the purpose of ... *social dialectology/lexical phonology* ...?
What was the main aim of ...?
What was the significance of ... *I promessi sposi by Alessandro Manzoni* ...?
Outline the developments leading up to ... *the outbreak of hostilities in 1939.*
If ... did not occur, what would be the implications?
Outline the different approaches that can be taken to the study of ... *Woman and society in Spanish drama of the Golden Age?*
Will this work in the same way at a larger/smaller scale?
How influential are ideas of ... *community in French Caribbean fiction.*?
What are the ... implications of this finding?
What is meant by ... *contextually dependent meaning* ...?
Why is ... *Kawabata* ... important in ... *Japanese post-1945 Literature*?

Do I agree that... *Le vingtième siècle est le plus grand siècle pour la France?*
Outline three types of ...?
Which examples would you cite when discussing ... *honour, jealousy and desire in Cervantes?*
Why study ... Confucian and Taoist texts?

Anagrams 4 p. 225

C	O	L	L	O	Q	U	I	A	L		I	N	F	L	E	C	T	I	O	N		S	P	O	O	N	E	R	I	S	M

D	O	G	G	E	R	E	L		M	E	T	A	P	H	O	R		W	H	O	D	U	N	I	T

Trivial Pursuit p. 230
c; b; a and c are both correct

Reasoning and Previous Knowledge Style p. 231
a Armenian, b Latvian, c Kurdish, d Romany.
a–h All of them are correct.

Writers Wordsearch p. 236
Aesop, Arnold, Asimov, Cervantes, Chekhov, Clare, Congreve, Dante, DeQuincy, Descartes, Dostoevsky, Dumas, Eliot, Galsworthy, Goethe, Greene, Grimm, Heine, Kafka, Keats, Kierkegaard, Mackenzie, Maupassant, Mcgonagall, Osborne, Pasternak, Pirandello, Pound, Pushkin, Rabelais, Sappho, Sassoon, Shute, Stein, Stendhal, Tutuola, Victor Hugo, Vidal, Voltaire, Wilde.

Try This 24.1 – Which of these are not members of the EU? p. 249
Israel, Hungary, Romania, Norway, Poland.

Language Cryptic Crossword 2 p. 256
Across 1 Collator, 6 Quarto, 9 Marginalia, 10 Team, 11 Scatterbrain, 13 Loci, 14 Voice-box, 17 Outstrip, 18 Prim, 20 Balladmonger, 23 Lilt, 24 Apolitical, 25 Séance, 26 Numbered.
Down 2 Oral, 3 Logistics, 4 Tinman, 5 Relative pronoun, 6 Quatrain, 7 Actor, 8 Tragi-comic, 12 Popularize, 15 Expertise, 16 Graduate, 19 Egoism, 21 Latin, 22 Page.

Language Links 2 p. 261
Thespian.

28 SKILLS: A MINI-BIBLIOGRAPHY

This is a mini-bibliography of skills texts. A compilation of the references from each chapter is at http://www.german.leeds.ac.uk/skillsbook/index.htm. We will update the web links regularly. Please let us know of other sites to link with.

Barnes, R. (1995) *Successful Study for Degrees.* (2nd edn.) London: Routledge.

Bucknall, K. (1996) *Studying at University: How to Make a Success of your University Course.* Plymouth: How To Books.

Buzan, T. (1989) *Speed Reading.* Devon: David & Charles.

Chambers, E. and Northedge, A. (1997) *The Arts Good Study Guide,* Milton Keynes: Open University.

Drew, S. and Bingham, R. (eds.) (1997) *The Student Skills Guide.* Aldershot: Gower.

Fairbairn, G.J. and Winch, C. (1996) *Reading, Writing and Reasoning: A Guide for Students.* (2nd edn.) Buckingham: Open University Press.

Marshall, L.A. and Rowland, F. (1983) *A Guide to Learning Independently.* Buckingham: Open University Press.

Payne, E. and Whitaker, L. (2000) *Developing Essential Study Skills.* Harlow: Financial Times/Prentice Hall.

Rowntree, D. (1993) *Learn How to Study: A Guide for Students of All Ages.* (3rd edn.) London: Warner Books.

Rudd, S. (1989) *Time Manage Your Reading.* Aldershot: Gower.

Russell, S. (1993) *Grammar, Structure and Style.* Oxford: Oxford University Press.

Saunders, D. (ed.) (1994) *The Complete Student Handbook.* Oxford: Blackwell.

Van den Brink-Budgen, R. (1996) *Critical Thinking for Students: How to Use your Recommended Texts on a University or College Course.* Plymouth: How To Books.

Generic Study Skills www sites (all accessed 30 November 2000) at:

http://units.ox.ac.uk/departments/english/undergra/studysch.html
The University at Oxford's English department: useful for essays and revision.

http://www.ucc.vt.edu/stdysk/stdyhlp.html A series of Study Skills self help information at Virginia Tech.

http://www.utexas.edu/student/lsc/The Learning Skills Center at the Universityof Texas at Austin. Click on the 'Our Favorite Handouts' link.

http://www.adm.uwaterloo.ca/infocs/Study/study_skills.html The Study Skills package at the University of Waterloo, Canada.

http://128.32.89.153/CalRENHP.html The CalREN Project study tips.

http://www.yorku.ca/admin/cdc/lsp/handouts.htm University of York, Ontario, Canada. Learning Skills Programme handouts.

http://www.campuslife.utoronto.ca/handbook/02-GettingGoodGrades.html Getting Good Grades at The University of Toronto, Canada.

http://www.edinboro.edu/cwis/acaff/suppserv/tips/tipsmenu.html Academic Survival Tips from Edinboro University, Pennsylvania.

INDEX